WORDPERFECT® 5.1 APPLICATIONS FOR BUSINESS STUDENTS

WORDPERFECT® 5.1 APPLICATIONS FOR BUSINESS STUDENTS

Peter R. Peacock

Wake Forest University

Prentice Hall, Englewood Cliffs, NJ 07632

Library of Congress Cataloging-in-Publication Data

Peacock, Peter R.
Wordperfect 5.1 applications for business students / Peter R. Peacock.
p. cm.
Includes index.
ISBN 0-13-964719-8
1. WordPerfect (Computer program) 2. Word processing--Computer programs. 3. Business writing--Computer programs. I. Title.
Z52.5.W65P43 1991
652.5'536--dc20 91-107
CIP

Editorial/production supervision and
interior design: *Anthony Calcara*
Acquisitions Editor: *Liz Kendall*
Cover design: Barbara Singer
Manufacturing buyer: *Ilene Levy (Pre-press)*
Ed O'Dougherty (Presswork and Binding)

A Simon & Schuster Company
Englewood Cliffs, New Jersey 07632

Printed in the United States of America

10 9 8 7 6 5 4 3 2 1

ISBN 0-13-964719-8

Prentice-Hall International (UK) Limited, *London*
Prentice-Hall of Australia Pty. Limited, *Sydney*
Prentice-Hall Canada Inc., *Toronto*
Prentice-Hall Hispanoamericana, S.A., *Mexico*
Prentice-Hall of India Private Limited, *New Delhi*
Prentice-Hall of Japan, Inc., *Tokyo*
Simon & Schuster Asia Pte. Ltd., *Singapore*
Editora Prentice-Hall do Brasil, Ltda., *Rio de Janeiro*

Contents

Preface

This book was written for the undergraduate or graduate business student who wants to use WordPerfect to produce letters, resumes, term papers, and written case analyses among other documents, but who doesn't have a week to set aside for WordPerfect[1] self-training and who really isn't interested in doing so anyway. The book is also intended for the student who writes well but isn't dead certain in matters of document planning and organization or the finer points of formatting and written communication effectiveness.

PURPOSE

The primary purpose of *WordPerfect Applications for Business Students* is to give the reader just described a set of task-specific instruction sets—i.e., instruction sets organized around a specific task such as writing a letter or memo—that are comprehensive enough to let him or her type attractive and readable documents without having to spend several days reading word processing training manuals designed for professional secretaries. A secondary purpose of the book is to help users plan, organize, and complete major writing projects such as term papers and management reports. The book's final purpose is to provide guidelines on the arrangement and format of customary business documents and to give tips on how to get a major writing project completed "on time and under budget."

[1]WordPerfect is a registered trademark of WordPerfect Corporation; All Rights Reserved.

The Nature of the Book

WordPerfect Applications has four major features:

- *A focus on the casual user.* The book meets the needs of the casual user with minimal WordPerfect experience and little time for training.
- *A focus on tasks.* The book focuses on helping readers complete specific, well-defined word processing tasks rather than on providing comprehensive training to the individual who wants to become professionally competent with WordPerfect.
- *A focus on the documents business students produce.* The book emphasizes the documents business students are expected to prepare and the word processing tasks they're most likely to take on.
- *Format examples.* Examples in the book follow standard written communication formats that most instructors would find acceptable.

The book has nine chapters. *Chapter 1* describes the purpose and structure of the book, presents assumptions about readers, and tells how to use the book most effectively.

Chapter 2 explains the keyboard, the mouse and pull-down menus, defines terminology, and prescribes the conventions used in the remainder of the book. The chapter also introduces the reader to the hidden formatting codes that control document format, emphasizes the importance of the codes, and tells how to reveal them. Finally, the chapter tells the reader with little personal computer or WordPerfect experience how to get started and how to preview finished work prior to printing. Chapter 2 is must reading.

Chapter 3 is devoted to document production tasks, focusing on correspondence applications—memos, letters, and resumes. It includes guidelines on format and the essential WordPerfect instructions needed to produce basic correspondence.

Chapter 4 is a set of supplemental instruction modules that supports all document production tasks but is most important for correspondence applications.

Chapter 5 is devoted to document production tasks but focuses on long documents—term papers, written case analyses, and management reports. The chapter's initial section includes guidelines on document construction and tips for producing a higher quality final product in a shorter period of time. The sections on term papers, case analyses, and management reports advise on conducting library research; and on planning, organizing, producing, and packaging each of the long document types. The final section in Chapter 5 is an instruction set that explains how to produce and package long documents using WordPerfect's powerful features.

Chapter 6 includes a collection of supplemental instruction sets that are most important for long document applications. Examples are "Constructing Tables," "Headers and Footers," and "Preparing a Title Page."

Chapter 7 focuses on important word-processing tasks that do not produce *documents* in the usual sense of that term. The chapter has three sections. The first section tells how to prepare outlines, the second explains how to perform several different merge operations; and the third explains how to prepare and print mailing labels.

Chapter 8 provides instructions for some advanced WordPerfect features that many readers may find useful. Among the features covered are macros, sorting, importing and exporting ASCII text, and column operations.

Chapter 9 instruction sets are in the nature of utilities and would be used only infrequently by most readers. Examples are instruction sets for installing WordPerfect and canceling print requests.

ACKNOWLEDGEMENTS

The book reflects the contributions of many people over a long period of time. Paul Arsenault, who worked with me on a similar project in the early 80s, had an important impact on my early thinking as have some of my more recent colleagues. In particular, I'd like to thank my colleague, Carolyn Browder, who carefully worked through two versions of the manuscript and provided insightful comments and suggestions and the all-important written communications perspective. Other colleagues who provided sound advice and welcome encouragement are Jean Hopson, Chuck Kennedy, and Ken Middaugh. I would also like to thank my graduate assistants, Rajesh Saggi and Ajay Sareen, who carefully and patiently tested the WordPerfect instructions and gave me all-important "student-user" reactions to the work. Tina Duvall is another good friend who patiently worked through early versions of this material. I also benefited greatly from the excellent and tireless product testing and secretarial assistance of Carolyn McDonald, a person of constant good humor and endless patience. I must also thank Bill Wicker and Liz Kendall at Prentice-Hall for their willingness to take a chance on an untried concept and wait a bit long for the finished product.

1

Introduction

1-1 THE CONCEPT

WordPerfect Applications for Business Students is a collection of modular instruction sets that lets the casual student user of WordPerfect create a document with little or no training or assistance. The book is designed so that a reader possessing basic keyboard skills and some experience with personal computers—but no prior WordPerfect experience—can complete a reasonably complex document creation task at a single sitting.

The book emphasizes documents that business students are most apt to prepare. It includes chapters on standard correspondence such as memos, letters, and resumes; on long course-oriented documents such as term papers, case analyses, and management reports; and on specialized documents such as outlines, merge letters, and labels. Detailed instructions are provided for each document type.

The book also provides guidance on document formats. If you aren't sure-footed on these matters, adopting the formats used here should enable you to produce documents that will pass muster in most business courses. The chapter on long documents provides additional guidance on document planning and construction.

The instruction set modules in *WordPerfect Applications* tell you how to type, edit, and print a document. They also tell you how to complete related support tasks such as preparing a table of contents.

The book's purpose is to provide you with just the bare essentials needed to produce an acceptable document or complete a supplemental operation. In the interest of getting you up and running as quickly as possible, we've taken a "no-frills" approach in the sense that we've omitted coverage of WordPerfect features most business students would be unlikely to use. Examples are "Type Through", "Concordance", and "Passwords".

Who Is the Casual User?

A *casual user* is defined to be anyone who uses word processing software on an occasional basis. The casual user is typified by the manager or professional who writes a long memo or report at night or on weekends when secretarial support isn't available. The college professor who types her own notes and research papers is another obvious example. So is the student who types term papers and correspondence because professional help is too expensive.

These characteristics typify casual users:

- They've usually had some previous experience with microcomputers or terminals, but they're word processing novices.
- They have severe time constraints and are only infrequent users of personal computers or terminals—a two-hour session once a week might be typical.
- They tend to forget the complex, patterned strings of instructions needed to create, edit, and print documents.
- They are highly task-oriented and want to complete specific, well-defined tasks such as producing a letter and envelope in a single session.
- They don't like the usual vendor training and user manuals and the massive "how to" books available through the mail and from large chain book stores.
- Finally, they are unsure of themselves in matters of format, style, and usage.

Design Principles

To meet the needs of casual users, the following design principles were adopted to guide development of the book.

- *Focus on Document-Creation Tasks. WordPerfect Applications* tells you how to perform well-defined word processing tasks such as preparing letters and envelopes, case analyses, resumes, and term papers.
- *Provide Standard Models.* A "no frills" *standard* model is adopted for each task included in *WordPerfect Applications.* Operationally, that means you are instructed how to perform a given task using a simple, direct approach.
- *Use Authoritative Examples.* The example documents included in *WordPerfect Applications* are authoritative in that they conform to guidelines found in leading source materials on written business communications.

- *Organize Instructions into Easily Located Modules.* Most instruction books on word processing software are *feature-* and *operator-oriented*: they emphasize special features of the software and have raising the reader's skill level to that of the reasonably competent secretary or word processing operator as their purpose. *WordPerfect Applications,* on the other hand, is *task-* and *casual-user*-oriented. It emphasizes the word processing features and operations needed to complete documents usually prepared by students. Common operations such as editing text, printing, and spell-checking are detailed in easily-located, stand-alone modules that are separate from the more or less unique instructions associated with specific document types.

  Four categories of instruction set modules were developed for *WordPerfect Applications*: (1) task-specific instructions, (2) support instructions, (3) advanced features, and (4) utility instructions.

  - *Task-specific Instructions* are instructions that are unique to a particular type of document. Examples are "Writing a Management Report" and "Preparing an Outline."
  - *General Support Instruction Sets* are modular instruction sets for operations that are common to most document types and are almost always required. Examples are "Printing Documents" and "Editing Text."
  - *Long Document Support Instruction Sets* show how to perform operations that are usually required to produce a finished document. Examples of Long Document Support Instruction Sets are "Using the Thesaurus," "Hyphenation," and "Preparing a Bibliography."
  - *Advanced Features* tell you how to perform operations that can improve productivity but that also require an additional time commitment. Examples are "Creating Macros" or "Sorting Text."
  - *Utility Instruction Sets* tell you how to configure your system, define a printer, or perform some other task having to do with setting up your work environment.

- *Employ Consistent Terminology.* Wherever possible, consistency of convention and terminology between *WordPerfect Applications* and WordPerfect's own training and reference manuals was maintained. This principle was adopted to ensure compatibility between *WordPerfect Applications* and standard WordPerfect user documentation.
- *Provide Basic Guidelines on Format, Usage and Style.* Many casual student users are not entirely comfortable writing letters and reports because they lack confidence in their writing skill and are uncertain about standard document formats. It seemed only natural to provide some help with these problems to accompany the more explicit instructions on WordPerfect.

Assumptions About Your Environment

We make the following assumptions about your word processing environment:

- You are using a personal computer equipped with the IBM standard or enhanced layout keyboard or a similarly equipped PC.
- Your PC is equipped with a hard disk drive and a floppy drive.
- The computer's operating system, MS-DOS/PC-DOS (henceforth referred to as "DOS") and WordPerfect are both loaded on the system and you know the name of the disk directory where WordPerfect resides. (If WordPerfect hasn't been installed, read the Utility Instruction Set in Chapter 9 called "Installing WordPerfect.")
- You have a dot matrix printer such as one of the IBM, Epson, or Okidata machines set for continuous form paper or you have a Hewlett-Packard LaserJet or compatible. If your printer hasn't been *defined* in your WordPerfect software, that is, if WordPerfect hasn't been told to recognize your particular brand and model of printer, read the Utility Instruction Set in Chapter 9 called "Defining and Selecting Printers."
- Your PC doesn't share WordPerfect on a local area network (LAN). If you *do* share WordPerfect on a LAN, ask a network user consultant for the commands needed to access the network version of the software.

To the extent that the assumptions listed aren't met, some translation between assumed and actual environments may be required. For example, if the key tops on your keyboard don't match those on the standard or enhanced IBM PC keyboards, modification of some of the instructions provided will be necessary.

1-2 FINDING MODULES

Several methods may be used to find the instructions needed to complete a particular task. One familiar method is to look for the required instruction module in the table of contents at the *front* of the book and then turn to the page indicated. Another familiar approach is to turn to the index at the *back* of the book, look up the words and phrases you'd expect to be included in a particular set of instructions, and then turn to the page or pages listed there. A third approach is to use the tabs at the edges of the pages in the book. Numbered tabs mark chapters; labeled tabs mark task-specific, support, and utility instruction sets as well as advanced features. A fourth approach is to follow the branching information included here and at the end of each task-specific instruction set. For example, the following branching information is at the end of the instruction set on creating a letter:

Task-specific Instruction Set	*Chapter and Section*	*Page*
Editing Text	4-1	44
Spell Checking	4-2	48
Printing documents	4-3	49

Finally, for each task-specific instruction set (writing a memo, for example), Fig. 1-1 shows page numbers of the support instruction sets and advanced features that pertain to the listed task. To use the figure, identify the task to be completed in the first column. Next, move across its row to find the support modules and advanced features that supplement the task specific instructions. Then find initial page numbers for the supplemental modules in the second or "page number" row. For example, observe that "Writing a Memo" is listed on the left side of the figure. Glancing across that row, note the check marks under "Editing Text," "Spell Checking," "Printing Documents," and "Leaving WordPerfect." They signal that the supplemental instruction sets checked are required for the completion of the document in question.

1- 3 WHAT ISN'T COVERED

Some operations are not addressed in *WordPerfect Applications* because they are outside the boundaries of WordPerfect. Examples are:

- Changing printer ribbons
- Changing daisy wheels
- Loading toner cartridges
- Loading paper

Some operations within the boundaries of WordPerfect have also been excluded from coverage. Examples are:

- Type through
- Concordance
- Redline and strikeout
- Document summaries
- Indexes
- Table of authorities
- Passwords
- Math

Support Instruction Sets and Advanced Features	Pages	Memo (23)	Letter (29)	Resume (37)	Term Paper (75)	Written Case Analysis (84)	Management Report (96)	Outline (172)	Merge Letters (182)	Membership Lists (195)	Mailing Labels (198)
Editing Text	45	✓	✓	✓	✓	✓	✓	✓	✓	✓	✓
Spell Checking	49	✓	✓	✓	✓	✓	✓	✓	✓	✓	✓
Printing Documents	51	✓	✓	✓	✓	✓	✓	✓	✓	✓	✓
Numbering Pages	55		✓		✓	✓	✓	✓	✓		
Creating, Editing, and Printing Envelopes	58		✓						✓		
Leaving WordPerfect	63	✓	✓	✓	✓	✓	✓	✓	✓	✓	✓
References to Other Work	117				✓	✓	✓				
Constructing Tables	122	✓	✓	✓	✓	✓	✓		✓		
Importing Figures	139	✓	✓		✓	✓	✓		✓		
Using the Thesaurus	144			✓	✓	✓	✓				
Hyphenation	146				✓	✓	✓				
Headers and Footers	150				✓	✓	✓				
Preparing a Bibliography	152				✓	✓	✓				
Listing Tables and Figures	157				✓		✓				
Preparing a Table of Contents	162				✓		✓				
Preparing a Title Page	167				✓		✓				
Working with Graphics	207				✓	✓	✓				
Sorting Lines and Paragraphs	226				✓	✓	✓		✓	✓	✓
Formatting Text in Columns	232				✓	✓	✓				
Drawing Lines and Boxes	239				✓	✓	✓				
Working with Equations	245				✓	✓	✓				
Importing and Exporting ASCII Text	257	✓	✓		✓	✓	✓		✓	✓	✓

Task-Specific Instruction Sets: Applications / Pages

Figure 1-1 Instruction Module Map

Instructions for these categories of operations were omitted because they are usually of little interest to the casual user and are performed rarely, if ever. The omitted operations are usually well explained by a vendor's own hardware documentation (printers), or covered in the WordPerfect workbook and reference manual (WordPerfect features) in any event.

2

GETTING STARTED

This is an *important chapter* because it's the foundation for *all* subsequent instructions; read it carefully before you attempt your first word processing task. The purpose of the chapter is to:

- Describe the keyboard and mouse
- Explain how the keyboard is used and how sequences and combinations of keystrokes are depicted in the instructions
- Explain how to select options from pull-down menus
- Explain the purpose of notes and warnings included in the instructions
- List and explain standard conventions applicable to all instruction sets
- Describe how to set up a user directory and how to run WordPerfect
- Describe how to reveal formatting codes
- Describe how to preview a printer image of a document

2-1 THE KEYBOARD AND MOUSE

If you're not sitting in front of a PC, examine the keyboard diagrams shown in Fig. 2-1. Then read the sections below.

Typing Keys

The typing keys are the character keys 1 through = on the top row, Q through] on the second row, A through ' on the third row, and Z through / on the bottom row.

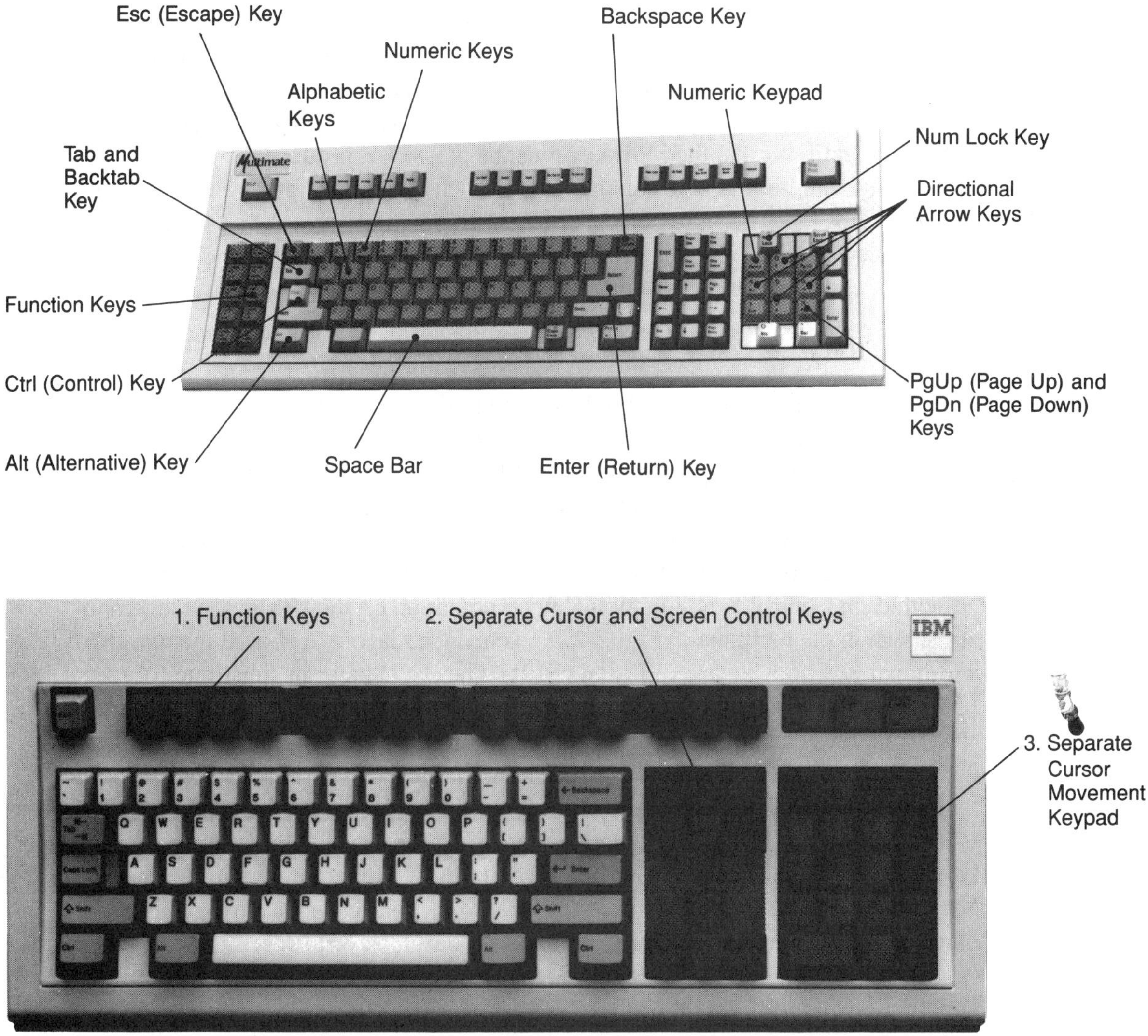

Figure 2-1 IBM Layout and Enhanced Layout Keyboards

These keys are more or less standard on manual, electric, and electronic typewriters and have been so for many years. Six other keys that perform many of the same functions in WordPerfect that they perform on a typewriter are “Tab,” “Shift,” “Back Space,” “Caps Lock,” “Space Bar,” and “Return” (or “Enter”). You’ll also find several keys on your keyboard that are not usually found on a standard typewriter: the "back slash" (\), "vertical bar" (|), and "tilde" (~) keys.

In most cases, PC keys work just like typewriter keys, but there are two important exceptions: (1) you must press the "1" key and *not* the "L" key to produce a 1, and (2) you must press the "0" key and *not* the letter "O" key to produce a zero. A third exception is that the Shift key must be pressed to produce the uppercase alternative of a non-alphabetic character even when the typing keys are locked in uppercase (Caps Lock is depressed). For example, you must press Shift and the 3 key to generate a pound sign (#). Likewise, you must press Shift and the semi-colon key to generate a colon.

Function Keys

Keys labeled (F1) through (F10) ((F1) through (F12) on the enhanced layout keyboard) are called "function keys" and are used either directly or in combination with Ctrl, Shift, or Alt keys to signal WordPerfect to perform important operations. For example, pressing (F4) tells WordPerfect that you'd like to indent text; pressing Shift and (F10) together prompts you for the name of a document file to be retrieved to the display screen from a hard disk or diskette. The operations associated with each Control Key/Function Key combination on the IBM layout keyboard are shown in the template in Fig. 2-2. The enhanced layout keyboard includes two additional functions keys: (F11) and (F12). The (F11) key can substitute for (Alt-F3), "Reveal Codes;" the (F12) key can substitute for (Alt-F4), "Block."

Four keys that control WordPerfect operations directly or in conjunction with other keys are "Ctrl" (Control), "Shift," "Alt," and "Esc" (Escape) keys. As the template in Fig. 2-2 indicates, the primary purpose of the Ctrl, Shift, and Alt keys is to modify the effect of the function keys. In WordPerfect, pressing the escape key lets you repeat the *next* keystroke several times. For example, if you press the Escape key, release it, and then press the space bar, you'll see the cursor (the small, blinking bar of light on your screen) jump to the right several spaces.

Delete, Insert, and Cursor Keys

The key marked "Del" or "Delete" deletes characters in a *forward* direction, one character at a time. The key marked "Backspace" deletes characters in a *backward* direction, one character at a time. (Keystroke combinations and sequences that delete words, sentences, paragraphs, and entire pages of text are described in Section 4- 1, "Editing Text.") Normally, WordPerfect is in *Insert* mode and typing new text pushes existing text to the right. Pressing the key marked "Ins" toggles WordPerfect into *Typeover* Mode so that typing new text *replaces* existing text. Additional keys on the right side of the keyboard with arrows and words like "Home," "End," "PgUp" and "PgDn" control the movement of the cursor. (The "Scroll

F1	**Shell** SETUP *Thesaurus* Cancel	**Spell** SEARCH <- *Replace* Search ->	F2
F3	**Screen** SWITCH *Reveal Codes* Help	**Move** -> INDENT <- *Block* -> Indent	F4
F5	**Text In/Out** DATE/OUTLINE *Mark Text* List Files	**Tab Align** CENTER *Flush Right* Bold	F6
F7	**Footnote** PRINT *Math/Columns* Exit	**Font** FORMAT *Style* Underline	F8
F9	**Merge/Sort** MERGE CODES *Graphics* Merge R	**Macro Def** RETRIEVE *Macro* Save	F10

Press Ctrl key (bold) and function key
Press SHIFT key (all caps) and function key
Press *Alt* key (*italics*) and function key

Figure 2-2 Function Key Template

Lock," "Prt Sc," and "5" keys have no direct cursor control function in WordPerfect 5.1.)

The Mouse

The mouse is a small, roll-around accessory device with two or three buttons used to select options from menus. Mice are also handy for moving your cursor around on your display screen, for drawing, and for other graphic work. Some PCs come equipped with a mouse as standard equipment; in other cases, the mouse must be purchased separately. If your PC has a mouse, we assume it has been installed properly and works the way it should. If you don't have a mouse already, buy one. The value of the time you'll save will quickly return your investment.

2-2 *NOTES AND WARNINGS*

When you prepare documents with these instruction sets, you'll see notes and warnings interspersed with instructions. *Notes* provide supplemental information explaining why what's on your screen may not be the same as what's on the printed page. Notes also contain practical advice and ideas about how a particular task might be accomplished in another way as well as information of a parenthetical nature. *Warnings* tell you that certain combinations and sequences of keystrokes may lead to trouble. Notes and warnings begin with the words, NOTE: or WARNING: in boldface type (darker, heavier type).

2-3 *CONVENTIONS AND TERMINOLOGY*

This section describes the book's conventions and terminology. For the most part, conventions and terminology are consistent with WordPerfect usage.

Conventions

The following conventions are adopted for all instruction sets.

- The wide key at the right of the "A" row is always referred to as the "Enter" key although it may be labeled "Return" or may be embossed with a left pointing arrow (←') on your own keyboard.
- Cursor control keys labeled with arrows are referred to as Up Arrow, Down Arrow, Right Arrow, and Left Arrow.
- Keys to be pressed are shown in boldface. For example,

  Shift means press the Shift key
  Home means press the Home key

  Letters or numbers to be typed are shown in boldface and surrounded by square brackets. An example would be "type [**3 1, 4**] to enter a date code."
- Examples of display screen prompts and messages from WordPerfect are shown in boldface (→ **Srch**, for example).

Terminology

Here are some frequently used terms:

- *CODES:* Codes are document formatting commands that WordPerfect uses to control the screen formatter and printer. For example, the codes, **[HRt]**, **[SRt]**, **[TAB]**, and **[Center]** translate to a hard return, a soft return, a tab, and center (the following) text. You can see the codes in the Reveal Codes screen (to be discussed below) by pressing (Alt-F3) (or (F11) if you have an enhanced layout keyboard).

NOTE: A *hard* return (**[HRt]**) is a return to the left margin on the next line down caused by pressing the Enter key. A *soft* return (**[SRt]**) is a return inserted by WordPerfect at the end of a line when it "wraps" text around to the left margin.

- *CURSOR:* The cursor is a small, blinking bar of light that indicates where the next character entered will appear on the screen. It's your type guide and can be moved by pressing the cursor control keys. You can also move the *blinking* cursor from place to place in the document displayed on your monitor by moving the *mouse* cursor (usually a small, highlighted rectangle) and pressing the left mouse button. The cursor can be located anywhere on the screen *where characters, tabs, and indents have been typed*; it can't be moved into blank screen space.
- *DOCUMENT:* A document is any electronic file stored on a hard disk or diskette in WordPerfect format.
- *NORMAL EDITING SCREEN:* The Normal Editing screen is the display screen area within which you create and edit reports, resumes, letters or other documents.
- *MESSAGES:* Messages are of four different types:
    - *Prompts:* Prompts appear at the bottom left side of the screen and signal an action to be taken by you. An example is the **Save document? Yes (No)** message that appears when you press (F7) to exit WordPerfect.
    - *System Action:* System action messages also appear at the bottom left side of the screen and describe what the system is doing during some operations. An example is the counter that reports on progress when a table of contents is being generated.
    - *Information Messages:* Are reminders such as Typeover that appear at the bottom left side of the screen.
    - *Error Messages:* Error messages appear at the bottom left side of the screen when you make a procedural error—specify the wrong drive, for example.
- *SCROLLING:* Scrolling is the visual phenomenon of text or data appearing to flow off the screen at the top, bottom, or sides. When screen images disappear from the top or bottom, the movement is called *vertical* scrolling. When they disappear from the sides, it's called *horizontal* scrolling.

2- 4 USING THE KEYBOARD AND MOUSE

This section explains that *key combinations* are multiple keys pressed simultaneously and that *key sequences* are multiple keys pressed sequentially. The section also describes key functions, that is, the actions that are performed when particular keys are pressed and explains how to use the *Microsoft* or compatible mouse with WordPerfect.

Key Combinations and Sequences

You will need to press *combinations* and *sequences* of keys to use WordPerfect effectively. A *key combination* is holding one key down and then pressing a second key. Key combinations are shown with the two keys separated by a hyphen and enclosed in parentheses. For example,

(Alt-F3)

means press and hold the Alt key and then press the F3 key. A *key sequence*, on the other hand, is pressing *and releasing* two or more keys in sequence. Key sequences are shown with the designated keys separated by commas. For example,

Home, Home, Up Arrow

means press and release the Home key twice and then press and release the Up Arrow key.

Frequently, you will press key combinations *and* key sequences. For example, to clear out the tab stops in a format line,

Press **(Shift-F8)**, type [L], [T], and press **Home**, **Home**, **Left Arrow**, and **(Ctrl-End)**.

Most WordPerfect features may be selected by pressing either number keys or letter keys. For example, the line format menu may be displayed by typing 1 or L after the (Shift-F8) combination is pressed. In *WordPerfect Applications* we've adopted the convention of always using mnemonic letters because that approach has become the standard for selecting options from a menu. Examples of popular software packages using the mnemonic approach are Harvard Graphics, Lotus 1-2-3, and the Norton Commander.

Key Functions

Key functions describe the operations of individual keys.

- *CANCEL* (F1): CANCEL tells WordPerfect to ignore or back out of the set of instructions you've just entered. (For multi-level tasks, you may need to press (F1) more than once.) IMPORTANT: *Pressing (F1) and then typing R also "undeletes" up to three prior deletions, restoring the lost text to your screen in doing so.*
- *ENTER:* The Enter key corresponds to the Return key on a typewriter (and on some personal computer keyboards). When you're working in the Normal Editing screen, pressing the Enter key generates a hard return. In response to a prompt, on the other hand, pressing Enter tells WordPerfect that you accept the action it proposes. In that role, the Enter key functions as an *Execute* key.
- *HELP* (F3): Pressing (F3) toggles on WordPerfect's help screens. Learning about Help is best done through experimentation and the instructions in the

help screens themselves. The help in WordPerfect is "context-sensitive." This means that the help message you see relates directly to a function key sequence or feature. For example, to get help on how to run a macro, press (Alt-F10) and then press (F3).

NOTE: Pressing (F3) twice in a row displays an image of the function key template on your screen. Very handy if you've misplaced your regular feature template.

- *NUM LOCK:* The Num Lock key is at the top right of your keyboard. Normally, Num Lock is inactive, meaning that the cursor control/numeric key group is controlling cursor movement. When the numeric key group is inactive, pressing Num Lock toggles the numeric keys on (and cursor control off). You can usually enter large numbers of numeric values more quickly and accurately with the numeric key group. Generally, it's best in WordPerfect to type numbers by using the keys in the top row of the typing group rather than the keys in the numeric key group.

  You may find that Num Loc is engaged when you start your PC. If so, a light will be lit on the key itself or on a nearby panel, and the word, "Pos," will be blinking at the bottom of your screen. If Num Loc is engaged when your PC boots (starts up), press the Num Loc key to disengage it.

  NOTE: Cursor control keys are separate from the numeric key group (or "key pad") on the enhanced layout keyboard (see Fig. 2-1).

Using the Mouse

If you have a mouse installed, you should see a small rectangle of light on your display screen, called a "Mouse Cursor," that moves about when you roll the mouse around on a desk or tabletop. In this book, we describe how to use a two-button *Microsoft* mouse with WordPerfect. Other, three-button mice operate in a similar fashion although you may need to experiment a bit to reveal the similarities and differences between the operation of your own mouse and that of the *Microsoft* mouse. In WordPerfect, the left button is used to *select* a menu option once the mouse cursor has been moved to that option. This action is often referred to as "pointing and shooting" or "clicking on" an option.

The *right* mouse button usually performs the same functions as the (F7) (Exit) key. That is, it terminates an activity, closes a menu panel, etc. The right button does *not* perform the same functions as the (F7) key when you are working in editing screens other than the Normal Editing screen—e.g., the Endnote, Footnote, or Header/Footer editing screens. The right button sometimes functions as an "Execute" key to activate options. For example, use the left button to select the "Forward" option from the panel that drops down when you click on "Search" in the menu bar. After you've typed some text in response to the -> Srch prompt, press the *right* button to *execute* the search (instead of pressing (F2) a second time as you'd have to do if you weren't using a mouse). Finally, the right button displays the menu bar if WordPerfect has not been set up to always display the menu bar. (Pressing the right button produces the same result as typing (Alt-=).)

2- 5 PULL-DOWN MENUS

Version 5.1 of WordPerfect includes a menu *bar* and pull-down menu *panels* that let you select options and features by using your cursor keys, by typing certain letter keys, or by "pointing and shooting" with a mouse.

There are three layers of menus in WordPerfect 5.1. At the first layer is a horizontal menu bar with nine options that can be displayed at the top of your screen. The menu bar is shown in Fig. 2-3.

If the menu bar isn't displayed automatically when you run WordPerfect, it can be made to appear by pressing and holding the Alt key and typing an equals sign (or by pressing the right mouse button if your PC is equipped with a mouse).

NOTE: If you'd like the menu bar to be visible all the time, run WordPerfect and take the next five steps. (If you aren't using a mouse, you'll still need to type (Alt-=) to activate the menu and *select* one of the nine options displayed.)

- Press **(Shift-F1)** for systems set up.
- Type [**D**] to select display options.
- Type [**M**] to select menu options.
- Type [**V**], [**Y**] to keep the menu bar visible whenever WordPerfect is running.
- Press **(F7)** to return to the Normal Editing screen.

After the menu bar has been activated, the second layer of menu *panels* can be displayed by highlighting one of the nine menu bar options and pressing Enter, by typing the boldfaced letter marking the desired option, or by moving the mouse cursor over the desired option and pressing the left button. For example, select the "Tools" options by typing t or the "Font" options by typing o. A panel of sub-options is displayed for each menu bar option. Should you inadvertently pull down

File Edit Search Layout Mark Tools Font Graphics Help

Figure 2-3 Menu Bar

the wrong panel, press the left or right cursor arrow key to highlight the correct option. Alternatively, move your mouse cursor to the preferred option and press the left button.

When the desired panel has been pulled down, select options by following the procedure for selecting menu bar options described above. Selecting some options from a panel will generate a prompt to make a yes-no decision (the "Save" option on the "File" panel, for example). Selecting other options displays a third menu level (the "Text In" option on the "File" panel, for example). Selecting still other options displays a numbered and lettered menu not incorporated in a panel (the "Document Summary" option on the "File" panel, for example). Finally, selecting some options causes WordPerfect to perform an action directly. An example is the "Reveal Codes" option on the "Edit" panel. When you type R in the edit panel (or select that option by pointing at it and shooting with your mouse), you immediately display the "Reveal Codes" split screen.

Menu Selections are Shown as Thick Bordered Boxes

We represent mouse or cursor key selection of menu options by displaying the option or options in a *box with thick borders.* Selection of a menu option from a *standard menu* (not a menu bar or pull down panel) is indicated by a bold capital letter, and typed input is shown in brackets. If the input is specific—e.g., the word "envelope," it is shown in roman (upright) style. If the input is general—e.g., "filename," it is shown in italic (slanted) style. Pressing a mouse button is indicated by the letter R (for right) or L (for left) within angle brackets. If you have a mouse, just click the mouse cursor on the lines in standard menus. The mouse cursor need not be on the specific letter indicated. When a function or control key is enclosed in angle brackets—e.g., <Enter>, <(F7)> press the key indicated. Here are several examples,

```
Tools
        Spell  D
```

Means select *Tools* from the Menu Bar, the *Spell* option from the Tools Panel, and spell check the full *d*ocument.

```
Layout
        Endnote
                Create
```

Means select *Layout* from the Menu Bar, *Endnote* from the Layout Panel, and *Create* from the Endnote Options.

File			
	Text In		
		Spreadsheet	
			Import F

Means select *File* from the Menu Bar, *Text In* from the File Panel, *Spreadsheet* from the Text In panel, *Import* from the Spreadsheet Options, and *F*ilename on the Spreadsheet: Import menu. As you use the instructions, you may at times have difficulty linking the text instructions and the menu box instructions. The key is the thick black line ■■■ in the left border. All instructions between the black line and the next menu box are included in the box. If you don't see a black line between two menu boxes, then all the instructions between the two boxes are captured in the second box.

Although you may get started in WordPerfect by selecting most options from the pull-down menus, you'll quickly learn that pressing function keys to use WordPerfect options and features is often more effective. There are exceptions to this general rule, of course: one is the Spell Checking feature. As you develop proficiency with WordPerfect, you'll undoubtedly use pull-down menus and function keys in unique combinations that best fit your own personal working style.

2- 6 SYSTEM SET-UP

We assume WordPerfect is on your disk in a subdirectory named WP51. If you're unsure about the disk location of WordPerfect, ask someone for help or re-install WordPerfect according to the instructions given in the Utility Instruction set in Chapter 9 called "Installing WordPerfect."

Switch on your PC and enter the date and time.

NOTE: It's important to enter the date and time when you boot your system because WordPerfect uses that information to generate the current date and time in your documents. (If your computer has a built-in, battery-operated clock, date and time may be set already.)

In response to the DOS prompt,

C:\>,

type [**MD USER**] and press Enter.

The DOS command, MD USER, creates a new subdirectory called "USER" to hold all the documents you produce using WordPerfect and *WordPerfect Applications for Business Students.* It's only necessary to create the "user" subdirectory once although you should switch to it every time you run WordPerfect.

Finally, type [**CD\USER**] and press **Enter** to switch to the "User" subdirectory. You should now be ready to begin producing and packaging documents with WordPerfect.

Before you read the next two sections, we suggest that you run WordPerfect and type a few sentences of free-form text just to get the feel of the program and the look of the Normal Editing screen. Follow the three additional steps below to do so.

- Type [**PATH WP51**] and press **Enter** to create a path to the WordPerfect directory. (If WordPerfect is in a directory other than WP51, substitute the name of the other directory for WP51 in the path command above.)
- Type [**WP**] and press **Enter** to run WordPerfect.
- Type your text sample, being sure to let some text "wrap around" to the left margin by typing text lines too long to fit on one line of your display screen. Also be sure to end some lines by pressing Enter before you reach the right side of the screen. Finally try pressing Tab at the beginning of one or two lines.

2-7 REVEAL CODES

Unlike some word processing software, WordPerfect hides formatting codes to show you a less cluttered display screen work area. Nevertheless, formatting codes are used by the program to perform essential functions such as centering, bolding, or underlining text. Special codes are also required to instruct your printer to center text vertically or to advance the print head away from the top left corner of the page.

Although formatting codes are usually hidden from view, you can make them appear when you need to. To see the codes in a WordPerfect document, press **(Alt-F3)**; to switch back to the full Normal Editing screen press **(Alt-F3)** again. (Press **(F11)** if you have an enhanced layout keyboard—it's easier.) When you reveal codes, the screen is split into two windows by a "tab ruler," a reverse-video bar with small triangles indicating the relative positions of tab stops. Your text is in the upper window clear of formatting codes; the same text with formatting codes revealed is in the lower window. *Codes may be deleted just like text characters.* It's also possible to search for and replace format codes just as you'd search for and replace letters, numbers, and punctuation marks.

2-8 VIEWING A DOCUMENT

WordPerfect also lets you check the appearance of a printed document without going to the trouble of actually producing a hard copy on a printer. By using this feature, you avoid the frustration of printing out a long but incorrectly formatted document.

If your PC has a graphics adapter, you can produce an attractive replica of your document on the display screen. To do so, press **(Shift-F7)** to select print options and then type [**V**] to view the printer image of your document. The full-page image (option 3 in the menu at the bottom of your display screen) will probably not be readable, but it still shows the format of your document including page number placement, footnotes, vertical and horizontal lines, and the positions of any graphic images you may have included. If you select options 2 or 3, you can read the text, but you won't see the entire document.

3

Correspondence Applications

This chapter contains instructions for producing memos, letters, and resumes. Each instruction set provides detailed, step-by-step guidance for constructing a model document following a generally accepted layout. Given that the purpose of *WordPerfect Applications* is to provide model documents, style and format guidance, and explicit WordPerfect instructions for constructing specific document types at widely-spaced time intervals, each primary instruction set is intended to be self-contained and independent of other *primary* instruction sets.

Each instruction set in Chapter 3 has Overview and Procedure subsections, and each is linked to other sets of *supporting* instructions in Chapter 4. Overview subsections indicate the purpose of the document type, describes its basic elements, present one or more examples of standard layouts, and provide useful hints and helps. Procedure subsections include detailed WordPerfect instructions for producing the particular document type. We provide guidance in the next three sections that applies to all documents, but especially to correspondence.

Create Documents Step by Step

When you produce documents, try to follow these simple steps.

- Plan the document on a piece of scrap paper, outlining the major points.
- Select an appropriate layout.
- Create text by composing your thoughts at the keyboard or by typing from a previously written draft.

- Edit your first draft to make it more concise and increase clarity and focus.
- Spell check the edited draft.
- Review the printer image of your document in the View Document screen.
- Print the draft and carefully proofread it again.

Don't Right Justify Text

In the document processing field, the term, "justification," refers to the precise alignment of text on the left side, right side, or both sides of a document. Justification on both sides of a document is referred to as "Full" justification and is the WordPerfect default condition. Not surprisingly, many newcomers to word processing favor full justification because of its book-like appearance and novelty. When full justification is used with "fixed-space" fonts, however, the printed document often has the appearance of a Martian landscape. (A fixed-space font is a set of characters all of equal width. Examples are the common fonts, Courier and Prestige Elite, both of which have crossed over from typewriters to the word processing world.)

Unless you plan to use proportionally spaced fonts for your correspondence, take the following steps to switch to left justification only (assuming WordPerfect is running and the Normal Editing screen is displayed),

- Press **(Shift-F8)** and type [L], [J], [L] to switch on left justification.
- Press **(F7)** to return to the Normal Editing screen.

```
Layout
        Line  J, L, <R>
```

NOTE: The last instructions toggle off full justification only for the document you're working on right now. Take the following additional steps to ensure that all your documents are left justified.

- Press **(Shift-F1)** to select Setup options.
- Type [I] and [C] to select Initial Settings and Initial Codes.

```
File
        Setup
                Initial Settings  C
```

- Press **(Shift-F8)**, type [L], [J], [L], and press **(F7)** to repeat the earlier instructions. By setting justification left in the system setup, you ensure that the instruction applies to all of your documents.

- Press **(F7)** twice to return to your document.

> Layout
> Line J, L, <R>, <(F7)>, <(F7)>

Pay Close Attention to Spelling and Grammar

Be especially careful to use every resource available to ensure that your grammar and spelling are *absolutely* correct. Documents that include easily avoidable errors attest loudly to carelessness and immaturity. Perhaps your most powerful support tool will be WordPerfect's own spell checker, but don't ignore grammar checkers such as *Grammatik* and *RightWriter.*

3-1 *WRITING A MEMO*

Instructions in this section show you how to write a simple business memo. The Overview subsection provides format and construction guidelines, while the Procedure subsection contains instructions on how to produce a memo with WordPerfect. If you haven't read Chapter 2 yet, do so now; it contains essential background information and instructions you should follow before you begin typing the memo.

Overview

Memos are internal business communications written to individuals who work for the same organization. Most memos have five elements:

- The *date,* usually written in month, day, and year format.
- The *to line,* showing the name of the individual (or group of individuals) to whom the memo is to be sent.
- The *from line,* showing your name and handwritten initials.
- The *subject line,* stating the purpose of the memo. Subject lines should be brief, to the point, and in the nature of a headline announcing the contents of the body. Don't use the subject line to summarize the body of the memo.

  NOTE: Write the subject line *after* the body of the memo is written.

- The *body,* containing the message you're attempting to convey.

Most memos follow one of the three layouts shown in Fig. 3-1. (There are frequent departures from these layouts from organization to organization.) The sample memo in Fig. 3-2 conforms to the second of the three layouts. No matter which layout you select, make your memo concise and to the point. Be sure each

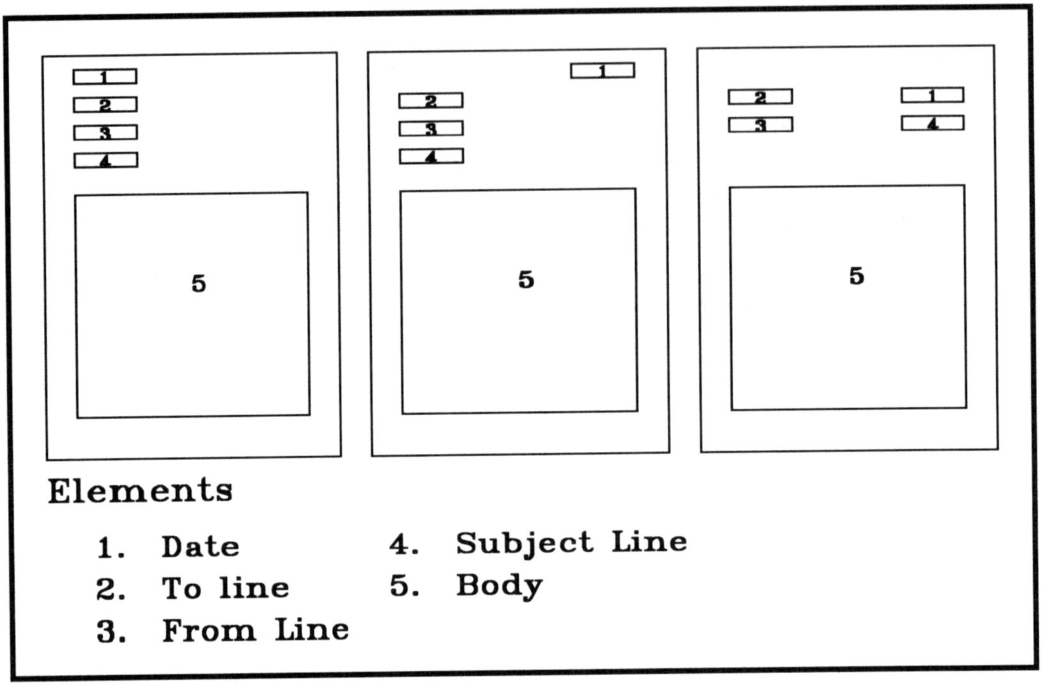

Figure 3-1 Memo Layouts

paragraph focuses on a single idea and begins with a topic sentence that tells the reader exactly what the paragraph is about.

Procedure

1. Type [**WP**] and press Enter to run WordPerfect. Before typing text, notice the status line at the bottom of the screen. From left to right, it shows document number (Doc 1 or Doc 2), page number (Pg), the *vertical position* of the cursor (Ln) measured in inches from the top of the page, and the *horizontal position* of the cursor (Pos) measured in inches from the left edge of the page.

   NOTE: You always have two Normal Editing screens active in WordPerfect at the same time. The first screen is called Doc 1; the second is called Doc 2. Press (Shift-F3) to switch back and forth.

   NOTE: If you're working on a document saved previously, the status line also shows document name (including drive designation and subdirectory names, if any).

   An important *menu* you don't see on your WordPerfect screen is used to set margins, tab stops, and line spacing. It's called the Format menu. Let's use it now to be sure margin settings are OK. To see margin settings, press **(Shift-F8)** and type [**L**]; to change them, type [**M**] once the menu is displayed.

Layout
Line M, [*left margin*], <R>, [*right margin*], <R>

NOTE: Margin settings of 1" left and right are good default settings for a memo.

To see tab settings (assuming you're still in the Format: Line menu),

- Type [**T**] for Tab settings, [**T**] for Type, and [**R**] for Relative.
- Since you only need tabs at 0.5" and 1", relative to the left margin, press **(Ctrl-End)** to delete any existing tabs. (The key combination, (Ctrl-End), also deletes the characters from the cursor to the end of a text line.)
- Type [**0.5**], press **Enter**, type [**1**], and press **Enter** again. Notice that "L"s appear at positions +.5 and +1 in the tab set line. (Be sure to type "0.5" and not "5". If you make a mistake, just delete the "R" and "L" by moving your cursor under each letter and pressing the delete key.)
- Press **(F7)** to return to the Format: Line menu.

T, T, R, <(Ctrl-End)>, [0.5], <R>, [1], <R>, <R>

If line spacing is set at 1 (single spacing), press **(F7)** to return to the Normal Editing screen. Otherwise, type [**S**], change the number to 1 and press **(F7)** twice to return to the Normal Editing screen.

S, [1], <R>, <R>

For a memo, good formatting rules of thumb are:

- Single spacing
- Left and right margins of 1 inch
- Top and bottom margins of 1 inch
- Tabs at 0.5 and 1 inches relative to the left margin

NOTE: The Format: Line menu displayed information called "initial settings" or "default settings." Generally, if these settings will meet your needs, don't alter them.

2. You should now be ready to type your memo, but look at Fig. 3-2 before you do so. Press **(Shift-F6)**, **(F6)**, **Caps Lock** and then type [**memorandum**] as

```
                         MEMORANDUM

DATE:        August 23, 1991

TO:          Charles Taylor
             Mary Neems
             Frank Brown

FROM:        Mark J. Rodgers

SUBJECT:     Payroll Software Package Evaluation


     It's time for us to meet and evaluate the five payroll package proposals
we've received from the vendors we solicited late last month. Therefore, please
mark your calendars for a meeting on Thursday, March 1, at 2:30 P.M., in the
board room.

     Gerry Lord and Bob Harrelson have been invited to sit in on our discussion.


cc:  John Role
```

Figure 3-2 Memo Example

you would on a typewriter. (Notice what happens to the information on the status line.) Then press **(F6)**, **Caps Lock**, and **Enter** three times.

3. To produce today's date in your memo, type [**DATE:**], press **Tab**, **Tab**, **(Shift-F5)**, and type [T]. Press **Enter** twice.

Tools	
	Date Text

4. Type [**TO:**], press **Tab**, **Tab** and type the addressee's name. Press **Enter** twice. (If there are additional addressees—as there are in this example—press **Tab**, **Tab**, type the name and press **Enter** for each additional addressee prior to pressing the second Enter.)
5. Type [**FROM:**], press **Tab**, **Tab**, type your own name, and press **Enter** twice.
6. This is a good place to toggle on Reveal Codes to see what WordPerfect's formatting codes look like. Press **(Alt-F3)** to do so (or **(F11)** if you have an enhanced layout keyboard). Press **(Alt-F3)** (or **(F11)**) to toggle Reveal Codes off again.

Edit	
	Reveal Codes

7. Type [**SUBJECT:**], press **Tab**, type the subject of your memo, and press **Enter** three times.
8. Press **Tab** and type the text of your memo.

   NOTE: You needn't press Enter every time you come to the end of a line because WordPerfect "wraps around" automatically to the beginning of the next line. But do press Enter when you want to end a paragraph or otherwise end a line of text prematurely.

If your memo is to be single spaced (the normal case), leave a blank line between paragraphs by pressing **Enter** twice at the end of each paragraph. Also press **Tab** at the beginning of each new paragraph to indent the first line five spaces.

If your memo is longer than a single page, break it up with side headings. They make it easier for the reader to digest your ideas and provide signposts for later reference. Starting at the end of a paragraph, here is how to create an underlined, sentence-style headline.

- Press **Enter** twice to move your cursor to the left margin.
- Press **(F8)** to toggle on underlining, type the headline sentence-style—that is, capitalize only the first letter of the first word—and then press **(F8)**, **Enter**, **Enter**, **Tab** to toggle off underlining, skip a line, and tab over to be ready to begin the first paragraph after the heading.

9. If a copy of your memo is to be sent to someone other than the person to whom it's addressed, press **Enter** three times at the end of the memo's text, type the letters, cc:, press **Tab** and then type the name of the person to whom the copy is to be sent. If several persons are to receive copies, add the other name or names directly below the first. Be sure to press **Tab** before each additional name.
10. Do the following to proofread your memo:

    10.1 Review the text to ensure that all necessary punctuation is included.

    NOTE: Two spaces follow a period, question mark, or exclamation point at the end of a sentence; single spaces follow punctuation marks within sentences—that is, commas, semicolons, and colons.

    10.2 Carefully examine the text, using Up Arrow and Down Arrow to move a line at a time, or the - and + keys at the right of the numeric keypad to jump to the top and bottom of the screen to scan for errors. To move to the top of your document—even if it has multiple pages—press **Home**, **Home**, **Up Arrow**; to move to the bottom, press **Home**, **Home**, **Down Arrow**.

Press either **Right Arrow** or **Left Arrow** to move a character at a time within a line. Press **(Ctrl-Right Arrow)** or **(Ctrl-Left Arrow)** to move a word at a time forward or backward; press **End** to move to the right end of the line; and press **Home**, **Home**, **Left Arrow** to move to the left end of the line before any text.

NOTE: Pressing Home, Home, Home, Left Arrow moves the cursor to the left of any codes at the left end of the line (codes are visible only when you reveal codes).

11. Turn to the instruction set called "Editing Text" (see Section 4- 1) for additional editing support.
12. Turn to the instruction set called "Spell Checking" (see Section 4- 2) to see how to use the WordPerfect spell checking feature.
13. When you've finished editing and spell-checking your memo, press **(F7).** WordPerfect prompts you with,

    Save document? Yes (No)

    with the cursor flashing under Y. Press **Enter** and WordPerfect requests a document name. Type a name—CATMEM01.W51, for example—and press **Enter**. Next, WordPerfect prompts you to exit. If you just want to clear your Normal Editing screen, press **Enter**; if you want to return to DOS, type [**Y**].

File
Exit Y, [*filename*], Y

NOTE: If you wish to save your memo on a floppy disk in drive A instead of on the hard drive, type [**A:CATMEM01.W51**] and press **Enter** when WordPerfect prompts you for a document name.

14. If you didn't complete your task in one sitting, recall your memo to the screen. Here's how.

    14.1 Assuming WordPerfect is still running, press **(F5)**, **Enter** to see a list of your files. If not, type [**WP**] and press **Enter** before pressing **(F5)**.

File
List Files <R>

NOTE: If you saved your memo on a diskette in drive A, type [**A:**] and press **Enter** after you press **(F5)**.

14.2 To recall your memo, press the cursor arrows or use your mouse to highlight its name and type [**R**].

NOTE: An alternative way to retrieve the memo is to press **(Shift-F10)**, and, in response to WordPerfect's prompt,

Document to be retrieved: ,

type [***document name***] and press **Enter**. If the document has been saved on a floppy disk, type [**A:*document name***] and then press **Enter.**

File
Retrieve [*filename*], <R>

15. Turn to the Instruction Sets listed below to complete the preparation of your memo.

Instruction Set	*Section*
Editing Text	4-1
Spell Checking	4-2
Printing Documents	4-3
Leaving WordPerfect	4-6

3- 2 WRITING A LETTER

Instructions in this section show you how to write a business letter. The Overview subsection provides format and construction guidelines, while the Procedure subsection gives detailed instructions on how to produce a letter using WordPerfect. If you haven't read Chapter 2 yet, do so now; it contains essential instructions you should follow before you begin typing the letter.

Overview

Letters are used for *external* written business communications, that is, communications to individuals working for organizations *other than their own.* All business letters have six basic elements:

- The *heading,* which includes a return address — if letterhead is not used — and the date the letter is signed.
- The *inside address,* which includes the name, title, and address of the individual to whom the letter is being sent (the addressee).
- The *salutation line,* which greets the addressee. For example,

  Dear Ms. Jones:

Dear Mr. Smith:
Dear Permissions Editor:
Dear Customer Service Representative:

NOTE: The last two forms avoid the sexism of "Gentlemen:" or "Dear Sir:"

- The *body,* which contains the message you wish to convey.
- The *close,* which is an expression such as,

  Sincerely yours,
  Very truly yours,
  Best regards,
  With warmest personal regards,
  Cordially,

  followed by three or four blank lines for your signature, your typewritten name, and your title (on the line below your name).
- The *References,* which include the initials of the typist or word processing operator, the word, "Enclosure," or "Enclosures" if the letter is accompanied by additional material, and the initials, "cc:" (for "carbon copy") or bc: (for "blind copy") followed by the name(s) of the individual(s) to whom copies are to be sent. If multiple enclosures accompany the letter, include the number to be enclosed following the word, "Enclosures"—e.g., Enclosures 2.

  NOTE: Don't include initials when you type your own correspondence.

A subject line stating the purpose of the communication is optional. If a subject line is included, place it just below the salutation line.

Most written communications authorities recognize three basic layouts for business letters: full-block, modified-block, and semi-block or traditional. The three layouts are shown graphically in Fig. 3-3. Semi-block layout was used for the sample letter in Fig. 3-4 because producing the letter in semi-block form is a more challenging exercise. We recommend the full-block layout for regular correspondence because it's the easiest of the three to produce.

Start your letters with a paragraph stating the purpose of the letter and end them with another paragraph stating the action you'd like the reader to take.

Procedure

1. Type [**WP**], and press **Enter** to run WordPerfect. Before typing text, notice the status line at the bottom of the screen. From left to right, it shows document number (Doc 1 or Doc 2), page number (Pg), the *vertical position* of the

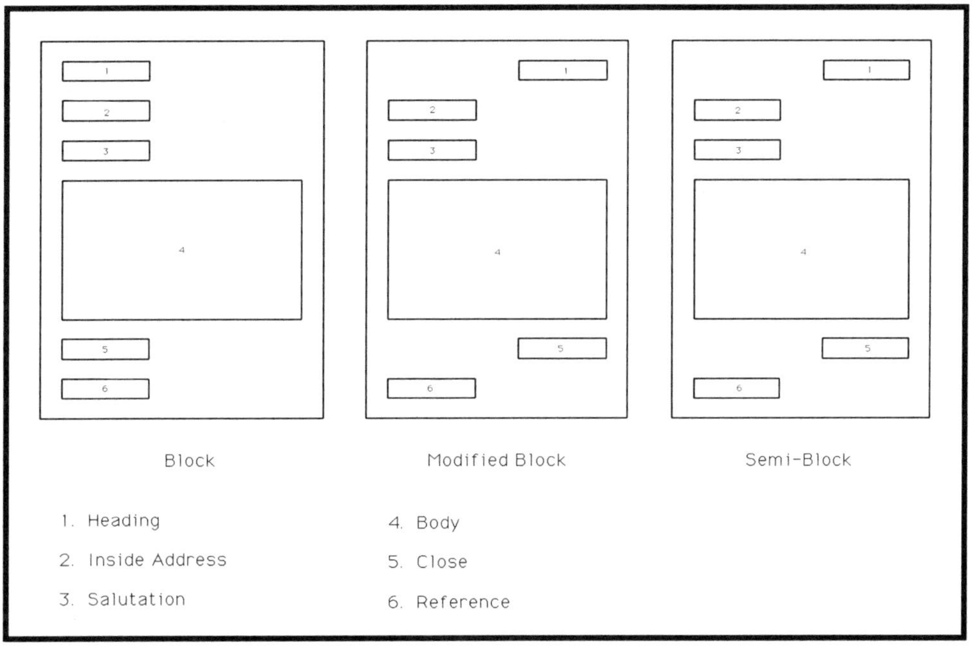

Figure 3-3 Business Letter Layouts

cursor (Ln) measured in inches from the top of the page, and the *horizontal position* of the cursor (Pos) measured in inches from the left edge of the page.

NOTE: You always have two Normal Editing screens active in WordPerfect at the same time. The first screen is called Doc 1; the second is called Doc 2. Press **(Shift-F3)** to switch back and forth.

NOTE: If you're working on a document saved previously, the status line also shows document name (including drive designation and subdirectory names, if any).

An important *menu* you don't see on your WordPerfect screen is used to set margins, tab stops, and line spacing. It's called the Format menu. Let's use it now to be sure margin settings are OK. To see margin settings, press **(Shift-F8)** and type [**L**]; to change them, type [**M**] once the menu is displayed.

Layout
Line M, [*left margin*], <R>, [*right margin*], <R>

February 8, 1991

Ms. Rachel King
322 Fleur De Lis Parkway
New Orleans, Louisiana 70124

Dear Ms. King:

Thank you so much for writing us about your recent happy experience at our Terrytown Brown & Bertram branch store.

I'm sure you'd be interested in learning that Mrs. Lavicheau has been with the Brown & Bertram organization for eighteen years. During that time, more than a score of customers like yourself have written letters in praise of the extraordinary service they've received from her. We like to think all Brown & Bertram employees are as personable and thoughtful as Mrs. Lavicheau, but of course, we're not quite so fortunate as that.

You may rest assured that Mrs. Lavicheau, her immediate supervisor, and the manager of our Terrytown store have all been provided with copies of your warm and funny letter.

We appreciate the opportunity to serve you and hope to merit your patronage for many years to come.

With best personal regards.

Sincerely yours,

Mark J. Rodgers
Manager of Customer Relations

ibm

Enclosure

cc: Bernadette M. Lavicheau
Brenda Smith-Tisdale
Frieda S. Kerlaza

Figure 3-4 Letter Sample

NOTE: Margin settings of 1" right and left are good default settings for a letter.

To see tab settings (assuming you're still in the Format: Line menu),

- Type [**T**] for Tab settings, [**T**] for Type, and [**R**] for Relative.
- Since you only need tabs at 0.5" and 3.25", relative to the left margin, press **(Ctrl-End)** to delete any existing tabs. (The key combination, (Ctrl-End), also deletes the characters from the cursor to the end of a text line.)

- Type [**0.5**], press **Enter**, type [**3.25**], and press **Enter** again. Notice that "L's appear at positions +0.5 and +3.25 in the tab set line. (Be sure to type "*0.5*" and not ".5". If you make a mistake, just delete the "R" and "L" from your tab line by moving your cursor under each letter and pressing the delete key.)
- Press **(F7)** to return to the Format: Line menu.

T, T, R, <(Ctrl-End)>, [0.5], <R>, [1], <R>, <R>

If line spacing is set at 1 (single spacing), press **(F7)** to return to the Normal Editing screen. Otherwise, type [**S**], [**1**], and press **(F7)** twice to return to the Normal Editing screen.

S, [1], <R>, <R>

For a letter, good formatting rules of thumb are:

- Single spacing
- Left and right margins of 1 inch
- Top and bottom margins of 1 inch
- Tabs at 0.5 and 3.25 inches relative to the left margin

NOTE: If you type your letters on embossed letterhead, allow for the space required by the embossed graphic in the layout of the first page. The solution to this problem is to use WordPerfect's "Advance" feature. Follow the instructions below to do so:

- Measure the distance in inches from the *top of the page* to a point two lines below the letterhead graphic.
- Press **(Shift-F8)** and type [**O**], [**A**], [**D**] to select the "Advance" option from the "Other" format options and signal WordPerfect that you wish to advance down the page.
- In response to the WordPerfect prompt,

  Adv. down 0,

  type the measured distance—e.g., [**1.5**]—and press **Enter**.
- Press **(F7)** to return to your document.

Layout
Other A, D, [*inches*], <R>, <R>

NOTE: The Format: Line menu displayed information called "initial settings" or "default settings." Generally, if these settings will meet your needs, don't alter them.

2. You should now be ready to type your letter. Look at Fig. 3-4 before you do so, however.

    2. 1 Press **Tab** twice to zip over to the position you've set for your return address and date.

NOTE: Omit steps 2. 2 and 2. 3 below if you're using letterhead stationery.

    2. 2 Type your own street address. Press **Enter** and then press **Tab** twice.
    2. 3 Type your city, state, and zip code. Press **Enter** and then press **Tab** twice.
    2. 4 Press **(Shift-F5)** and type [T] to produce today's date. Press **Enter** twice.

```
Tools
        Date Text <R>, <R>
```

    2. 5 Type the inside address, ending each line with **Enter**. Press **Enter** again to leave a blank line between the inside address and the salutation line.
    2. 6 Type the salutation line (for example, Dear Ms. King:).

    NOTE: Use the title, "Ms. King" unless you know she prefers either "Miss King" or "Mrs. King".

    2. 7 Press **Enter** twice following the salutation line to insert a blank line before the first paragraph of the letter.
    2. 8 Press **Tab** to indent the first line of the paragraph.

3. This is a good place to toggle on Reveal Codes to see what WordPerfect's formatting codes look like. Press **(Alt-F3)** (or **(F11)**) on the enhanced layout keyboard) to do so. Press **(Alt-F3)** (or **(F11)**) to toggle Reveal Codes off again.
4. Type the text of your letter.

    NOTE: You needn't press Enter every time you come to the end of a line because WordPerfect "wraps around" automatically to the beginning of the next line. But do press Enter when you want to end a paragraph or otherwise end a line of text prematurely.

If your letter is to be single spaced (the normal case), leave a blank line between paragraphs by pressing **Enter** twice at the end of each paragraph. Also press **Tab** at the beginning of each new paragraph.

5. When the body of the letter is complete, press **Enter** twice. Then press **Tab** twice and type your complimentary closing (for example, Sincerely yours,). After that, press **Enter** four times to leave space for your signature.
6. Now press **Tab** twice and type your name. Press **Enter** and then press **Tab** twice.
7. Type your title and press **Enter.**
8. If an enclosure is to be included with your letter, press **Enter** twice and type the word, "Enclosure," and press **Enter**.
9. If a copy of your letter is to be sent to someone other than the person to whom it's addressed, press **Enter** three times at the end of the text, type the letters, cc:, press **Tab** and then type the name of the person to whom the copy is to be sent. If several persons are to receive copies, add the other name or names directly below the first. Be sure to press **Tab** before each additional name.
10. Do the following to proofread your letter:

    10. 1 Review the text to ensure that all necessary punctuation is included.

    NOTE: Two spaces follow a period, question mark, or exclamation point at the end of a sentence; single spaces follow punctuation marks within sentences—that is, commas, semicolons, and colons.

    10. 2 Carefully examine the text, using Up Arrow and Down Arrow to move a line at a time, or the - and + keys at the right of the numeric keypad to jump to the top and bottom of the screen to scan for errors. To move to the top of your document, press **Home**, **Home**, **Up Arrow**; to move to the bottom, press **Home**, **Home**, **Down Arrow**.

    Press either **Right Arrow** or **Left Arrow** to move one character at a time within a line; press **(Ctrl-Right Arrow)** or **(Ctrl-Left Arrow)** to move a word at a time forward or backward; press **End** to move to the right end of the line; and press **Home**, **Home**, **Left Arrow** to move to the left end of the line.

    NOTE: Pressing **Home**, **Home**, **Home**, **Left Arrow** moves the cursor to the left of any codes at the left end of the line (the codes are visible only when you reveal codes).

11. Turn to the instruction set called "Editing Text" (Section 4- 1) for editing support.
12. Turn to the instruction set called "Spell Checking" (see Section 4- 2) to see how to use the WordPerfect spell checking feature.

13. When you've finished editing and spell checking your letter, press **(F7)**. WordPerfect prompts you with,

    Save document? Yes (No)

    with the cursor flashing under Y. Press **Enter** and WordPerfect requests a document name. Type a name—MRRKLE01.W51, (for *M*ark *R*odgers *le*tter number *01* to *R*achel *K*ing) for example—and press **Enter**. Next, WordPerfect prompts you to exit. If you only wish to clear your Normal Editing screen, press **Enter**; if you want to return to DOS, type [**Y**].

    NOTE: To save your letter on a floppy disk in drive A instead of on the hard drive, type [**A:MRRKLE01.W51**] and press **Enter** when WordPerfect prompts you for a document name.

14. If you didn't complete your task in one sitting, recall your letter to the screen. Here's how.

    14.1 Assuming WordPerfect is still running, press **(F5)**, **Enter** to see a list of all your files. If not, type [**WP**] and press **Enter** before pressing **(F5)**.

File
List Files <R>

NOTE: If you saved your letter on a diskette in drive A, type [**A:**] and press **Enter** after you press **(F5)**.

14.2 To recall your letter, press the cursor arrows or use your mouse to highlight its name and type [**R**].

NOTE: An alternative way to retrieve the letter is to press **(Shift-F10)** and, in response to WordPerfect's prompt,

Document to be retrieved: ,

type [***document name***], and press **Enter**. If the document has been saved on a floppy disk, type [**A:*document name***] and then press **Enter**.

File
Retrieve [*filename*], <R>

15. Turn to the instruction sets listed below to finish your letter and the envelope to stuff it in.

Instruction Set	*Section*
Editing Text	4-1
Spell Checking	4-2
Printing Documents	4-3
Numbering Pages	4-4
Creating, Editing, Printing an Envelope	4-5
Leaving WordPerfect	4-6

3- 3 WRITING A RESUME

Instructions in this section show you how to write a resume. The Overview subsection provides format and construction guidelines, while the Procedure subsection gives instructions on how to produce the resume using WordPerfect. If you haven't read Chapter 2 yet, do so now; it contains essential background information and instructions you should follow before you begin typing your resume.

Overview

The resume is a sales piece for yourself, and it should suggest to a potential employer that you'll contribute more to the organization than you'll cost. A prospective employer searches your resume for evidence that you have good potential or that adding you to the organization team will increase the productivity of others. At a minimum, your resume should show sufficient promise to make it worthwhile for a company to take you to the next round in the recruiting process—the interview. As you plan your resume, think about how each additional piece of information can enhance the perception of your potential. Also realize that any errors in grammar, spelling, style, or organization will be seized upon immediately as evidence of your lack of fitness. *Be sure your resume is perfect.*

A resume should include the following four sections:

- The *Career Objective* is a short, focused statement of what you'd like to do in your next job. There's some disagreement among authorities as to whether a job objective should be included. On the plus side, the job objective signals your interests to the potential employer, helping ensure a better fit between you and the job. On the minus side, the career objective may close doors to positions you might find quite acceptable.
- The *Education* section describes your college experience (including graduate school if appropriate). It gives the name(s) and location(s) of the college or colleges you attended, dates of attendance and the degree or degrees earned. The school attended most recently should be listed first. It also indicates your major, any honors you may have earned, and other significant accomplishments.

- The *Experience* section describes your work experience, listing the names and locations of employers and dates of employment. It also shows your responsibilities and accomplishments and describes important skills you learned or sharpened on the job. Your most recent position is listed first.
- The *Personal Information* section includes information attesting to your employability. It may describe a special strength such as language fluency; infer your competitiveness (prizes or awards in sports, music, or art), or indicate that you have ample experience working with others toward a common goal (community service, for example).

Procedure

The memo and letter examples in Sections 3- 1 and 3- 2 were formatted in WordPerfect as standard documents with horizontal spacing defined with tabs and spaces. It would be cumbersome to do that with the resume shown in Fig. 3-5. Instead, we construct the resume as a two-column document. Treating the resume as a two-column document is a faster, more effective way to produce a good-looking finished document.

1. Type [**WP**] and press **Enter** to run WordPerfect. Before typing text, notice the status line at the bottom of the screen. From left to right, it shows document number (Doc 1 or Doc 2), page number (Pg), *vertical position* of the cursor (Ln) measured in inches from the top of the page, and the *horizontal position* of the cursor (Pos) measured in inches from the left edge of the page.

   NOTE: You always have two Normal Editing screens active in WordPerfect at the same time. The first screen is called Doc 1; the second is called Doc 2. Press **(Shift-F3)** to switch back and forth.

   NOTE: If you're working on a document saved previously, the status line also shows document name (including drive designation and subdirectory names, if any).

   An important *menu* you don't see on your WordPerfect screen is used to set margins, tab stops, and line spacing. It's called the Format menu. Let's use it now to be sure margin settings are OK. To see margin settings, press **(Shift-F8)** and type [**L**]; to change them, type [**M**] once the menu is displayed.

Layout Line M, [*left margin*], <R>, [*right margin*],<R>

MARK J. RODGERS
14 Del Monte Drive
Winston-Salem, NC 27103
(919) 766-5555

OBJECTIVE	A managerial position in marketing with a major corporation, leading to senior management responsibility.	
EDUCATION	BABCOCK GRADUATE SCHOOL OF MANAGEMENT Wake Forest University	Winston-Salem, NC
	<u>Master of Business Administration</u>, May 1991. Followed a general management curriculum with emphasis on marketing and operations. Awarded second year Food Service Scholarship.	
	THE UNIVERSITY OF NORTH CAROLINA	Chapel Hill, NC
	<u>Bachelor of Arts</u>, May 1986. Majored in economics and business administration. Member of honorary economics fraternity.	
EXPERIENCE	PIEDMONT MASTER CATERERS	Winston-Salem, NC
June 1989 to Present	Planned, organized, and implemented major marketing program that launched the firm into new markets and doubled sales within one year of the program's inception.	
	THE BULL IN THE MOON	Winston-Salem, NC
April 1988 to August 1989	Managed a large, full-service restaurant with thirty staff members. Instrumental in developing new food products and menu choices. Responsible for scheduling all employees and ordering food. Reduced employee turnover by fifty percent and food costs by ten percent.	
	LEO'S RESTAURANTS, INC.	Raleigh, NC
May 1986 to March 1988	Implemented cost controls, wrote employee job descriptions, and developed a marketing plan for a regional restaurant chain. Developed a planning system to reach sales growth and profit objectives.	
PERSONAL	Fluent in Spanish. Enjoy tennis, traveling, skiing, and long distance running.	

Figure 3-5 Resume sample

NOTE: Margin settings of 1" right and left are good default settings for a resume.

If spacing is set at 1 (single spacing), press **(F7)** (or the right mouse button) to return to the Normal Editing screen. Otherwise, type [**S**], change the number to 1 and press **(F7)** twice to return to the Normal Editing screen.

S, [1], <R>, <R>

For a resume, good formatting rules of thumb are:

- Single spacing
- Left and right margins of 1 inch
- Top and bottom margins of 1 inch

NOTE: The Format: Line menu displayed information called "initial settings" or "default settings." Generally, if these settings will meet your needs, don't alter them.

2. You should now be ready to type your resume. Look at Fig. 3-5 before you do so, however. Press **(Shift-F6)**, **Caps Lock**, **(F6)** to center, set in uppercase, and bold the text. Type your name just as you would on a typewriter.
3. Press **(F6)**, **Caps Lock**, **Enter** to toggle off boldface, shift back to lowercase and return the cursor to the left margin.
4. Press **(Shift-F6)**, type your street address, and press **Enter** to center your street address.
5. Press **(Shift-F6)**, type your city, state, and zip code; and press **Enter**.
6. Press **(Shift-F6)**, type your phone number, and press **Enter** three times.
7. Now set up the rest of your resume as a two-column document. (See Section 8- 4, "Formatting Text in Columns," for additional help if you need it.)

NOTE: If you forgot to press **(Shift-F6)** *prior to* typing one or more of the first four lines so that lines are left justified, move your cursor into the left justified line and then press **Home**, **Home**, **Left Arrow** to move the cursor to the left margin. Finally, press **(Shift-F6)** to center the line.

WARNING: Be careful when you edit column-formatted documents such as this resume. It's easy to delete one of the formatting codes that control column structure and the appearance of your document. We strongly advise you to do your editing with Reveal Codes toggled on so you can see control codes and thereby avoid deleting them.

7. 1 Press **(Alt-F3)** (or **(F11)**) to toggle on Reveal Codes.

NOTE: Avoid deleting these codes by mistake: **[HPg]**, **[Col On]**, **[Col Off]**, **[Col Def]**. If you do delete a control code by mistake, press **(F1)** and type [**R**] to "undo" your error.

7. 2 Press **(Alt-F7)** and type [**C**], [**D**] to define columns.

7. 3 Type [**T**], [**B**] to select parallel columns with block protect.

7. 4 Type [**N**], [**2**], and press **Enter** to select 2 columns and then type [**M**] to alter the display on the lower part of your screen so the settings are the same as those shown below. Press **Enter** to move from number to number and **Enter** again to return your cursor to the bottom of the screen.

Column	*Left*	*Right*
1:	1"	2.25"
2:	2.35"	7.5"

7. 4 Press **(F7)** and type [**O**] to set columns on. Your cursor should be in column 1. Note that the status line now displays "Col 1" on the left.

8. Press **Caps Lock**, type [**objective**], and press **Caps Lock** again.

Layout
Columns
Define T, B, [N], [2], <R>, M, [1], <Enter>, [2.25], <Enter>, [2.35], <Enter>, [7.5], <Enter>, <R>, O

9. Press **(Ctrl-Enter)** to switch to column 2 and type your career objective. Press **(Ctrl-Enter)** to skip a line and switch back to column 1.
10. Press **Caps Lock**, type [**education**], and press **Caps Lock** again.
11. Press **(Ctrl-Enter)** and type the name of the last college or university (or school) you attended.
12. Press **(Alt-F6)** to position your cursor flush right and type the location of the school. Press **Enter**.
13. If appropriate, type the university name and press **Enter** twice. Otherwise, press **Enter** a second time to skip a line.
14. Press **(F8)** to toggle on underlining, type the name of your latest degree, and press **(F8)** again to toggle *off* underlining. Then type a comma, a space, the month and year the degree was granted, a period, and two spaces. Type a brief description of the educational experience following the example in Fig. 3-5. Press **Enter** twice.

NOTE: Don't press Enter at the end of a line that continues on the next line down because WordPerfect automatically "wraps around" to the beginning of the next line for you. Do press Enter when you want to end a paragraph or otherwise end a line of text prematurely.

15. Type your earlier educational experience, continuing the process for the rest of your educational background. At the end of your education section, press **(Ctrl-Enter)** to jump back to column 1.
16. Press **Caps Lock**, type [**experience**], press **Caps Lock** again and then press **(Ctrl-Enter)** to jump to column 2.
17. Type the name of the last company you worked for, press **(Alt-F6)** to move your cursor flush right and type the company's location (city and state). Press **(Ctrl-Enter)** to jump back to the column 1.
    17.1 Type the months and years of work experience.
    - Type the first date, press **Enter** and type the word, "to."
    - Center "to" by pressing **Home**, **Home**, **Left Arrow** to move the cursor flush left.
    - Press **Space Bar** to push "to" to the right, press **End**, and then press **Enter**.
    - Type the second date.

    17.2 Press **(Ctrl-Enter)** and type your job responsibilities for that company. When you finish, press **Enter** twice.
18. Repeat these steps for the rest of your work experience. Remember that dates are in column 1 while the company name and work experience descriptions are in column 2. Be sure to press **(Ctrl-Enter)** after the state abbreviation on the company name line to switch back to column 1. Be sure to press **(Ctrl-Enter)** after the ending date to jump to column 2. When you've entered all your work experience, press **(Ctrl-Enter)**.
19. Next, press **Caps Lock,** type [**personal**] and press **Caps Lock** again. Press **(Ctrl-Enter)** to jump to column 2 and type any additional information about your interests, hobbies, special talents, etc.
20. Press **(Alt-F7)** and type [**C**], [**F**] to toggle columns off.

```
Layout
        Columns
                Off
```

21. Do the following to proofread your resume:
    21. 1 Review the text to ensure that all necessary punctuation is included.

NOTE: Two spaces follow a period, question mark, or exclamation point at the end of a sentence; single spaces follow punctuation marks within sentences—that is, commas, semicolons, and colons.

21. 2 Carefully examine the text, using Up Arrow and Down Arrow to move a line at a time, or the - and + keys at the right of the numeric keypad to jump to the top and bottom of the screen to scan for errors. To move to the top of your document, press **Home**, **Home**, **Up Arrow**; to move to the bottom, press **Home**, **Home**, **Down Arrow**.

    In either the right or left column, move your cursor *within* a line by pressing **Right Arrow** or **Left Arrow** to move a character at a time. Press **(Ctrl-Right Arrow)** or **(Ctrl-Left Arrow)** to move a word at a time; press **End** to move to the right end of the line; and press **Home**, **Home**, **Left Arrow** to move to the left end of the line before any text. Press **(Ctrl-Home)**, **Right Arrow** to move from the left to the right column; press **(Ctrl-Home)**, **Left Arrow** to move from the right column to the left. (If you have a mouse, move from column to column by moving the mouse cursor over to the adjacent column and then pressing the left button.)

22. Turn to the instruction set called "Editing Text" (Section 4- 1) for additional editing support. Be aware that the operations described there apply *within* column boundaries. For example, if you delete text, only text in the column where your cursor is blinking will be affected. Turn to Section 8- 4 for additional guidance on formatting text in columns.
23. Turn to the instruction set called "Spell Checking" (see Section 4- 2) to see how to use the WordPerfect spell checking feature.
24. When you've finished editing your resume, press **(F7)**. WordPerfect prompts with,

    Save document? Yes (No)

    with the cursor flashing under Y. Press **Enter** and WordPerfect requests a document name. Type a name—RESUME01.W51, for example—and press **Enter**. Next, WordPerfect prompts you to exit. If you only want to clear your Normal Editing screen, press **Enter**; if you want to return to DOS, type [**Y**].

File
Exit Y, [*filename*], <R>, Y

NOTE: If you wish to save your resume on a floppy disk in drive A instead of on the hard drive, type [**A:RESUME01.W51**] and press **Enter** when WordPerfect prompts you for a document name.

25. When you first work with columns, it's easy to scramble your format by keying in too many returns in the wrong column or by making other mistakes.

Should you scramble the format, press **(Alt-F3)** and reveal codes to see how WordPerfect arranges your columns.

Once you open the Reveal Codes screen, you can delete troublesome codes such as extra hard returns (**[HRt]**) in a forward direction by pressing Delete or in a backward direction by pressing Back Space. Experiment to see the effect of code deletion by toggling open the Reveal Codes screen, deleting some codes, toggling it closed by pressing **(Alt-F3)** a second time and then pressing **(Shift-F7)** and typing [**V**] to view the printer image of the resume. Be sure to save your resume before you start experimenting, however.

26. If you didn't complete your task in one sitting, bring your resume back to the screen. Here's how.

    26. 1 Assuming WordPerfect is still running, press **(F5)**, **Enter** to see a list of your files. If not, type [**WP**] and press **Enter** before pressing **(F5)**.

```
File
        List Files <R>
```

NOTE: If you saved your resume on a diskette in drive A, type [**A:**] and press **Enter** after you press **(F5)**.

    26. 2 To recall your resume, use the cursor arrows to highlight the name you gave it and type [**R**].

NOTE: An alternative way to retrieve the resume is to press **(Shift-F10)**, and then in response to WordPerfect's prompt,

Document to be retrieved: ,

type the document name, and press **Enter**.

```
File
        Retrieve [filename], <R>
```

27. Turn to the instruction sets listed below to complete the preparation of your resume.

Instruction Set	*Section*
Editing Text	4- 1
Spell checking	4- 2
Printing documents	4- 3
Leaving WordPerfect	4- 6

4

General Support

Three of the six instruction sets in this chapter are *required* to complete correspondence *or* long documents successfully. They are "Editing Text," "Printing Documents," and "Leaving WordPerfect." Instructions in two other modules are important enough to the preparation of high quality documents that they should be followed for virtually every document you prepare. In this category are "Spell Checking," that should be used for all but your most informal documents and "Numbering Pages," whose instructions should be followed whenever you prepare a multiple-page document. The other module in the chapter, "Creating, Editing, and Printing an Envelope," is required only when you need to type an envelope. We included it here because you'll probably use it frequently in conjunction with the preparation of correspondence.

4- 1 EDITING TEXT

This module describes the keys, key combinations, and key sequences required to edit documents. Turn here if you need to insert text, delete text, or move blocks of text from one section of a document to another. These instructions also show you how to search for and replace text. Global search and replace is handy for making changes such as replacing all occurrences of "salesman" with "sales person."

These instructions also show you how to move (or copy) text from one document to another. For example, you may have typed a term paper in one WordPerfect document and a set of quotations in another. WordPerfect lets you keep two documents (called Doc 1 and Doc 2) in memory at the same time. Retrieve the term paper draft into Doc 1 and the quotations into Doc 2. Then, switch from Doc 1 (the default) to Doc 2, "block" a quote, copy it into a temporary holding location in computer memory called a "buffer," switch back to Doc 1, and then drop it into your term paper at the designated spot. Edit text by pressing Insert and typing over existing characters or by using the keys described next.

NOTE: Normally, WordPerfect is already in *insert* mode, so that characters typed at the cursor position push existing text to the right.

NOTE: You can insert Tabs, Indents, Hard Returns, and other formatting codes in addition to characters. Tabs shift the first line of a paragraph to the right while Indents shift all lines in a text block to the right. Indents are produced by pressing **(F4)**; Hard Returns are produced by pressing **Enter.**

NOTE: If you get into trouble, *cancel* an operation by pressing **(F1)**. If you delete text by mistake, recover it by pressing **(F1)** and typing [**R**].

Deleting text

1. *Delete Characters Forward* [(Delete)]
   This key deletes single *characters* in a forward direction. Move the cursor under the first character or space you want knocked out and press **Delete** to delete text.
2. *Delete Characters Backward* [Back Space]
   This key also deletes single *characters* in a backward direction.
3. *Delete Words Forward* [(Ctrl-Back Space)]
   This key combination deletes single *words.* Move the cursor anywhere in the word to be purged, press and hold the **Ctrl** key, and then press **Back Space**.
4. *Delete to End of Line* [(Ctrl-End)]
   This key combination deletes text from the cursor position to the end of the line. Move the cursor to the character where deletion is to begin, press and hold **Ctrl**, and then press **End.**
5. *Delete to End of Page* [(Ctrl-PgDn)]
   This key combination deletes entire pages or parts of pages. Move the cursor to the point in the page where deletion is to begin and press and hold **Ctrl** and then press **PgDn**. WordPerfect prompts you with,

   Delete Remainder of page? No (Yes).

Type [**Y**] to delete the rest of the page, or press **Enter** to cancel the operation.

NOTE: WordPerfect warns you if you attempt to delete a formatting code such as **[BOLD]** or **[Center]** by pressing Delete or Backspace. Press **Enter** if you don't want to delete the code, and type [**Y**] if you do. You won't see the warning when you delete text using other key combinations—e.g., (Ctrl-End).

Replacing text

6. *Replace Text* [(Alt-F2)]

This key combination performs insert and delete operations simultaneously. To replace material, press and hold **Alt** and then press **(F2)**. WordPerfect prompts you with,

w/Confirm? No (Yes)

Type [**Y**] to confirm each replacement (a wise choice for the first time user). WordPerfect then prompts you with,

-> **Srch**: .

Type the text to be replaced and press **(F2)**. WordPerfect then prompts you with the message,

Replace with: .

Type the replacement text and press **(F2)** one more time. If you selected replacement with confirmation, respond to the prompt,

Confirm? No (Yes),

by typing [**Y**] (to replace) or by pressing **Enter** (to leave the original character string intact).

Search
Replace Y, [*old text*], <R>, [*new text*], <R>, Y

Moving text within documents

7. *Move Sentences, Paragraphs, and Pages* [(Ctrl-F4)]

This key combination transfers a sentence, paragraph, or page from one location in a document to another location *in the same document* (or to *another document* in the Doc 2 Normal Editing screen). Text is deleted from the original location and appears in the new location. Position the cursor anywhere in the sentence, paragraph, or page to be moved and press **(Ctrl-F4)** to start the move.

A menu appears at the bottom of the screen:

Move: 1 Sentence; 2 Paragraph; 3 Page; 4 Retrieve: 0

Type or click on the appropriate option mnemonic—S for Sentence, for example—and WordPerfect highlights the block of text and responds with the sub-menu,

1 Move; 2 Copy; 3 Delete; 4 Append: 0

Type [**M**], move your cursor to the point where the text is to be inserted, and press **Enter**.

WARNING: If your text contains periods within a sentence—e.g., the title Mr. or Ms.—you can't move the complete sentence. In that situation, move the sentence as a block of text (see instructions below).

NOTE: The *copy* feature corresponds to the *move* feature except that the source text remains in place in its original form, while an *image* of the source text is placed elsewhere.

8. *Move Sections of Text*

To move (or copy) a *section* of text (a portion of a sentence, for example), first "block" the text. Here's how:

8. 1 Place your cursor at the beginning of the word, phrase, etc. to be moved.
8. 2 Press **(Alt-F4)** (or **(F12)**) to toggle on the block feature.
8. 3 Highlight the text to be moved or copied by moving the cursor forward with the Right Arrow, Down Arrow, Space Bar, or Enter.

NOTE: After you've toggled block on, you can also highlight text by keying in a specific character. Highlight a whole sentence by typing a period, for example. Try it and see.

NOTE: If you go too far while highlighting, move the cursor *backward* with the Left Arrow or Up Arrow keys.

Press **(Ctrl-F4)** to see a menu of options for moving and copying blocks, columns, and rectangles of text. Type [**B**] and [**M**] to move the block of text (or [**B**] and [**C**] to copy it). When you type M or C, the text you've blocked is moved temporarily into a storage location in memory called the "Move/Copy buffer." Now, move your cursor to the place where you want the block to reappear and press **Enter**.

Moving text between documents

9. *Copying Text from One Document to Another*

9. 1 If you've already saved the document on your screen, press **(F7)**, and type [**N**], [**N**] to clear the Normal Editing screen. If you haven't

yet saved your document, press **(F10)**, type a document name in response to the WordPerfect prompt and then press **Enter**. Retrieve the document *to which* text is to be moved into the Doc 1 Normal Editing screen (let's call this document the *destination document*). To do so, press **(Shift-F10)**, type [***destination document name***], and press **Enter**.

```
File
        Retrieve [filename], <R>
```

NOTE: If you're not sure about the spelling of the name of the destination document:

- Press **(F5)**, **Enter** to list files.
- Highlight the name of the destination document by pressing the cursor arrows and type [**R**] to retrieve it.

```
File
        List Files R
```

9. 2 Press **(Shift-F3)** to switch to Doc 2.

9. 3 Press **(Shift-F10)**, type the name of the document *from which* text is to be moved (the *source document*), and press **Enter**.

```
File
        Retrieve [filename], <R>
```

9. 4 Use the procedures described in instructions 7 and 8 above to move (or copy) a sentence, paragraph, page (or pages), or block of text to the Move/Copy buffer.

9. 5 Press **(Shift-F3)** to switch back to the destination document in Doc 1, move your cursor to the target location for the block of text and press **Enter**.

4- 2 SPELL CHECKING

The instructions here show you how to spell check a WordPerfect document. The Overview subsection explains how the spell check feature works and advises you when and how to use it. The Procedure subsection includes the few simple steps required to use this feature.

Overview

As it steps through your document word by word, WordPerfect's spell checker highlights words not found in its "common" or "main" word lists or in an optional word list containing the words you add to the dictionary yourself. Unless a highlighted word is quite unusual, the spell checker will list several words as replacement options.

For many WordPerfect users (including those of us who aren't particularly good spellers) the greatest benefit of WordPerfect's spell checker *is finding and correcting typographical errors.* Perhaps your experience will be similar. Here's a tip: Add frequently used technical terms, acronyms, and names of individuals and places each time you verify spelling. It's a good habit to develop. Adding new words is accomplished with instruction 4. 2 below.

Procedure

1. If your document isn't already on the screen, retrieve it by pressing **(Shift-F10)**, typing the name of the document, and then pressing **Enter**.

```
File
        Retrieve [filename], <R>
```

2. Press (**Ctrl-F2**) to actuate the spell checker.
3. Type [**D**] for "Document."

```
Tools
        Spell D
```

4. If the highlighted word *is* a proper name—e.g., Rodgers,
   4. 1 select (or click on) options 1 or 2 to *skip* one or all instances of the name in the document, or
   4. 2 select (or click on) option 3 to *add* the name to your optional dictionary.
5. If the highlighted word *is not* a proper name, and
   5. 1 its correct spelling is shown in the list under the tab ruler, swap words by typing the letter matching the correct spelling. (If you have a mouse, just click on the correct word.)
   5. 2 its correct spelling is *not* shown in the list under the tab ruler, select option 4, "Edit," to correct the highlighted word.

4- 3 *PRINTING DOCUMENTS*

The instructions included in this module tell you how to print single- and multiple-page documents and how to center short, single-page documents vertically. They also tell you how to view a printer image of your document prior to producing hard copy, how to print selected pages from the document on your screen or a document on disk, and how to use Printer Control should you run into trouble.

Overview

Before you attempt to print a newly created, first-time document, you must have *defined* a printer, and the defined printer must be *selected* for the instructions given below to work properly. If you aren't sure whether a printer has been defined in your version of WordPerfect, run WordPerfect, press **(Shift-F7)** to display the Print menu, and then type [S] to display the Print: Select Printer screen. If a printer has been *defined,* it's displayed there.

Your display screen should look like the example in Fig. 4-1. Your screen may list more or fewer printer names, and, of course, the names shown on your screen may differ from the ones in the example. (To *select* a printer, just highlight it with your cursor control keys, and then mark it by typing [S].) Press **(F7)** twice to return to the Normal Editing screen. If a printer has not yet been defined, see Section 9- 5, "Defining and Selecting Printers" for instructions on printer definition. Do that now and then come back here to print the document.

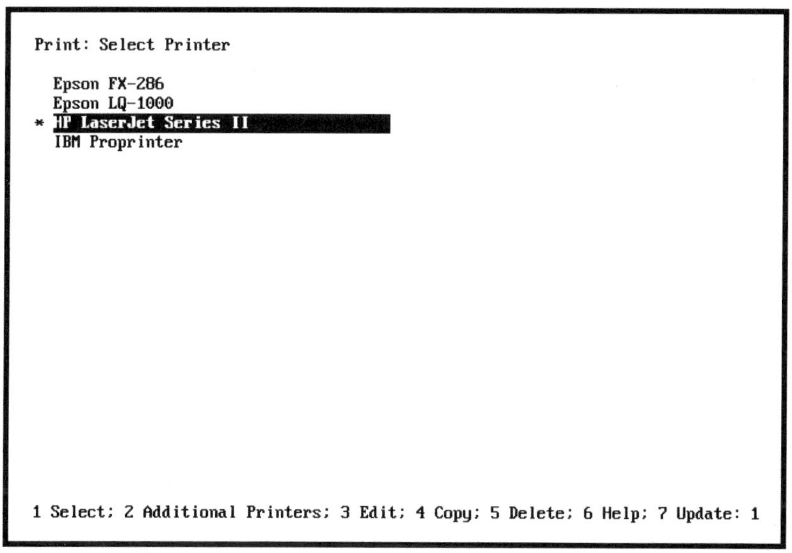

Figure 4-1 Select Printer Screen

File
    Print S, [N], [*printer name*], <R>, S, <R>

Procedure

1. If your document isn't already displayed on the screen, retrieve it by pressing **(Shift-F10)**, typing the document name, and then pressing **Enter**.

File
    Retrieve [*filename*], <R>

NOTE: If your document is already on the screen, press **Home**, **Home**, **Up Arrow** to move your cursor to the top of the document.

2. Press **(Shift-F8)** and type [**P**] to see page formatting options.
3. Type [**C**] and [**Y**] to "Center Page (top to bottom)."

NOTE: This feature centers the document on the *printed* page—not on your screen. (Don't use this feature for a document longer than a single page.)

4. Press **(F7)** to return to the Normal Editing screen.

Layout
    Page C, Y, <R>

5. Press **(Shift-F7)** to display printing options.
6. Type [**V**] to select the View Document feature to see what your document will look like when it's printed. If you're satisfied with the format, press **(F1)** and type [**F**] (for "Full Document"). If not, press **(F7)** to return directly to the Normal Editing screen to make appropriate changes.

File
    Print V, <(F1)>, F

Type [**1**] to enlarge the image in the View Document Screen to 100 percent of the full-page image and type [**2**] to increase it to 200 percent; enlarging the image enables you to see fine detail. Move about the enlarged View Document screen by using the same key sequences you'd employ to move about the Normal Editing screen. When you've seen enough of the printer image of your document, press **(F1)** to return to the Print menu or **(F7)** to return to the Normal Editing screen.

> **NOTE**: It's not *necessary* to "view" your document prior to printing, but we strongly advise you to do so—especially if the printed document includes headers or footers, graphics, or multiple fonts. Your PC must be equipped with a graphics adapter before you can use the View Document feature, however.

Occasionally you may wish to print selected pages rather than printing an entire document. Four options are available for doing so, two of which print pages from the document on your screen, and two of which print pages from a document on disk.

Printing one on-screen page from the Print menu

1. Press **(Shift-F7)** to display the Print menu.
2. Type [**P**] to select the "Page" option.

```
File
     Print P
```

Printing selected on-screen pages from the Print menu

1. Press **(Shift-F7)** to display the Print menu.
2. Type [**M**] to select the "Multiple Pages" option.
3. In response to the prompt,

   Page(s): ,

   type the desired page numbers and press **Enter**.

```
File
     Print M, [page numbers], <R>
```

Type the beginning and ending pages of the block separated by a hyphen to print a block of pages in sequence ([**23-28**], for example). If the pages to be printed aren't in sequence, separate the page numbers with commas. For example, type the character string, [**10,13,17**], to print pages 10, 13, and 17. (Enter page numbers the same way for options three and four.)

Printing selected on-disk pages from the Print menu

1. Press **(Shift-F7)** to display the Print menu.
2. Type [**D**] to select the "Document on Disk" option.
3. In response to the prompt,

   Document name: ,

   type the name of the document from which the subset of pages is to be printed and then press **Enter**.
4. WordPerfect then prompts you with,

   Page(s): (All).

   Type the desired page numbers and press **Enter** in response. Press **(F7)** to return to the Normal Editing screen.

```
File
        Print D, [filename], <R>, [pages], <R>, <R>
```

Printing selected pages from the List Files screen

1. Press **(F5), Enter** to display the List Files screen.
2. Highlight the name of the document from which the subset of pages is to be printed.
3. Type [**P**] to select the "Print" option. When you do so, WordPerfect prompts you with, **Page(s): (All)**. Follow the instructions in step 11 above in response and press **Enter**.

```
File
        List Files <R>, N, [filename], <R>, P, [pages], <R>, <R>
```

Printer Control

Sometimes, nothing happens when you try to print a document even though the printer image of your document checks out OK on the View Document screen. What do you do in such cases? Your first action should be to press (**Shift-F7**), and then type [**C**] for printer control.

```
File
        Print C
```

After you take these steps, you should see the Print: Control Printer menu displayed on your screen. Note that it provides information about the "Current Job," a "Job List" with one or more jobs listed, and a Printer Control menu. Often, the Current Job section of the screen displays a message and suggested action that will help you trouble shoot your printer problem.

Notice the options in the menu at the bottom of your screen. "Cancel Jobs" lets you delete any jobs waiting in the queue. "Rush Job" lets you move a particular job up in the queue if you need to print it right away. The "Go" option lets you start your printer by typing [G] when you've instructed WordPerfect to prompt you for a manual feed. The "Stop" option lets you stop your printer to change paper or clear a jam.

4- 4 NUMBERING PAGES

In these instructions, we show you how to create a page numbering header for a multiple-page letter and a term paper. We also show you how to use WordPerfect's page numbering feature to add page numbers to long documents using a somewhat simpler approach. Finally, we show you how to use the *page numbering* style to print your name and the page number at the top right side of each page of a long document.

Overview

Get into the habit of numbering all multiple-page documents, even relatively short ones. But before attempting to paginate long documents, such as term papers and written case analyses, you should understand their structure. All term papers, case analyses, and management reports are divided into three sections: (1) the *front matter,* such as a table of contents or preface, (2) the *text,* and (3) the *back matter,* such as a bibliography, appendices, or endnotes. For any given document, the front matter, back matter, or both may be omitted; the front matter or back matter may also be divided into subsections.

Front matter is paginated with consecutive small Roman numerals (i, ii, iii) centered at the foot of each page. Text and back matter are paginated consecutively at the top right of each page with Arabic numerals (1, 2, 3). Some authorities also recommend that the initial pages of major sections of a long document—chapters or sections that begin on new pages, for example—be numbered at the foot of the page with centered Arabic numbers in sequence with upper-right-corner page numbers.

Procedure

Be sure your cursor is at the top of the page prior to inserting page numbering codes. If you follow the steps in this section carefully, your cursor will always be at the top of the page. To be sure your cursor is at the top of any page in one of your own applications, press **(Ctrl-Home), Up Arrow**.

Creating a page numbering header for a letter. Follow the steps below to create a header that numbers the second and third pages of a three-page letter to Mr. Smith. (We assume WordPerfect is running and that the letter to Mr. Smith is displayed in the Normal Editing screen.)
NOTE: We show how to create a *header* in these instructions. Corresponding approaches are used to create a page numbering *footer.*

1. Press **Home**, **Home**, **Home**, **Up Arrow** to move to the top of page 1.
2. Press **(Shift-F8)** and type [**P**], [**H**], [**A**], [**P**] to display the Header/Footer editing screen.
3. Type [**Mr. Smith**] and press **Enter** to insert Mr. Smith's name and move down a line.

Layout
Page H, A, P, [Mr. Smith], <Enter>

4. Press **(Shift-F5)**, type [**T**], and press **Enter** to insert the date and move down a line.
5. Now type [**Page**], and press **Space Bar**, **(Ctrl-B)**, **(F7)** to increment the page number automatically and return to the Format: Page menu.
6. Type [**U**], [**H**], [**Y**], and press **(F7)** to suppress header A on the first page and return to the Normal Editing screen.

Tools
Date Text, <Enter>, [Page], <(Ctrl-B)>, <(F7)>, U, H, Y, <R>

Numbering a document with a title page but no other front matter. Follow the next five instructions when there's no front matter other than a title page.

1. Press **Home**, **Home**, **Up Arrow**, and then press **PgDn** twice to move your cursor to the top of page 2. Your cursor should be at the top of your third *physical* page (or at least its electronic representation).
2. Press **(Shift-F8)** and type [**P**], [**N**] to select page numbering.
3. Type [**P**], [**3**] to place the page number at the top right corner of each page.
4. Type [**N**], [**2**], and press **Enter** to begin numbering at *page 2* with number 2. Remember: You moved to the top of page 2 (physical page 3) in step 6 above.

NOTE: The first page of a report or paper *without a title page* also is not numbered. Therefore, page numbering begins on page 2 with number 2.

5. Press **(F7)** to return to the Normal Editing screen.

Layout
Page N, P, 3, N, [2], <R>, <R>

Numbering a document with front matter. If your document contains a title page and additional front matter, follow these instructions:

1. Press **Home**, **Home**, **Up Arrow**, **PgDn** to move to the top of page 2.
2. Press **(Shift-F8)** and type [**P**], [**N**] to select page numbering.
3. Type [**P**], [**6**] to place the page number at the bottom center of each page.
4. Type [**N**], [**ii**] and press **Enter** to begin numbering pages with lowercase roman numerals starting with "ii" on the second page of the front matter. (Be sure the i's are *small* i's.)
5. Press **(F7)** to return to the Normal Editing screen.

Layout
Page N, P, 6, N, [ii], <R>, <R>

6. Press **(Ctrl-Home)**, type the number of the physical page where the text of your document begins, and press **Enter**. Complete the following instructions:
   - 6. 1 Press **(Shift-F8)** and type [**P**], [**N**] to select page numbering.
   - 6. 2 Type [**P**], [**3**] to position the page number at the top right corner of the page.
   - 6. 3 Type [**N**], [**1**] and press **Enter** twice to reset page numbering to the usual arabic form and return to the Format: Page menu.
   - 6. 4 Type [**U**], [**P**], [**Y**], and press **(F7)** to suppress the page number on the first page of the text section and return to the Normal Editing screen.

Layout
Page N, P, 3, N, [1], <R>, <Enter>, U, P, Y, <R>

Creating a Page Number Style for a term paper. Some instructors may require that you type a page number *and* your name at the top of each page of a term paper or other written assignment to ensure that papers can be reassembled correctly should they come apart and the pages be scrambled together. The instructions below show you how to meet this requirement using WordPerfect's Page Number Style feature.

1. Press **Home**, **Home**, **Up Arrow** to move to the top of page 1.
2. Press **(Shift-F8)** and type [**P**], [**N**], [**S**], to select the Page Number Style option.
3. Type your last name and press **Space Bar** and **Enter**.
4. Type [**P**], [**3**] and press **Enter** to set page numbering at the top right side of the page and return to the Format: Page: menu.
5. Type [**U**], [**P**], [**Y**], and press **(F7)** to suppress the page number on physical page one and return to the Normal Editing screen.

> Layout
> Page N, S, [*name*] <Enter>, P, 3, <Enter>, U, P, Y, <R>

4- 5 CREATING, EDITING, AND PRINTING ENVELOPES

The instructions included here tell you how to create, edit, and print standard, 9-1/2" by 4", #10, business envelopes. The Overview subsection explains how to lay out an envelope with and without a return address. The Procedure subsection presents explicit WordPerfect instructions for formatting and typing the envelope. Instructions are also provided for viewing a printer image of the document and then printing it on either a Hewlett-Packard LaserJet Series II or Epson FX printer. The LaserJet and Epson printers were chosen because they are widely available and because they've become standards for most other printer manufacturers.

Overview

If your envelopes already have a return address, place the addressee block (name, title, company, etc.) 1-3/4 inches from the top edge of the envelope and 4 inches in from the left edge. If the envelope is to include a typed return address, begin it 1/4 of an inch down from the top and 1/4 inch in from the left edge. To save you from having to include large numbers of tabs and returns in the final envelope document, we've incorporated the WordPerfect "Advance" feature in these instructions. Another benefit of the Advance feature is that you can use different font sizes and still maintain consistent placement of the envelope's address element(s). That wouldn't be the case if you used tabs and returns to place the address elements.

In the procedure section, we show you how to complete the following tasks:

- Change page and line formats to conform to an envelope layout
- Select an envelope "paper type"
- Define an envelope paper type (optional)

- Set up the envelope format for situations when you do and don't want to include a return address
- Print an envelope on a Hewlett-Packard LaserJet Series II printer
- Print an envelope on an Epson FX-286 dot matrix printer

Procedure

1. Assuming WordPerfect is running, press **(F7)** and type [**N**], [**N**] to clear your screen.
2. Change the format to fit an envelope. For the standard 9.5" by 4" (#10) envelope, good formatting rules of thumb are single spacing and:

	Return Address	*No Return Address*
Left margin:	0.25"	4"*
Right margin:	0"	0"
Top margin:	0.25	1.75"*
Bottom margin:	0"	0"

NOTE: In the example developed in this section, we obtain the starred settings by using the WordPerfect Advance feature.

2. 1 To create *line format* settings, press **(Shift-F8)**, type [**L**], and then modify the following line format characteristics:
   - spacing: Type [**S**], [**1**], and press **Enter**. (optional)
   - margins: Type [**M**], [**.25**], press **Enter**, type [**0**], and press **Enter** twice to return to the Format menu.

```
Layout
        Line  S, [1], <R>, M, [.25], <R>, [0], <R>, <R>
```

2. 2 Type [**P**] to select the Format: Page menu.

2. 3 Type [**M**], [**.25**], press **Enter**, type [**0**], and press **Enter** to create *page format* settings.

2. 4 Type [**S**], [**N**], [**Envelope**], press **Enter**, type [**S**], and press **(F7)** to select the "Envelope" option from the Format: Paper Size/Type: menu and return to the Normal Editing screen.

```
Layout
        Page  M, [.25], <R>, [0], <R>, S, N, [Envelope], <R>, S, <R>
```

NOTE: If the "Envelope" paper type was not listed among the options on the Format: Paper Size/Type menu, follow the instructions below to define the envelope type. Otherwise, go to Step 3.

Defining an envelope paper type. You may find that the Envelope type is not listed among the paper type options for your printer. If not, take the following additional steps to include it. *This is a one-time only operation.* After an envelope type is added to your paper type list, it remains there so long as you don't reload WordPerfect. (We assume you're in the Normal Editing screen.)

- Press **(Shift-F8)**, and type [**P**], [**S**]
- Type [**A**], [**E**], to select the envelope type.
- Type [**S**], [**E**], to add the envelope size.
- If you're using a *dot matrix or daisy wheel printer,* type [**R**], [**Y**], [**L**], [**M**] to toggle on a prompt and audible signal to load your envelope and signal WordPerfect that you will insert the envelope *manually.*
- If you're using a *laser printer,* type [**F**], [**L**], [**L**], [**M**] to set font type to landscape and signal WordPerfect that you will insert the envelope *manually.*
- Press **(F7)** twice to return to the Format: Page menu. Now you can select the envelope form from the Format: Paper Size/Type menu following instruction 2. 4 above.

```
Layout
      Page  S, A, E, S, E, R, Y, L, M, <R>
```

[Dot Matrix Printer]

```
Layout
      Page  S, A, E, S, E, F, L, L, M, <R>
```

[Laser Printer]

NOTE: The "Font Type" option on the Format: Edit Paper Definition menu should be set to "Portrait" for dot matrix printers and "Landscape" for HP Laserjet or compatible printers. *Portrait orientation* is the normal or long way you'd hold a standard 8-1/2" by 11" sheet of paper. When you turn the sheet sideways, that's *landscape orientation.*

3. Now you're ready to type text. Before you do, however, check the status line to be sure the cursor is .25 inches from the top and left edges of your imaginary page. Follow the directions in instruction 4, omitting those in 5, to cre-

ate an envelope *with* a return address. Follow the directions in instruction 5, omitting those in 4, for an envelope *without* a return address.

4. Preparing an envelope *with* a return address.
   4. 1 Type your own name and press **Enter**.
   4. 2 Type your address and press **Enter**.
   4. 3 Type your city, state, and zip code and press **Enter**.
   4. 4 Press **(Shift-F8)**, type [**L**], [**M**], [**4**], press **Enter**, type [**0**], and press **Enter** twice, to set the left margin at four inches, the right margin at zero and return to the Format menu.

Layout
  Line M, [4], <R>, [0], <R>, <R>

   4. 5 Type [**O**], [**A**], [**I**], [**1.75**] and press **Enter**, **(F7)** to advance to a point 1.75 inches from the top of the envelope and return to the Normal Editing screen.

Layout
  Other A, I, [1.75], <R>, <R>

   4. 6 Type the addressee's name and press **Enter**.
   4. 7 Type the street address and press **Enter**.
   4. 8 Type the city, state, and zip code.
   4. 9 Proofread and edit your envelope and then go to step 6.

5. Preparing an envelope *without* a return address.
   5. 1 Press **(Shift-F8)**, type [**L**], [**M**], [**4**], press **Enter**, type [**0**], and press **Enter** twice to set the left margin at four inches, the right margin at zero, and return to the Format menu.

Layout
  Line M, [4], <R>, [0], <R>, <R>

   5. 2 Type [**O**], [**A**], [**I**], [**1.75**] and press **Enter**, **(F7)** to advance to a point 1.75 inches from the top of the envelope and return to the Normal Editing screen.

Layout
  Other A, I, [1.75], <R>, <R>

5. 3 Type the addressee's name and press **Enter**.
5. 4 Type the street address and press **Enter**.
5. 5 Type the city, state, and zip code.
5. 6 Proofread and edit your envelope.

6. When you're satisfied with your creation, press **(Shift-F7)** and type [**V**] to see a printer image of your envelope and then press **(F7)** and **(F10)** to save the envelope as, say, JSENPH01.W51 (for *J*ob *S*earch *e*nvelope number one going to *P*izza *H*ut).

File
    Print V, <R>

File
    Save [*filename*], <R>

Printing the envelopes. If the envelope isn't displayed on the Normal Editing screen, retrieve it by pressing **(Shift-F10)**, typing its filename, and pressing **Enter**.

File
    Retrieve [*filename*], <R>

7. Press **(Shift-F7)** and **(F1)** to tell WordPerfect you want to print the "Full Document." Because you set "Prompt to Load" to *yes* and "Location" to *manual* earlier, WordPerfect will beep and prompt you with,

    Action required in Printer Control.

File
    Print F

Press **(Shift-F7)** and type [C], [**G**] in response to display the Printer Control panel and send a "Go" to the printer.

File
    Print C, G, <R>

NOTE: If you're printing on a LaserJet, adjust the paper tray to feed envelopes and then insert an envelope in the adjustable slot at the top of the paper tray so that the envelope flap is to the left and down. Also open the side of the printer opposite the paper tray to feed the envelope straight through.

When you see the message, "PE FEED COM-10" on your printer's display panel, push the envelope into the slot until you feel a little resistance. The machine will take the envelope and print the address, and your printed envelope will soon roll out on the other side.

4- 6 LEAVING WORDPERFECT

This brief module tells you how to save your document and leave WordPerfect properly. The Overview subsection tells why you shouldn't switch off your PC until you've exited WordPerfect correctly. The Procedure subsection includes instructions for saving documents under old and new filenames and for ending the WordPerfect session.

Overview

Getting out of WordPerfect is really simple, but you should go through the steps below *every time* you return to DOS. If you switch off your PC without taking the normal departure steps listed below, WordPerfect leaves two backup files called WP{WP}.BK1 and WP{WP}.BK2 on your hard disk. (The backup files are a precaution against losing files in case of a power failure that shuts down your PC unexpectedly; WordPerfect deletes them when you make a normal exit.) If you do happen to make an abnormal exit from WordPerfect, you'll also see the message,

Are other copies of WordPerfect currently running? (Y/N)

displayed at the foot of your screen the next time you run WordPerfect. If you see this message, type [**N**] and [**D**] to erase the old backup files and restore the situation to normal.

This is a good place to stress the importance of file backup. Get into the habit of backing up all new or updated documents to a floppy disk if you normally store them on a hard disk, or to a *backup* floppy if you normally store them on a floppy. Over the years, we've listened to the tearful entreaties of many students who have failed to follow this advice. Don't put yourself in their place—back up your documents religiously.

Procedure

1. Press **(F7)**.
2. WordPerfect prompts you with **Save document? Yes (No).**
3. Press **Enter** to save the document. Assuming you've saved this document previously (a good habit to get into), WordPerfect displays the name used last.

4. Press **Enter** to save the document under the old name. WordPerfect prompts you to replace the existing document. Respond by typing [**Y**] if you want to replace the old document and **Enter** if you don't.
5. If you do press Enter, meaning that you *don't* want to write over the existing document, WordPerfect displays the document name again.
6. In response, edit the existing document name or type a new name and then press **Enter**.

   NOTE: Edit file information by deleting or typing over the drive designation, subdirectory name, or filename displayed. You can also insert characters to alter existing file information. For example, you can append an extension to an existing filename by adding a period and one, two, or three more characters.

7. WordPerfect prompts you to exit. If you want to clear the Normal Editing screen to begin work on a new document, press **Enter**. To return to DOS, type [**Y**] instead.

File
Exit Y, <R>, Y, Y

5

Long Document Applications

This chapter has five sections:

1. The long document overview you're reading now.
2. "Preparing a Term Paper," which includes general guidelines for term paper construction with emphasis on planning the document production process.
3. "Writing a Case Analysis," which includes general guidelines for case analysis and preparation of the written case report.
4. "Writing a Management Report," which includes general guidelines for writing a management report.
5. "Long Document Procedures," which includes detailed WordPerfect instructions for constructing long documents.

Some of the format and construction guidelines in this chapter are common to all long document types. Examples are identifying reader needs, budgeting your time, and making actionable recommendations. Other guidelines are specific to particular document types. For example, since the written case analysis is the only long document that includes an action plan, advice pertaining to the preparation of action plans is confined to that particular section.

The general guidelines included in this first section are organized into the following subsections:

1. Preliminaries
2. Planning the Writing Project

3. Construction Guidelines
4. Helpful Hints
5. Avoiding Plagiarism

Preliminaries

Whether you're preparing a term paper, a written case analysis, or a management report, the long document production process incorporates an *analysis* stage and a *writing* stage. We examine the analysis stage briefly here, although it's covered more fully in Section 5- 2, "Writing a Case Analysis." The writing stage is examined a little later in this section.

Analysis. Before you begin your analysis, decide whether the purpose of your paper or report is to be descriptive or prescriptive. The two types call for different approaches to the analysis and result in final documents that are somewhat differently structured. Because the differentiation is important, we take a few sentences here to explain the meaning of the terms, descriptive and prescriptive.

A *descriptive* study describes an existing problem (or situation), and its purpose is to illuminate and clarify the problem so that a good solution can be prescribed at *some point in the future.* An example of a descriptive study would be a report written following a comprehensive inventory of computer hardware, software, data communications equipment, personnel, and associated facilities. The report would describe the existing situation and perhaps draw conclusions but *would not* include recommendations for change.

On the other hand, a *prescriptive* study describes an existing problem *and* includes one or more recommendations for action. Its purpose is to provide background information about a problem, as in the example above, draw pertinent conclusions, *and* propose a solution. An example of a prescriptive study would be a report presenting an inventory of information processing resources (like the example above) that also proposes one or more alternatives to improve the existing system. A term paper or management report can be descriptive or prescriptive in purpose. A written case analysis is almost always prescriptive.

If a study is *descriptive,* the *analysis* steps required are usually grouped into four primary tasks:

1. State the problem and dimensions of the analysis.
2. Select an appropriate research methodology.[1]
3. Conduct the analysis and produce findings.
4. Draw conclusions based on the findings.

If a study is *prescriptive,* a fifth task must also be completed:

5. Make recommendations supported by the findings.

Identify Reader Needs. From the very start, focus on the target audience and think how your reader might use the information you're getting ready to provide. At the same time, place a value on your reader's time and let that assessment guide your organization and the level of detail to be included. Also be sure to determine ahead of time reader preferences for format, level of detail, and supporting documentation so you can zero in on the appropriate writing level. Focusing on the needs and habits of your reader helps you tailor your writing style and identify important points and issues for coverage. For example, if your primary reader is a course instructor and the assignment is a term paper, he or she will probably read the entire paper carefully and will want to see it organized in the classic arrangement of: (1) problem, (2) background, (3) findings, and (4) conclusions. On the other hand, if your primary reader is a local business executive, he or she probably won't have much time to spend reading your report. Therefore, use management report style (which is essentially a reversal of the classic arrangement).

Finally, ask yourself how much the reader knows about the subject of your long document. If he or she is fully knowledgeable of background, technical terms, practices, and customs, don't spend much time filling in the background, and you can use relatively technical language. On the other hand, if your reader isn't familiar with the situation you're addressing and doesn't understand industry jargon, provide adequate background development at the beginning of your document and be sure to use lay terminology or carefully define the technical terms you can't do without.

Treat your assignment as a project with a modular structure. Begin writing only after you've completed your analysis and reached a conclusion. Your analysis should be one well-defined project, and the writing of the results should be a second well-defined project. This guideline doesn't mean you shouldn't keep notes as you work or that you shouldn't sketch draft tables or figures. It simply means that your analysis should be complete with all results available before you begin writing the first draft.

Producing and packaging a long document is analogous to constructing a building. The complete project can be divided into modular subtasks or groups of subtasks, some of which can be completed at the same time while others must be completed in sequence. Obvious examples of modular subtasks are: (1) preparing a bibliography, (2) adding footnotes or endnotes, (3) creating figures, and (4) constructing tables. Moreover, writing the individual sections of the paper may also be treated as distinct work modules.

Depending on the length, purpose, complexity, and formality of your writing assignment, the mix of subtasks will differ substantially from one document type to another and within documents of the same type. Usually, the longer the document, the larger the *number* of sets of subtasks. As a long document's complexity or technical sophistication increases, moreover, we frequently observe a somewhat different *mix* of subtask sets as well.

In recognition of these characteristics, a complete project can be divided into modules, each in a separate WordPerfect document that you can work on more or less independently of the contents or stage of completion of related modules in other WordPerfect documents. Indeed, if the project is a group effort, it is especially important that you conceptualize the group's total effort as a collection of modular components.

The writing order. Write the body of your document before you write the introduction, conclusions, or summary. That is, first write the report of the analysis of the situation and your findings. The body may also include a description of your research methodology if the analysis incorporated formal research.[2] As you write the body, prepare sketches of the tables and graphs you plan to use to support your findings. Your sketches can be rudimentary back-of-the-envelope tabulations or drawings, or you can create them directly and electronically in a spreadsheet or graphics package for later inclusion in the report.

After you've written the body of the report, write the introduction; it answers the *what, why,* and *how* questions pertaining to your assignment. The introduction states *what* the document is about—that is, the problem or situation being addressed—*why* it has been written, and *how* it is organized. After you've completed the introduction and added supporting exhibits, write the management summary (if your document is a management or case report), prepare endnotes (if included), bibliography, appendices, lists of tables and figures, the table of contents and, finally, a title page. Depending upon the practice at your college or university, you may also be required to prepare a cover letter to accompany your submission.

When you *package* a term paper, that is, put all the pieces together in your final draft, the arrangement should correspond closely to the analysis stages listed above.[3] When you package a case analysis or management report, however, the written account of the study is usually arranged differently than the stages of analysis. Instead of describing problem and research methodology first, lead off with the information of greatest importance to the reader: conclusions and recommendations. More specifically, the standard management report arrangement is:

1. Principal results and conclusions
2. Recommendations (if called for in the study request)
3. Findings
4. Methodology
5. Background
6. Interpretive discussion[4]

When you consult the individual sections of this chapter, you will see that the arrangement for the written case analysis varies somewhat from the arrangement for the management report, but the differences are mostly in the placement and em-

Activity	Hours	Total
1. Topic identification		10
1.1 Read text, other course material	3	
1.2 Write working hypothesis	1	
1.3 Draft preliminary outline	1	
1.4 Talk to instructor and others	1	
1.5 Read encyclopedias, magazines	2	
1.6 Fine tune working hypothesis	2	
2. Library research		30
2.1 Search for sources	4	
2.2 Read sources	15	
2.3 Write notes	10	
2.4 Revise working hypothesis	1	
3. Organizing notes		5
3.1 Arrange note cards	2	
3.2 Organize the structure	3	
4. Writing		25
4.1 Revise outline	1	
4.2 Write first draft	9	
4.3 Revise to second draft	5	
4.4 Revise to final draft	5	
4.5 Prepare references	2	
4.6 Prepare tables, figures	3	
Total		70

Figure 5-1 Term Paper Project Activities and Time Budget (Time in Hours)

phasis given to each subsection rather than in the general approach. Both the case and the management report are structured to present results first.

Make Actionable, Realistic, Recommendations. When your paper, report, or written case analysis is prescriptive, don't simply state that a problem exists. Explain the source of the problem and describe the likely consequences if it isn't solved. State exactly why and how the situation will adversely affect the organiza-

	WEEKS													
Tasks	1	2	3	4	5	6	7	8	9	10	11	12	13	14
1. Select topic				XXXX										
2. Identify sources					XXXX									
3. Conduct research						XXXX	XXXX							
4. Organize notes								XXXX						
5. Create outline								XXXX						
6. Write first draft									XXXX					
7. First revision										XXXX				
8. Second revision											XXXX			
9. Packaging											XXXX			

Figure 5-2 Term Paper Gantt Chart

tion, providing details to undergird your conclusion. After the problem has been carefully dissected, recommend one or more courses of action to correct the situation (you will have evaluated other courses of action in your analysis, of course).

Guidelines for planning the writing project and construction tips are provided in the next two subsections; helpful hints are given in the fourth subsection; the final subsection treats plagiarism.

Planning the Writing Project

Planning tools such as budgets, schedules, network diagrams[5] and Gantt charts[6] are essential for the timely completion of major projects such as buildings and marketing campaigns. Although you may not realize it at first, these tools can also be applied to major writing projects such as term papers, written case analyses, and management reports. Indeed, applying these tools to smaller and more manageable projects permits you to hone your planning skills inexpensively and early in your career. In these subsections we focus on three long document planning tools: (1) time budgets, (2) project schedules, and (3) outlines.

Budget your time. One of the most important elements of project planning is time management—that is, assigning a total block of time to a project and then allocating the assigned time to project activities so that the finished project is of "high quality, on time, and under budget." As a first step, establish the *total* amount of time you think you should spend on the project. Your allotment might be 40, 60, 80, or even 100 hours, depending on the nature of the assignment, the time you have available, and your own work habits and efficiency. To give you some perspective, a good-quality, ten- to fifteen-page term paper might require as much as 70 hours of effort from a reasonably efficient student. After you've decided on the total amount of time you can afford to spend on the writing project, identify and categorize the activities that constitute the project. An example of an activity list with sample completion times for a term paper is shown in Fig. 5-1.

After you've identified and categorized the major activities required to write the paper or report, allocate the total project time to the activities identified. Base the first-cut allocation on your own past experience and the shared experiences of your fellow students. You will probably adjust time allocations (and perhaps your first estimate of total time) to bring both into line with the actual total time you think you can afford to spend on the project. Not surprisingly, the more you practice budgeting your time, the better you become at doing it.

Schedule the production tasks. Once you've prepared your time budget, schedule the completion of the major tasks over the semester or quarter using a simple Gantt chart like the one shown in Fig. 5-2. Note that the Gantt chart in the example allocates more time to library research than to any other activity. Also note that organizing notes and creating the outline, and writing the final draft and packaging the paper for submission are represented as parallel activities—activities that can be completed in the same week. The structure of the Gantt chart, like the structure of the time budget, will depend heavily on your own work habits and research and writing strengths and weaknesses. For the purposes of generating the relationships in Figs. 5-1 and 5-2, we assume a good-quality, 15-page paper based on library research.

One major benefit realized from constructing a Gantt chart is that you quickly realize how important it is to work on the project throughout the term rather than leaving it until the last moment. Preparing the chart also forces you to realize that you *must* start the project early and work on it steadily to produce a first-class result.

Prepare an outline. Undoubtedly the most useful tool for long document planning is the outline (see Section 7- 1 for detailed instructions on creating an outline with WordPerfect). Prepare a preliminary skeletal outline when you have a firm enough grasp of your topic to formulate a working hypothesis. The preliminary outline can be quite simple—five to ten phrases, all at the same level, or it can be quite detailed. In any event, you will surely modify it as your work progresses.

Construction Guidelines

This subsection presents several construction guidelines:

1. Plan your document carefully and use an outline.
2. Select a document format appropriate to your writing task.
3. Use three levels of headings.
4. Reference exhibits ahead of time and interpret their contents.

We elaborate upon these guidelines in the paragraphs that follow.

Plan Your Document. When you take the time to carefully prepare an outline and then write directly from it, you are applying one of the most fundamental and useful of management precepts: "plan your work and then work your plan." When you adopt this precept, your long document is constructed more quickly and with fewer errors. (Section 7- 1 shows how to construct an outline with WordPerfect.)

Select An Appropriate Document Format. Format refers to the general arrangement of the major elements of your document. You have undoubtedly observed that the *Wall Street Journal* and the *Harvard Business Review* have a distinctive "look" that sets them apart from other periodicals. That's their format. Well-packaged term papers, case reports, and management reports also have a distinctive "look" (although perhaps not quite so distinctive as the formats of the *Wall Street Journal* or the *Harvard Business Review*).

You will feel more comfortable and write more quickly if you write to a format. To make your job easier, format guides are provided for the long document types covered in this chapter. Although we've attempted to ensure that the format guides conform to recommended standards in authoritative reference materials, we advise you to double check to see if format requirements for coursework or job-related submissions have been specified by your course instructor or business school policy.

Use Three Levels of Headings. The heading standard adopted for this text has three levels. At the first level, text is centered and in full capitals; at the second level, text is left justified, underlined, and typed headline style (all words other than articles, conjunctions and prepositions are capitalized); at the third level, paragraph headings are underlined and typed sentence style. Whether you use the approach adopted here or another style, follow it consistently and be sure to include at least two headings at each level.

To avoid having two different levels of headings without intervening text, write some explanatory prose in a brief paragraph or two immediately following a heading at one level and introducing the heading of the next subdivision. The explanatory prose can provide an overview of the following section, suggest what is to be included there, and define unfamiliar terms used for the first time in the section.

Placing, referencing, and interpreting tables. If you include tables (and these guidelines apply equally well to figures), the text reference to each table should precede the table, and if possible, the table referenced should be located on the same page as its reference. When you explain the meaning of a table, don't repeat the table's information in the text. Instead, use the accompanying text to interpret or draw inferences from the table's contents.

Helpful Hints

This section contains general guidelines for attacking the writing project straight on and using your time to maximum effectiveness. We recommend that you complete your analysis before you start writing, set deadlines and then meet them, write complete blocks of text before editing, and regularly set aside large blocks of writing time.

Write the first draft in one block of time. Compose your complete first draft in one block of time if your paper or report is relatively short—say, ten or fewer pages. When your project is longer than ten pages, compose it in well-defined chunks of five to ten pages, each of which should have a natural beginning and end. Prepare a schedule of the large blocks of time required for the actual writing, and try not to let other activities alter your schedule.

Set and meet writing deadlines. Set deadlines for completion of each major component of your long document and then meet the deadlines. Accomplishing this goal straight off may be difficult if you've not developed good habits of working to completion of a given task. If you do have trouble completing extended tasks, start by breaking a complete project into chunks that you think can be completed in a single sitting. Then, start working through them, a chunk at a time. Discipline yourself to stay at the task until it's finished.

If this approach doesn't work at first, your chunks are probably too big. Cut them down to a more manageable size and then go back to work. After you've trained yourself to consistently finish the smaller chunks, however, start increasing their size so that the time spent on each chunk increases from an hour to an hour-and-a-half, then to two hours, and so on. Keep trying to reach your goal before quitting to go on to something else.

Another helpful strategy is to try to write every day for a specified number of hours without interruption. In doing so, set a goal for yourself in terms of numbers of pages written, sections completed, or diagrams or tables prepared.

Don't grope for words. Don't stop writing to grope for the perfect word. If you can't think immediately of an ideal word for a given situation, pop in a reasonable substitute or simply leave a blank space to be filled in later. As you edit your draft, the ideal word often jumps to mind; if it doesn't, turn to WordPerfect's on-line thesaurus and experiment with its recommended substitutes. (See Section 6- 4 for instructions on using the WordPerfect thesaurus.)

Don't edit as you write. Many of us edit our work as we write; this bad habit wastes time and blurs the focus of a writing project. A better approach is to try to complete an entire section without giving much thought to stylistic, grammatical, and spelling niceties. Follow this rule no matter how depressingly bad your draft looks; take comfort in the fact that most of us are better at editing than we are at writing. By writing the first draft quickly with little thought given to grammar and style and then following up with a careful editing job, we play to our strengths.

After completing the first draft and letting it age for several days (or even weeks), then edit it. You will probably rewrite heavily in the process, and some of your material will end up in the trash can, but that's an outcome all writers experience.

Illustrate concepts with examples. Use examples to explain complex concepts and issues; the redundancy inherent in examples increases the likelihood that your readers will understand your arguments. It's also useful to remember that some readers seem to learn best by being exposed to abstract information, while others seem to learn best by being exposed to concrete information, by "doing," as it were. Using examples to illustrate abstract ideas helps you communicate effectively with both types of readers.

Ask a friend to review your work. You are probably your own best critic, but if you have time to do so, turn to others for a critical assessment of your work. Before you ask a friend for suggestions, however, be absolutely sure that you've done your best to eliminate obvious errors of organization, grammar, spelling, and style. *Always* spell check your document in WordPerfect itself (see Section 4- 2), and use a writing assistant such as *RightWriter* or *Grammatik* to help with grammar and style.

Avoiding Plagiarism

Plagiarism is presenting the ideas of others, whether directly or indirectly, as your own, that is, without attribution. *Direct plagiarism* is lifting the words of other writers and incorporating them in your own work without including them in quotation marks or indenting them and without properly citing the original source. Substituting a few synonyms in a paragraph of someone else's text doesn't make you intellectually honest! You must give credit to those whose work you include in your own. *Indirect plagiarism* is paraphrasing the original *ideas* of others without giving proper credit to the source of the ideas. For example, you might be intrigued by Michael Jensen's ideas about the societal value of leveraged buyouts[7] and want to include those ideas in the paper you're planning to write for a finance course. Even if you capture the essence of Jensen's thesis *in your own words,* you must give him credit.

The only conditions under which you need not cite the work of others is when text represents your own thinking strictly or when it clearly contains elements of general knowledge, that is, information available in the reference section of the average size municipal library.

For additional guidance on matters of construction, format, and style, consult the following references:

Communibook. The University of Western Ontario School of Business Administration, London, 1979, Number 9-83-L003.

Keithley, Ervin F., and Marie E. Flatley, *A Manual of Style for Business Letters, Memos and Reports,* 4th ed. Carlsbad, CA: SouthWestern Press, 1988.

Strunk, William, and E. B. White, *The Elements of Style.* New York: MacMillan Publishing Company, 1979.

Williams, Joseph M., *Style.* Chicago: University of Chicago Press, 1990.

ENDNOTES

1. Research methodology may be restricted to library research of existing sources. (These are secondary data.) Research may also involve collection and statistical analysis of original data including interviews and reviews of policy and procedure documents. (These are primary data.)
2. A written case analysis differs from a term paper or management report in the nature and extent of the "research" conducted. Usually, the research for a case analysis is confined to the case text and exhibits, although some instructors request that students search for supplemental information in other sources.
3. Richard C. Huseman, James M. Lahiff, and John M. Penrose, *Business Communications,* 3rd ed. (Hinsdale, IL: The Dryden Press, 1988), chs. 9, 10.

4. A. S. C. Ehrenberg, "Writing Technical Papers or Reports," *The American Statistician,* 36, No. 4 (November 1982), 326-29.
5. The Project Evaluation Review Technique (PERT) and Critical Path Method (CPM) employ network diagrams for large project control.
6. A Gantt chart is a two-dimensional table that lists tasks to be accomplished in the left-most column and weeks, months, or some other time period along the top. The combinations of tasks and time periods show the planned sequence of completing the entire project.
7. Michael C. Jensen, "Eclipse of the Public Corporation," *Harvard Business Review,* 89, No. 5 (September-October 1989), 61-74.

5- 1 WRITING A TERM PAPER

Writing term papers is a tedious, painful, and drawn-out undertaking for most business students because they're unsure about how to do library research; lack confidence in matters of format, construction, and style; and often don't have the typing skills required to produce a polished document. The instructions in this module show you how to avoid some of these problems. Writing a term paper involves six stages of production:

1. Finding a topic
2. Planning the writing project
3. Conducting library research
4. Preparing to write the paper
5. Writing the paper
6. Adding the optional extras

In the following subsections we provide suggestions and tips for completing stages 1, 3, 4, 5, and 6. The planning process was addressed in the overview section of this chapter.

Finding a Topic

Given that you'll probably spend one to two weeks of work producing and packaging each term paper you write, it's important to get a good start on every one you do. Always follow three simple guidelines:

- Know where you're going.
- Choose a topic that will hold your interest.
- Construct a working hypothesis.

This subsection tells you how to put these guidelines to work.

Know where you're going (the thesis statement). The introductory paragraphs of a well-constructed term paper contain a thesis statement that sets the tone for the remainder of the paper and alerts the reader to its purpose and direction. Following the statement of the paper's thesis, the remaining sections marshall evidence and argument to support it. The thesis statement is similar to the conclusions (and/or recommendations) in a management report or the recommendations in a written case analysis; it's the culmination of all the effort that goes into a term paper.

The sentence below is a thesis statement from a term paper describing an analysis of leveraged buyouts. Notice that it makes a positive statement about the expected economic impact of leveraged buyouts.

> Contrary to popular opinion, leveraged buyouts tend to strengthen the U.S. economy by ensuring that management is more responsive to resource owners.

If the thesis statement is the end point of the term paper production process, the first critical step is the selection of a fruitful *topic* from a broad *subject* area. An example of a subject area would be *leveraged buyouts;* a potential topic might be the *macroeconomic impact of leveraged buyouts.* When you choose your topic well, your thesis statement should develop naturally from your research.

Choose a topic that will hold your interest. Choose a topic that will stimulate and hold your interest. That usually means a topic you already know something about, one you want to know something about, or one that can be generalized to courses you plan to take in the future—that is, a topic area you can develop further and build upon in later courses. By selecting a stimulating topic, you economize on search, maintain your level of interest, and produce a better final product. Another good rule is to select a topic that has not yet been clearly defined (this would be a *descriptive* focus) or one about which authorities disagree (this would be a *prescriptive* focus). If you adopt a prescriptive focus, take an objective, balanced approach in your research but be sure to come down on one side of the issue or the other in your thesis statement.

Your course instructor, course text, and assigned reference materials are good potential sources for topics. Other potential sources are general encyclopedias such as the *Encyclopedia Britannica,* specialized encyclopedias such as the *Encyclopedia of Management,* and dictionaries such as the *Dictionary of Business and Economics* and the *McGraw-Hill Dictionary of Economics.* The latter is particularly useful because most entries give references should you want to know more about a particular subject. In addition, atlases and geographical dictionaries provide some coverage of business and management subjects that may be of interest. Don't overlook business publications such as *Barrons, Forbes, Business Week, Fortune,* and newspapers such as the *Wall Street Journal* and the *New York Times*. (See Walker[1] and Weidenborner and Caruso[2] for guides to sources.)

Construct a working hypothesis. After you select a promising topic, do some general reading in your topic area—that is reading in your textbook or other assigned course materials, specialized reference materials, or current issues of business publications. Then construct a *working hypothesis,* which is a statement you think you can either prove or disprove with your research. If you were writing a paper on the macroeconomic effects of leveraged buyouts, for example, your working hypothesis might be:

> Leveraged buyouts tend to increase the danger of recession by increasing the risk of domino-like, large-scale business failures.

The working hypothesis is a step crucial to the success of your total writing effort.

As your investigation broadens and deepens, you can expect to modify and refine your working hypothesis which will evolve naturally into the thesis statement. As you conduct your library research you may identify many sources with something to say about your preliminary hypothesis. If so, consider narrowing the topic and tightening your hypothesis; on the other hand, if you identify too few sources, consider broadening the topic and loosening your hypothesis. The primary purpose of your hypothesis is to focus your research effort on those sources that pertain directly to your research problem. Use it as a screener; if a particular source doesn't relate to the hypothesis, put it aside; if it appears pertinent to the hypothesis, investigate it in depth.

Conducting Library Research

Conducting library research involves six distinct but related areas:

1. Learning how your university library is organized
2. Locating reference material
3. Preparing source notes
4. Screening potential sources
5. Taking and identifying notes
6. Creating a WordPerfect notes document

This subsection presents guidelines for each of these areas.

Learn how your library is organized. Before you begin searching for books and newspaper, magazine, and journal articles, find out how your university library is arranged physically and how its collections are organized.[3] Perhaps the most effective way of doing so is to spend some time with a reference librarian. He or she can explain how the card catalog is organized and then teach you how to use it. A reference librarian can also tell you how materials are classified and where materials are located in specific buildings and rooms.

Locating reference materials. After learning about the library's physical arrangement and the organization of its collections, locate the books, magazines, newspapers, and journals you will need. To find books, search by subject, author, or title; to find magazines, newspapers, and journals, search by title or subject. If your library has a computer output microfilm catalog or an on-line catalog accessible via terminal, ask your reference librarian to show you how to use them. If they aren't available, search in the traditional card catalog.

Once you know where magazines, newspapers, journals, and books are located, select the materials. You can "ease your way" in this process by the manner in which you take notes from the catalog. Catalogs are arranged in alphabetical order, book collections are not. Libraries in this country use either the Dewey Decimal or the Library of Congress classification schemes and arrange books on the shelves in the order designated by the system. If you take your notes from the catalog on individual cards (3 by 5, 4 by 6 — select your favorite size) you have the flexibility of arranging the cards to correspond with the arrangement of the books on the shelves. In a large library with several floors, doing so can save time when you go to retrieve your materials.

To locate articles in journals is at best a two-step process. First, you need to consult standard periodical indexes, whether in print, on CD-ROM, or on-line.[4] When you've identified articles you think offer promise, determine if the library you're using subscribes to the journals containing the articles. If your library doesn't subscribe to a needed journal, it can secure a copy of the article from another library. (Doing so may require several days, however, so avoid doing your library research at the last minute.)

For business students, there are several good indexes to articles appearing in the business press. A leading one is ABI-INFORM which is available both in CD-ROM and on-line. It indexes approximately 800 business journals and each reference it provides contains an abstract. *Business Periodicals Index* is a well-established index in the field and is available in print, on CD-ROM, and on-line. It indexes around 300 journal titles. A third leading title is *Predicasts F & S Index.* This title comes out in U.S. and international versions and is particularly good for its company approach. Its print edition is published weekly. Other important indexes for researching business and economic issues are *Public Affairs Information Service Bulletin* (better know as PAIS), *Social Sciences Index,* the *New York Times Index,* and the *Wall Street Journal Index. Reader's Guide to Periodical Literature* may be of some use for subjects with broad general interest. Additional leads to reference material in business are the *Journal of Economic Literature* that indexes articles in marketing and finance as well as in the different branches of economics, bibliographies from articles you've read, and of course, your instructor.

Prepare source cards. If you followed earlier advice and took notes from the catalog on individual cards, you now have the beginnings of source cards. Document the sources of ideas and all quoted material included in your paper.[5] You need not record a great deal of information when you document sources, and ordinary 3" by 5" index cards will do nicely, but do be sure to include complete source information (see Section 6- 1, "References to Other Work"). Complete a card for each source, even if you don't use all the sources in the preparation of your final draft.

Record the source information using the documentation style to be employed in the paper itself so that typing footnotes and bibliography is simply a matter of typing the contents of your cards. By writing your bibliography cards in the required documentation style from the start, you save time and cut down on errors and missing information later on in the production process. See Section 6- 1 for instructions on documenting sources. More extensive coverage of the popular documentation styles can be found in Walker[6] and in Weidenborner and Caruso.[7]

Write the call number on the back of each source card in case you need to find a particular reference again. Also summarize the content of the source, and note where the information might fit in to your paper. Finally, assign a grade to the source. A good grade signals that the reference may provide additional useful material; a poor one means that the source is barren and shouldn't be examined again.

Screen potential sources. Use your time wisely, recalling the allocations in your time budget; don't over-read sources at the outset. When you first examine a new source, scan it, don't read it. If scanning is fruitful, then read only the pages pertaining to your hypothesis. Quickly examine a new book's table of contents and index. If they show promise, read the introduction, conclusion, and the section headings. Also, scan tables and figures carefully and read the topic sentence in each paragraph. Use your hypothesis as a screener. If a source appears to support, refute, or tighten the hypothesis, plan to read it. If not, rule it out, assign a low rating to the source card, and place it in an inactive stack.

Do similar detective work on newspaper, magazine and journal articles. Read the abstract of the article (if one is included) and the introductory and concluding sections. Follow up by reading the section headings and topic sentences in each paragraph. If the material is promising, assign a high rating on the source card.

After you've identified all books, articles and other material pertaining to your topic, read carefully and take detailed notes. As you begin investigating a new area, read magazine and newspaper articles before you read journal articles and books because magazine and newspaper articles are written for a wider audience and tend to be easier to understand. Having cut your teeth on newspaper and magazine articles, you should then be more at ease with the material in journals and books.

Take and identify notes. Generally, a note can be categorized as: (1) a direct quote, (2) a paraphrase of the sense of the material, (3) information of general knowledge, or (4) your own thoughts and ideas. Customarily, most of your notes will paraphrase the work of others with credit given at the end of the material paraphrased.[8] Since paraphrasing takes considerable time and mental effort, be certain that the matter being paraphrased is relevant to your work. Normally, your paper will also include direct quotes. Restrict quoted material to no more than 20 percent of the total paper content, however.[9]

If you're not so fortunate as to have a laptop PC you can take to the library, two good options for taking notes are available: traditional note cards and xerographic copies. Let's look at note cards first.

Four by six or five by eight cards have been used for decades by countless students to take notes on the content of books, articles, and other materials. Cards are easy to organize; they can be quickly sorted into meaningful groups and subgroups, and they're inexpensive.

At the top left side of the card write the subtopic heading. In the top right corner, record author name and an abbreviated title if your references include two or more works by a single author; this is the source identifier. (Also use an abbreviated title if the work cited doesn't have an author.) Record the source call number and page numbers beneath the source identifier. Then write your notes—one note per card.

Be sure to indicate whether your note is a direct quotation, a paraphrase, information of general knowledge, or a thought wholly your own. One way to do so is to use a different colored card for each of the four types of notes. Write paraphrased material on white cards, quotes on yellow cards, information of general knowledge on pink cards, and your own observations on blue cards. An alternative approach is to key the type of note with a code in the lower left corner: "P" for paraphrase, "Q" for quote, "GK" for general knowledge, and "O" for your own observations. A third approach is to identify each note type with a colored, stick-on dot affixed to one of the corners of the card. Sheets of stick-on dots may be purchased at most stationery stores.

Photocopying source materials eliminates the intermediate step of writing notes on cards. Using a copier also increases your flexibility because you can read the copies at a more convenient time, make marginal notes on them directly, and highlight matter to be quoted in a distinctive color. If citation information and page numbers are not shown on your copies already, be sure to jot them down before you leave the library. Organizing copies is obviously more difficult than organizing note cards, however.

Create a notes document in WordPerfect. Type the card or copy contents into a "notes" document in WordPerfect as you go along, ensuring that each note has a heading and source identifier. On the first line of each note entry, record a subtopic heading within a pair of braces. On the second line record the author's name, an abbreviated title (if needed), page numbers, and date. Having done so, you can cut and paste the notes into your outline at the appropriate points to prepare your first draft. By using WordPerfect's search feature, it's easy to find the braces after the notes have been copied into the draft.

NOTE: To use the search feature to find a left brace:

- Press **(F2)**.
- Type [{].
- Press **(Alt-F2)** again.

Consider developing codes as substitutes for heavily used word combinations. Doing so speeds up your note taking. For example, if you were writing a term paper on the impact of information technology on business strategy, you might substitute the abbreviations "OS," "MF," and "DC" for the word combinations, "operating system," "mainframe," and "data communications." Having done so, you can then use WordPerfect's Replace feature to swap words and phrases for the codes. Be careful, however. This time saver must be applied judiciously or you may end up inadvertently replacing unanticipated letter combinations *within* ordinary words with other words and phrases. For example, had you unwittingly chosen the letters, "os" as an abbreviation for "operating system" and then typed the phrase,

> . . . the os reduces computer chaos and lost data.

a global search and replace that substituted "operating system" for "os" would produce the confusing result,

> . . . the operating system reduces computer chaoperating system and loperating systemt data.

To guard against being inconvenienced by this sort of error, take some simple precautions. First (and most important), always save your document just prior to performing the global search and replace operation so you can easily recover should you get into serious trouble. Second, specify full caps for your codes. Third, include a space at the beginning of the search string so that you search for " OS" rather than "OS," and, fourth, perform the search and replace operation with confirmation. (See Section 4- 1, "Editing Text," for details on the search and replace feature.)

Preparing to Write the Paper

The list below summarizes the major steps required to prepare for the writing stage of your project. See Fig. 5-3 for a production schedule and a model arrangement of the final paper. (The optional elements are marked with asterisks.)

1. Identify the major subtopics.
2. Revise your preliminary outline.
3. Sort your notes into the major subtopics.
4. Review your notes and relate them to the original hypothesis.

Production Schedule	Arrangement of Final Draft
1. Text	1. Title Page
2. Notes	2. Table of Contents
3. References	3. List of Tables*
4. Appendix*	4. List of Figures*
5. List of Tables*	5. Text
6. List of Figures*	6. End Notes
7. Table of Contents	7. References
8. Title Page	8. Appendix*

Figure 5-3 Arrangement of the Production Schedule and Final Draft

5. Modify the hypothesis if necessary.
6. Identify any gaps remaining in the research.
7. Return to original sources or find additional information to fill remaining gaps.
8. Write a preliminary thesis statement.
9. Sort the notes into major and minor supporting topics within each subtopic identified at step 1.
10. Within minor topics, order ideas logically into major details first and minor details second.
11. Expand your preliminary outline into a detailed outline.

When you type your notes directly into WordPerfect, sorting them into major and minor subtopics is easy: number them, perform a paragraph sort (see Section 8- 3) and then delete the numbers. If you don't key your notes directly into WordPerfect, use a large table to sort and organize the note cards. Whichever method is adopted, be sure to order the groupings in some meaningful fashion.

Next, order your notes within major topics. If you discover gaps in the narrative, return to your sources. After all gaps have been filled, "test" your hypothesis:

1. Is it supported by your findings?
2. Should it be modified or even replaced with an entirely new hypothesis?
3. Can you state a thesis?

If you can translate your hypothesis into a thesis statement, write it down. It may be as short as a sentence or as long as a paragraph and can either be descriptive or prescriptive. A *descriptive* thesis statement simply tells what the paper is about—for example, "This paper describes Yield Management: a set of pricing and space allocation strategies designed to maximize revenue that was first adopted in the airline industry." A *prescriptive* thesis statement takes a definite position—for example, "LBOs improve the competitiveness of American industry by forcing management to be more responsive to owners." Having reached this point, prepare your final detailed outline.

Writing the Paper

Your term paper should have three major sections: (1) introduction, (2) body, and (3) conclusions. Each major section should be introduced with a centered, first-level heading in full caps. The introduction section presents your thesis statement, briefly describes the subtopics you've selected, and provides a general description of your information sources. The body of your paper should be the largest section. There, you present enough historical or background information so your reader can readily grasp the problem being attacked, a discussion of the problem itself, an analysis of the problem, and the findings of your analysis. The conclusion re-states the thesis in terms of the evidence presented in the body and sums up what you think the research has accomplished.

Before beginning to write the first draft, carefully review your notes within the framework of your outline. Here, you should also draw conclusions, adding them to your outline, and develop linkages between ideas. This stage is like a pre-rough draft; if you do a good job here, writing the first draft should require just filling in the outline.

As concerns the process of putting words on paper or into a WordPerfect document, write the first draft quickly, getting everything down with a minimum of delay and interruption. Insert simple marker phrases for the tables and figures you plan to add in the second draft. For example, insert lines such as,

"—Table X about here—"

at the approximate location of each table and figure. Include quotations of three lines or less in running text and be sure to include them within quotes. If a quotation is longer than three lines, indent it from the left margin five spaces and set it single spaced. If the long quotation is a paragraph, indent the first line an additional four spaces.

After you've completed your second draft and allowed it to age for a day or two, check spelling and grammar. Use the WordPerfect Spell Check feature to check spelling (see Section 4- 2) and analyze your writing with a grammar software package such as *Grammatik* or *RightWriter*. Next, incorporate your tables and figures using WordPerfect's Graphics Feature, replacing the marker phrases included in your first draft (see Sections 6- 2, 6- 3, and 8- 1). Finally, incorporate parenthetical references or numbered footnotes or endnotes to replace the reference codes incorporated in your first draft (see Section 6- 1).

Adding the Optional Extras

When the final draft of your paper is complete, compose appendices, endnotes or footnotes, a table of contents, and a title page. Then, make a final spelling check, View Document, and proofread and replace any pages that still contain problems.

When you're ready to type your term paper, turn to Section 5- 4, "Long Document Procedures."

For additional guidance on the preparation of term papers, consult the following references:

Turabian, Kate L., *A Manual for Writers of Term Papers, Theses, and Dissertations* (5th ed.). Chicago: University of Chicago Press, 1987.

Walker, Melissa, *Writing Research Papers: A Norton Guide* (2nd ed.). New York and London: W. W. Norton & Company, 1987.

Weidenborner, Stephen, and Domenick Caruso, *Writing Research Papers: A Guide to the Process* (2nd ed.) New York: St. Martin's Press, 1986.

ENDNOTES

1. Melissa Walker, *Writing Research Papers: A Norton Guide*, 2nd ed. (New York and London: W. W. Norton & Company, 1987), appendix B.
2. Stephen Weidenborner and Domenick Caruso, *Writing Research Papers; A Guide to the Process*, 2nd ed. (New York: St. Martin's Press, 1986), pp. 25-31.
3. Newspaper and magazine articles are written for general audiences and terminology is usually understandable to the lay person. Journals, on the other hand, are written by professionals for professionals using language and terminology quite appropriate for the knowledgeable professional but often unintelligible to the lay person.
4. "CD-ROM" stands for *Compact Disk, Read Only Memory.* The technology required to produce CD-ROMs is similar to the technology used to produce music compact disks. "On-line" refers to information search services that are accessed via telephone line and modem.
5. You *need not* document ideas that are wholly your own, or information considered to be "general knowledge," that is, information which is readily available in the reference collections of most municipal libraries.
6. Walker, *Writing Research Papers,* ch. 8.
8. A paraphrase is a statement in your own words of the exact sense of a source passage.
9. Weidenborner and Caruso, *Writing Research Papers,* pp. 88.

5- 2 WRITING A CASE ANALYSIS

If your course instructors teach by the "case method," you may be asked to write case reports as regular assignments or take-home exams. Instructions in this module show you how do so. The module includes the following subsections:

1. Overview
2. Approaching the Case Assignment
3. Analysis
4. Organizing the Case Report
5. Writing the Case Report

These five subsections describe the structure of a case report, explain its purpose, and provide general guidelines for analyzing the case, organizing your notes in preparation for writing and then writing the case report itself. Turn to Section 5- 4, "Long Document Procedures," for detailed WordPerfect instructions on completing the operation.

Overview

Business students are often required to write analyses of business cases (called WACs at Harvard and other case method business schools). As you begin the task of "writing up a case," be aware that a single, standard format for a written case analysis doesn't exist. Nonetheless, there is a general approach to the task that most case instructors recommend and that the guidelines below attempt to capture. Although the approach described here is general and should suffice for most assignments, individual course instructors may specify the coverage, organization, and format of your written submission in some detail. Alternatively, you may discover that established case analysis guidelines are specified at the broader, school level. If either situation holds, modify the instructions included here accordingly.

Approaching the Case Assignment

As you approach a written case analysis assignment, observe these three guidelines: (1) assume the role of a manager or consultant, (2) supplement your case analysis with evidence from library research (unless the instructor prefers that you not do so), and (3) plan your analysis carefully. We expand upon the guidelines in the following paragraphs.

Take on the role of the manager. When you prepare to analyze a particular case, cast yourself in the role of a manager who must sort out a problem, develop alternative solutions, and recommend the best among the set of alternatives. Learn to work fast and don't waste time groping for "the one right answer" because a single right answer usually doesn't exist. (The ability of an effective manager to "champion" his or her solution to a particular problem and make it happen often results in a successful outcome even though he or she may not have adopted a "textbook" approach.)

An alternative approach for grappling with a written case assignment is to place yourself in the role of a consultant who thoroughly understands the underlying corporate culture and constraints faced by management but who is, nonetheless, tough-minded in proposing courses of action.

Bring in additional data. If the company is easily identifiable, extend your analysis beyond the data in the case. Most business libraries can provide additional background material on the important issues, and back issues of financial periodicals such as the *Wall Street Journal* and *Barrons* or more general business media such as *Fortune, Forbes,* and *Business Week* may have featured the subject company at the time the case research was conducted. Your analysis will be stronger if you can bolster the information drawn from the case with supplemental exhibits from outside sources. Be sure to document sources when you supplement case information with additional material, however (see Section 6- 1 for guidance in doing so). Remember that recommended courses of action should be framed in light of the information available to decision makers *at the time of the case,* not the information available when you analyze the case.

Plan for the analysis. Before you begin the written case analysis assignment, budget between 15 and 25 hours for all phases of the project. Then, working backward from the final revision of the written case report to the first reading of the case, allocate budgeted hours to each activity in the project. Finally, work according to the plan implicit in your time budget.[1]

Analysis

Generally, cases are analyzed in six stages:

1. Identification of problems and issues
2. Situation analysis and identification of appropriate evaluation criteria
3. Identification and assessment of alternative courses of action
4. Selection of one or more courses of action to be recommended
5. Development of an action plan for implementation of the recommended course(s) of action
6. Identification of controls to ensure successful implementation

These six stages comprise the principal elements of your analysis plan and should guide your efforts throughout. We discuss each stage in the following paragraphs.

Identify problems and issues. Carefully read the first few paragraphs of the case to familiarize yourself with the company and situation. Then quickly scan the remaining pages, asking the following questions:

- What is the case about?
- What are the significant issues, problems, and decisions impinging upon the situation described?
- What information am I being given?

This is your orientation reading. After the orientation reading, write what you recall on scratch paper, or key some preliminary notes directly into WordPerfect. Include the names and titles of the principal actors and their relationships to one another, apparent problems and issues, and possible courses of action for addressing them. In addition, jot down the major *points of focus,* that is, the particular criteria that appear to control the situation. For example, the situation faced by a newly launched restaurant chain may depend upon the strength of short-run product demand and the cash flow stream with all other considerations being secondary. Thus, projected short-run demand and cash flow should be the points of focus of the analysis.

After the initial analysis, read the case again, but more carefully this time, highlighting key facts and making marginal notes on the case itself. Ask yourself these questions:

- What are the problems facing this company at this time and why do they exist? Alternatively, identify the decisions that must be made and why.
- Who are the protagonists? What are their roles and responsibilities? To whom do they report and who reports to them?

State the problem or problems in written form, recognizing that the problem statement may be modified in the process of conducting the analysis. If multiple problems surface, rank them in the order of their relative importance. Also make notes on the company's objectives and strategies and try to understand the personality of the company, its management structure and style, and the organizational climate. Then link or relate problems to these characteristics.

If the case contains exhibits, be sure to analyze them thoroughly when they're referenced in the text. It's usually a good idea not to take exhibits at face value, for some critical information may be obtained from them by "massaging" the numbers.

Finally, summarize the important information gleaned from your reading. List all the facts, opinions, estimates, and assumptions of the case protagonists and be sure to identify all the pieces of information in your list as fact, opinion, assumption, conjecture, etc. Then add your own assumptions and reasoning. But be sure your assumptions are reasonable and consistent with the industry, environment, and time period of the case.

Perform a detailed situation analysis. Your objective in the situation analysis is to gain a complete and in-depth understanding of the situation so that your generation and analysis of alternative courses of action is unforced and rapid. At this point, try to prepare a preliminary outline whose elements are the primary and secondary headings in Fig. 5-4 (which is based on the ideas of Porter[2] and Strickland and Thompson[3]). As you take working notes, insert them into the outline, expanding it as you proceed and deleting elements for which you have no data. Constructing the outline will speed the process of writing later on and give you a bet-

1. Profitability and financial situation
2. Product situation:
    - 2. 1 Product line
    - 2. 2 New product development process
    - 2. 3 Vulnerability to substitutes
3. Competitive position relative to:
    - 3. 1 Rivals
    - 3. 2 Suppliers
    - 3. 3 Customers
    - 3. 4 Potential entrants
4. Operations—with particular attention paid to:
    - 4. 1 Production
    - 4. 2 Personnel
    - 4. 3 Organization structure
    - 4. 4 Controls
5. Markets and Customers
6. Quality of top management:
    - 6. 1 Past performance
    - 6. 2 Current performance
    - 6. 3 Future potential
7. Information technology
8. Prospects for the future

Figure 5-4 Case Analysis Checkpoints

ter final product. (See Section 7- 1 for guidelines and detailed instructions on constructing an outline.)

Generally, your analysis should separate symptoms from problems, rank the problems in terms of importance, and then show how they're related. The analysis should also incorporate appropriate quantitative assessments such as break-even, cash-flow, and pro forma models together with references to exhibits included at the end of your case.[4] Try to apply appropriate models to help yourself understand the situation better. For example, you may find that a microeconomic model might be appropriate for one type of situation while a behavioral model might be appropriate for another situation. Other models that may prove fruitful are systems models[5] and Michael Porter's "Competitive Forces" model.[6] Remember, general managers "wear many hats" so multidisciplinary approaches and integration of several models may be useful in the analysis of the case. Ask yourself other questions to a gain a better understanding.

For example, ask:

1. Why does this situation exist?
2. What will happen if no action is taken?
3. Are "hidden agendas" driving this situation? How might I infer what the agendas are?

4. Can I characterize the organization as a system with inputs, outputs, processes, standards, and a control mechanism? Can I gain useful insights by doing so?

Look for patterns in the data, and try to evaluate the situation from the point of view of each of the major protagonists in the case. You may gain some novel insights when you do. Try asking yourself, why would a rational individual behave in this fashion? If a process is involved, try breaking the process into its component parts and show how they're related by drawing a flow chart or other type of structure diagram.[7]

At this point, carefully reexamine all the exhibits in the case and make sure you calculate rates of return and appropriate financial ratios (when the data permit you to do so). In order to identify *feasible* alternative courses of action, assess the company's strengths and weaknesses and identify past courses of action that have been successes and failures. Also identify the firm's critical success factors[8] and look for distinct competencies. Doing so will help channel your efforts productively when you propose courses of action.

Identify the company's basic corporate strategy and ask whether it remains viable given the company's resources and the changes taking place in its competitive environment.

For example, ask:

- Is the company the industry's low cost producer?
- Does it compete through product differentiation?
- Is it a niche marketer?

Then match the strategy you've identified with resources, management, and competitive forces to assess its viability. The analysis should state your assumptions and indicate the major focus points governing the later evaluation of alternative courses of action. The final product of the analysis is a set of conclusions about the situation that are the criteria upon which the alternatives will be evaluated.

Identify alternative courses of action. Following your analysis of the case, identify a set of three to five *realistic,* alternative courses of action to match the problems identified in the problem-finding stage of your analysis. The alternatives should be unrelated and should flow from the analysis. Each alternative should also be feasible in the sense that a competent manager whose assessment of the situation differed from your own could still achieve success by implementing one of the alternative courses of action you have *not recommended.* (Doing nothing could be one of the alternatives considered, of course.) Don't consider alternatives that are obviously unworkable in the absence of extreme good fortune. Successful managers take carefully calculated risks, but they're not gamblers—at least not for long.

Alternative courses of action should be numbered and identified with appropriate labels. As you discuss alternatives, present advantages, disadvantages, and

Evaluative Criteria	Alternative #1	Alternative #2	Alternative #3
Criterion 1			
Criterion 2			
Criterion 3			
Criterion 4			
.			
.			
.			
Criterion n			
Overall Evaluation			

Figure 5-5 Alternative Analysis Table

your evaluation; finally, make a statement of acceptance or rejection, and briefly describe the criteria leading you to accept or reject. Explain why this set of criteria was chosen. For example, tie them in with strategy or critical success factors.

So far as organization is concerned, list your least preferred alternative first, then your next least preferred, and so on, progressing to the alternative you prefer most.

A concise but informative approach for evaluating alternatives is to complete a summary table like the one in Fig. 5-5. To use the table, list the evaluation criteria in the left-most column in order of their importance. Then list the alternatives across the top. The next step is to summarize the pluses and minuses associated with each criterion for the first alternative. After you've listed all the pluses and minuses for the first alternative, repeat the process for the second and subsequent alternatives. Record your overall evaluation of each evaluation at the foot of each column. (Tables like the one in Fig. 5-5 help you sort things out; don't include them in your written analysis.)

Recommend a "best" course of action. From the set of alternative courses of action, designate the alternative (or alternatives if they are not mutually exclusive) that represents the "best" choice given your view of the situation confronting management. The recommendation(s) should follow logically from your analysis, of course, and should possess the following characteristics:

- Affordable — The company possesses the financial resources to implement the alternative.
- Natural — It should fit corporate strategy, structure, and style.
- Ethical — It should be ethically and environmentally sound.

State your recommendation(s) in detail and don't hedge. Your proposal should be decisive, specific, and operational. Also indicate the most likely results if the recommended course of action is taken. Limitations to the recommended course of action should be identified, *but* show why they do not materially affect your decision. Finally, incorporate a contingency plan that can be implemented if the situation anticipated in your recommended course of action doesn't hold.

Prepare an action plan. Tell how to implement the recommended course or courses of action. Prepare an action plan to accompany your recommendation(s), outlining tasks to be accomplished, setting dates by which they should be complete, and identifying the individuals responsible for carrying out the actions recommended. Your action plan should also address the disadvantages of your recommended course of action, specifying in detail how they can be minimized.

Identify controls. Also specify appropriate management controls to help ensure that your action plan will be implemented effectively (assuming your situational assessment is correct). Incorporate the following components in your control section:

- Specific target benchmarks (e.g., market share, employee turnover)
- Performance measures
- A program of scheduled performance measurement
- Comparison of expected and actual results
- Evaluation of discrepancies
- A program of corrective action

If your situational assessment turns out to be in error, controls trigger the abandonment of the original plan and a switch to a contingency plan.

Organizing the Case Report

The format in Fig. 5-6 should be satisfactory as an organizing framework. This is a *model* format; and need not be followed slavishly, however. The *actual* structure of the case report should be determined by the needs of your audience, the content of the report, and the nature of the assignment itself. If your institution or instructor specifies a format differing from the format in Fig. 5-6, use the specified format instead.

Title Page

The "title page" should be a simple memorandum summarizing your recommendations addressed to an appropriate officer in the client organization—not your course instructor. (The title page is an executive summary and corresponds to the management report "Synopsis.") The subject line of the title page memo should be longer than the subject lines of memos with which we communicate on a day-to-day basis because it must provide more information. (The subject line of a standard memo need only provide simple cues as to the purpose of the memo.) The text in the body of the title page memo is limited to your recommendation(s).

Introduction

The introduction provides a brief background statement, a statement of the case report's purpose, a summary of the primary problem or problems, the focus

A. Memorandum-style title page
    1. To, from, date lines
    2. Subject line
    3. Recommendations
B. Introduction
    1. Background
    2. Purpose of report
    3. Problem statement
    4. Limits of the analysis
C. Analysis
    1. Major points of focus
    2. Assumptions
    3. Interrelationships
D. Alternatives
    1. Advantages
    2. Disadvantages
    3. Conclusion
E. Recommendation
F. Implementation
    1. Action plan
        a. Tasks
        b. Dates
        c. Individuals responsible
    2. Contingency plan
G. Controls
H. Conclusion
I. Exhibits

Figure 5-6 Organization of a Written Case

point or points of the analysis and a list of the areas to be covered. This is where you tell why the problem surfaced and why it's important to the organization. Customarily, the introduction does not have a heading and is limited to one or two concise, *hard-hitting* paragraphs.

Analysis

The analysis section is usually the longest section of a case report and is introduced by the centered heading, "ANALYSIS," set in full caps. Depending on the depth of your analysis, second and third level headings are also appropriate in this section. Remember that at least two subordinate headings should be included at each level below a superior heading. If you prepared a sentence-style outline built around topic sentences during your analysis of the case (see Section 7- 1), your outline can provide the structure for this section, with topic sentences defining paragraphs.

Alternatives

Begin the alternatives section with a new centered heading set in full caps. The alternatives discussed within the section are numbered and titled, and each paragraph in the section describes the advantages and disadvantages of a single alternative, concluding with your statement as to its acceptability.

Recommendation

The recommendation section also begins with a centered heading in full caps and then presents the recommended course(s) of action. Following the presentation of the proposed best course(s) of action, justify your selection, linking back to the analysis section to provide the detailed logic necessary to convince the reader that you've considered all sides of the issue, weighed the evidence appropriately, and provided a workable solution to the problem identified at the beginning of the report.

Implementation

The implementation section is also introduced by a primary-level, centered, fully capitalized heading. The plan for implementing your recommended course(s) of action is presented here. It includes reasonable levels of detail on the tasks to be performed, expected completion dates, and the individuals responsible for seeing that required tasks are completed. Also include a contingency plan that can be implemented should the basic program(s) falter because of unanticipated events.

Controls

The controls section describes the benchmarks you recommend for assessing the degree of success of your recommended program. Potential measures are market share, sales volume levels, quality levels, costs, or brand awareness stated quantitatively as objectives on a time line. Benchmarks should be tied to the implementation plan.

Conclusion

The concluding section is at most a paragraph in length and can be as brief as a single sentence. The conclusion should be positive and upbeat, reflecting the decisiveness of your recommendation(s). Here's an example:

> By accepting this recommendation, the company gains a position in government markets without establishing price points that are so low that margins in traditional markets become unacceptable to the dealer network.

As a matter of custom (but surely not of reader convenience), exhibits are located at the end of a case report. Examples of exhibits are financial statements, plant layouts, advertisements, flow charts, organization charts, and cash flow spreadsheets. They enable you to present supporting detail economically. All exhibits are listed in numerical order—beginning with arabic numeral 1; all must have appropriate descriptive headings, and all must show sources when it is appropriate to do so. Each exhibit must be referenced somewhere in the text and the reference must be accompanied by interpretive commentary. *Don't pad your written analysis with exhibits that are not discussed in the body of the report.* A common practice is to include financial statements only. Although exhibits should be explained and interpreted in the text, don't overburden your reader by explaining the methods used to obtain the numbers in the exhibits. If necessary, an appendix can be included (for methodological details, extended calculations, computer programs, or questionnaires, for example). If a single appendix is included, label it as "APPENDIX." If two or more appendices are included, label them as "APPENDIX A," APPENDIX B," Etc.

Writing the Report

For the average written case analysis, try to limit the body of your report to five to ten double-spaced pages with ample headings and white space for readability and instructor comments. If the nature of the case requires that you support your analysis with numbers or quantitative models, incorporate them in tabular or graphical exhibits because tables and figures permit you to summarize information efficiently.

Don't state that the data are inadequate to the formulation of a course of action. Instead, take a stand based on a logical interpretation of *the facts you do have.* If necessary, make appropriate, *defensible* assumptions. It is a rare case that omits information central to proper analysis, and you will certainly face situations in real life requiring that decisions be made on the basis of incomplete or questionable information. Prepare yourself now to cope effectively with that situation. A related tip: don't recount case facts and history; your instructor is well aware of those details.

When you write your case report, remember a point made in the overview section of this chapter: Be sensitive to the value of your reader's time. It has been estimated[9] that the average instructor spends between 15 and 20 minutes per case while grading written case analyses. Thus, you have little time to make a good impression. Don't waste it; be sure your report is focused, direct, concise, and easy to read. Ask a friend to read your second or third draft if there's time available. Alternatively, read the report aloud yourself to check for awkward construction. Finally, take care to avoid using one-sided arguments to support your recommendation(s). Adopting an even-handed writing style will force you to consider alternative viewpoints and be more persuasive.

When you're ready to type your case analysis using WordPerfect, turn to Section 5- 4, "Long Document Procedures."

For additional guidance on the preparation of written cases, consult these references:

Haywood-Farmer, John, "Note on Case Analysis." The University of Western Ontario School of Business Administration, London, 1979, Number 9-81-L002.

Haywood-Farmer, John, "Note on Report Writing." The University of Western Ontario School of Business Administration, London, 1979, Number 9-81-L005.

Raymond, Thomas J., "Written Analysis of Cases." In *The Case Method at the Harvard Business School,* ed. Malcolm McNair, 139-163. New York: McGraw-Hill, 1954.

Ronstadt, Robert, "Tactics: Writing a Case Report," *The Art of Case Analysis.* Dover, MA: Lord Publishing Company, 1978.

Stopford, John M., Derek F. Channon, and John Constable, "Writing Case Reports," *Cases in Strategic Management.* New York: John Wiley & Sons, 1980, 529-541.

Strickland, A. J., and A. A. Thomas, "Case Analysis: Its Role and Method," *Strategic Management, Concepts and Cases* (3rd ed.). Plano, TX: Business Publications, Inc., 1984, 273-289.

ENDNOTES

1. See the long document overview at the beginning of Chapter 5 for a more detailed treatment of scheduling and time allocation for a major writing project.
2. Michael E. Porter, "How Competitive Forces Shape Strategy," *Harvard Business Review,* 57, No.2 (March-April 1979), 137-145.
3. A. J. Strickland and A. A. Thomas, "Case Analysis: Its Role and Method," in *Strategic Management, Concepts and Cases,* 3rd ed. (Plano, TX: Business Publications, Inc., 1984), pp. 273-289.
4. A model is a highly simplified representation of a real-world process or relationship with all nonessential features stripped away to aid the user in understanding the fundamental nature of the process or relationship. Models are expressed in many ways, but mathematical, verbal, and graphical models are most commonly used in business applications.
5. Raymond Mcleod, Jr., *Management Information Systems,* 3rd ed. (Chicago: Science Research Associates, Inc., 1986), ch. 4.
6. Porter, "Competitive Forces," 137-145.
7. Jeffrey Whitten, Lonnie Bentley, and Vic Barlow, *Systems Analysis and Design Methods,* 2nd ed. (Homewood, IL: Richard D. Irwin, 1989).
8. John F. Rockart, "Chief Executives Define Their Own Data Needs," *Harvard Business Review,* 57, No. 2 (January-February 1989), 81-93.
9. Robert Ronstadt, "Tactics: Writing a Case Report," in *The Art of Case Analysis* (Dover, MA: Lord Publishing Company, 1978).

5- 3 *WRITING A MANAGEMENT REPORT*

The instructions in this section show you how to use WordPerfect to write a management report. Follow them when you're preparing to write up a field project with a local company or the results of a summer internship. They'll also be useful if you take a course involving a consulting engagement with a local company or non-profit organization. The paragraphs below provide a general approach to report organization and make formatting recommendations. Turn to Section 5- 4, "Long Document Procedures," for detailed instructions on using WordPerfect to complete the management report.

Overview

No attempt is made here to differentiate between short reports (called memo or letter reports) perhaps three or four pages in length, and the longer, more formal reports that might include a title page, a table of contents, and some exhibits. No matter how long the report, however, principles of style, format, and construction are similar. Long reports and short reports differ only in numbers of pages and in the inclusion or exclusion of optional components such as title page, lists of tables and figures, a management summary, glossary, appendices, references, and footnotes and endnotes.

Reports, like term papers, can be classified as descriptive or prescriptive in purpose. A *descriptive* report describes a situation and draws pertinent conclusions but *does not* make recommendations for change. A *prescriptive* report, describes a situation, draws conclusions and *does make* recommendations for change.[1] No matter whether a report is *descriptive* or *prescriptive,* the writer must include some discussion of four primary analytical steps:

1. Problem identification
2. Method of analysis
3. Findings
4. Conclusions

A fifth element, "Recommendations," is added to the list above when the report is *prescriptive.*

Be Sure the Report Re-States the Problem, Method, Findings, Conclusions, and Recommendations Several Times

Management reports should incorporate several repetitions of problem, method, findings, conclusions, (and recommendations if the report is prescriptive). Usually, all four (or five) components are addressed in the cover letter, the management summary, the findings, and the report summary; they should also be reflected in major section headings and in the topic sentences of paragraphs. As we point out below, the final report *package* reverses the order of *producing* the components of the report.

Adopt an Effective Writing Production Schedule

Fig. 5-7 is a production schedule for *writing* the individual components of the report. It shows how to organize the production process to make the most efficient use of your time.[2] The figure also includes references to supplemental sections in *WordPerfect Applications* that provide detailed instructions for producing the components indicated.

After your analysis of the situation or problem under investigation, write the body of your report in the order shown. Start with a brief background statement for less knowledgeable readers. Follow up by describing the methodology in sufficient detail so readers will understand how your analysis was conducted and will be able to judge the quality of your work without getting bogged down in statistical terminology. Next, present your findings and results.

As you write about background, methodology, and findings, prepare thumbnail sketches of the tables and figures you plan to use in support of your findings. You

PRODUCTION SCHEDULE	SUPPLEMENTAL SECTIONS
A. Body	4- 1, 4- 2, 4- 6
1. Background	
2. Methodology	
3. Findings and results	
4. Tables [preliminary]	6- 2
5. Figures [preliminary]	6- 3
6. References [preliminary]	6- 1
7. Conclusions	
8. Recommendations [Prescriptive]	
9. Evaluative Discussion	
10. Introduction	
a. Historical material	
b. Criteria	
c. Assumptions	
B. Executive Summary	
C. Pagination (text and back matter)	4- 4, 6- 6
D. Appendices	
E. Exhibits	8- 1 6- 2, 6- 3
F. Reference material	
1. Endnotes	6- 1
2. Bibliography	6- 7
G. List of Tables and Figures	6- 8
I. Table of Contents	6- 9
F. Title Page	6-10
J. Pagination (front matter)	4- 4, 6- 6
K. Cover letter or memo	3- 1, 3- 2

Figure 5-7 Management Report Production Schedule

may also decide to create more or less finished graphics at this point, storing them in a separate WordPerfect document for later polishing and inclusion in the report.

Also try to prepare rough source and content footnotes and bibliographic entries as you write the text of your report. If you compose in WordPerfect, create the list of sources in Doc 2 using bibliographic reference format and then copy the individual source listings from Doc 2 into the Footnote/Endnote Editing screen in Doc 1. After switching back to Doc 1, change the source listing from bibliographic format to footnote/endnote format and return to work composing text. (We illustrate a similar operation in the "Long Document Procedures" subsection. See Section 5- 4.) Alternatively, you may wish to write the source and content notes on cards or separate sheets of paper to be typed at a later point.

When you finish describing and interpreting your findings, write your conclusions and recommendations (if the report is prescriptive). At this point you may also wish to write some evaluative commentary on the limitations of your research and analysis, including caveats governing the interpretation of your results, or suggesting future research directions.[3]

After the evaluative discussion, go back and write the introductory paragraphs. This brief section should include the following coverage:

1. Historical background
2. A brief discussion of the present situation
3. The criteria used in the analysis
4. The major assumptions framing the analysis
5. A description of how the report is organized

Next write the executive summary. This is a one-page, single-spaced description of the problem or situation, methodology, findings, and conclusions and recommendations. After you've drafted the executive summary, type your whole draft into WordPerfect (if you didn't compose at the keyboard at the outset). Then go back and edit all the material you've written to this point. Some of your editing will involve correcting typos and spelling errors; some will involve substituting words and phrases for existing text and moving blocks of material from place to place. And, of course, some will involve extensive re-writing and expansion of draft text. When your second draft is finished, read it aloud to check the coherency of your construction.

Now, organize the material to be included in the appendix or appendices. If your exhibits are not yet in final form, finish them at this point, melding them into the body of the report, or grouping them into a separate "Exhibits" section at the end of the report.

Prepare your endnotes (or footnotes) and bibliography in final form. If you composed your notes as you wrote the text of the report, all you need to do at this point is edit existing text.

Finally, turn to sections 6-10, 6- 8, 6- 9, and 3- 1 or 3- 2 to prepare your title page, lists of tables and figures (optional), table of contents, and memo or letter of transmittal.

Package Your Report for Efficient Reading

The outline in Fig. 5-8 is a guideline for *organizing the components of the final report.* It shows how all the major components that *might be* included should be organized; it also shows the composition of each component. (Components with asterisks are optional.) *Note that the order of the major components differs from the order in the production schedule displayed in Fig. 5-7.* The layered, repetitive arrangement illustrated in Fig. 5-8 ensures that the report can be read efficiently. Top-line information is immediately accessible in the first few pages (the cover letter and executive summary); additional detail emerges at levels further down in the structure as the reader progresses from the report's first page to its last.

A. Cover letter or memo
    1. Authorization or occasion
    2. Scope
        a. Problem
        b. Method
        c. Findings
        d. Conclusion
    3. Acknowledgements
    4. Closing

B. Title Page
    1. Report title
    2. Recipient's name and title
    3. Name of organization
    4. Writer's name, title, affiliation
    5. Place and date

C. Table of Contents
D. List of Tables and Figures*
E. Executive Summary
    1. Problem statement
    2. Major decision criteria
    3. Conclusions
    4. Recommendations
    5. Supporting evidence

F. Body
    1. Introduction
        a. Historical background
        b. Purpose of the report
        c. Statement of criteria
        d. Assumptions
    2. Conclusions
    3. Recommendations [Prescriptive Report]*
    4. Findings
    5. Methodology
    6. Background
    7. Evaluative discussion*

G. Glossary/Definition of Terms*
H. Appendices*
    1. Tables of data
    2. Samples of forms
    3. Questionnaires
    4. Articles
    5. Financial statements

I. Exhibits*
    1. Tables
    2. Figures

K. Reference Material*
    1. Bibliography
    2. Endnotes

Figure 5-8 Report Format

Inclusion or exclusion of the individual components listed in Fig. 5-8 depends on your report's length, on its technical complexity, and on the document formatting standards of the organization for which it is written.

Format the Report According to Accepted Standards

Most of the space in a management report should be used to present the study findings, and subsections within the findings section should be organized according to the principal criteria used to evaluate the situation being investigated. For example, if you were writing a report to propose an advertising program for a local symphony orchestra, organize your findings as you would an advertising plan. That is, include subsections on audience, objectives, media, copy, schedule and budget. On the other hand, if you were reporting on the evolution of a client company's management information system, a chronological arrangement would probably be most appropriate.

Relatively little space should be devoted to a description of methodology in a management report because readers are primarily interested in the findings and the conclusions you've drawn from them. If *details* on methodology are included at all, confine them to an appendix. (This advice should *not* be interpreted to suggest that methodological *rigor* is unimportant.)

The executive summary should be written last and confined to a single-spaced page. Identify the summary with a one-word heading, "SUMMARY," "SYNOPSIS," or "ABSTRACT," and be sure that the headings included in the summary match the headings in the report itself. When you adopt this last guideline, the reader can switch directly from the summary to related material in the detailed findings section.

With the exception of the executive summary, the report should be double-spaced with paragraphs indented five spaces from the left margin. Lengthy quoted material should be used only sparingly. If quoted material is included, however, type it single-spaced and indented five spaces from the left margin. Incorporate lists of tables and figures only if many tables and figures are included.

If the number of tables and figures is limited (say one or fewer in every two pages), include them directly in the body of the report and number them consecutively with Arabic numerals (see Section 6- 8). If a large number of tables and figures is to be included (say more than one in every two pages), place them at the end of the report, refer to them as "Exhibits," and identify them with Roman numerals and descriptive titles.

When you're ready to type your management report using WordPerfect, turn to Section 5- 4, "Long Document Procedures."

For additional guidance on the preparation of management reports, consult the following references:

Collett, Howard M., "Getting That Report Off the Ground," *WordPerfect*

Magazine (May 1989): 31-34.

Ehrenberg, A. S. C., "Writing Technical Papers or Reports," *The American Statistician* 36, No. 4 (November 1982): 326-29.

Himstreet, William C., and Wayne Murlin Baty, *Business Communications* (8th ed.), chs. 16-19. Boston: PWS-Kent Publishing Company, 1987.

Holcombe, Marya W. and Judith K. Stein, *Writing for Decision Makers: Memos and Reports with a Competitive Edge* (2nd. ed.). New York: Van Nostrand Reinhold Company, 1987.

Hoop, Kenneth W., and Thomas E. Pearsall, *Reporting Technical Information,* (6th ed.) New York: MacMillan, 1988.

Huseman, Richard C., James M. Lahiff, and John M. Penrose, *Business Communications* (3rd ed.), chs. 8-10. Hinsdale, IL: The Dryden Press, 1988.

Lesikar, Raymond V., and Mary P. Lyons, *Report Writing for Business* (7th ed.) Homewood, IL: Irwin, 1986.

Munter, Mary, *Business Communication: Strategy and Skill,* pp. 165-173. Englewood Cliffs, NJ: Prentice-Hall, Inc., 1987.

Ruch, William V. and Maurice L. Crawford, *Business Reports: Written and Oral*. Boston: PWS-Kent Publishing Company, 1988.

ENDNOTES

1. Descriptive and prescriptive approaches are contrasted in the introductory section of this chapter.
2. See the long document overview at the beginning of Chapter 5 for a more detailed treatment of scheduling and time allocation for a major writing project.
3. A. S. C. Ehrenberg, "Writing Technical Papers or Reports," *The American Statistician,* 36, No. 4 (November 1982), 326-29.

5- 4 LONG DOCUMENT PROCEDURES

Producing and packaging a long document using WordPerfect usually requires the completion of between 15 and 25 separate procedures with the number of procedures required depending on the length and complexity of the document. A list of twenty procedures involved in the preparation of a written case or management report of average complexity is shown in Fig. 5-9. Several of the procedures required are described fully in this subsection; others are described in supplemental instruction modules in Chapters 4, 6, and 8. Let's get started.

1. *Prepare the first draft.* Type [WP], and press Enter to run WordPerfect. Before typing text, notice the status line at the bottom of the screen. From left to right, it shows the document number (1 or 2), the page number (Pg), the *vertical position* of the cursor (Ln) measured in inches from the top of the page,

1. Prepare the first draft

    a. Body text
    b. Headings
    c. Quotations

2. Import tables and figures
3. Check your spelling
4. Number pages
5. Block protect headings
6. Edit your WordPerfect document on-screen
7. Print the first draft
8. Edit the first draft
9. Use the WordPerfect thesaurus
10. Prepare footnotes or endnotes
11. Hyphenate your text
12. Prepare and append your list of references
13. Add exhibits
14. Add appendices after exhibits
15. Generate lists of tables and figures
16. Generate the table of contents
17. Construct and insert a title page
18. Assign page numbers to the front matter
19. Spell check the full document
20. View and print the final document

Figure 5-9 Long Document Procedures

and the *horizontal position* of the cursor (Pos) measured in inches from the left edge of the page.

NOTE: If you're working on a previously saved document, the status line also shows the document name (including drive designation and subdirectory names, if any).

An important *menu* you don't see on your WordPerfect screen specifies margin settings, tab stops, and line spacing. It's called the Format menu. Let's use it now to make sure margin settings are OK. To see margin settings in the Format: Line menu, press **(Shift-F8)** and type [**L**]; to change them, type [**M**] when the menu is displayed.

NOTE: Margin settings of 1" left and right are good default settings for a long document. If your long document will be bound, leave some extra space on the left side of the page. Since an extra half inch is usually enough, set the left margin at 1.5" instead of 1".

Layout
    Line M, [*left margin*], <R>, [*right margin*], <R>, <R>

To see tab settings (assuming you're still in the Format: Line menu),

- Type [**T**] for Tab settings. The default WordPerfect tab settings starting at 0.5" with a tab every half inch thereafter are probably best. If you see these settings (they appear as "L"s every half inch), press **(F7)** (or the right mouse button) to return to the Format: Line menu. If not,
- Type [**T**] for "Type", and [**R**] for "Relative".
- Press **(Ctrl-End)** to delete existing tabs.
- Type [**0, 0.5**] and press **Enter** (be sure to type "0.5" and not ".5"). Press **Home**, **Home**, **Home**, **Left Arrow**, **(Ctrl-End)** to delete tabs if you make a mistake.
- Press **(F7)** to return to the Format: Line menu.

T, T, R, <(Ctrl-End)>, [0,0.5], <R>, <R>

If spacing is set at 2 (double spacing), press **(F7)** to return to the Normal Editing screen. Otherwise, type [**S**], change the number to 2 and press **(F7)** twice to return to the Normal Editing screen.

S, [2], <R>, <R>

For a long document, good formatting rules of thumb are:

- Double spacing
- Tabs starting at .5 inches and every half-inch thereafter
- Left and right margins of 1 inch
- Top and bottom margins of 1 inch

NOTE: You saw that the Format: Line menu displayed settings already; these are called "initial settings" or "default settings." If default settings will meet your formatting needs, don't alter them.

The first page

1. 1 You should now be ready to type your long document; let's start at the top of the first page. Look at Fig. 5-10, an excerpt from a management report, before you do. Press **(Shift-F6)**, **Caps Lock**, and then type the title of your long document as you would on a typewriter. (Notice what happens to the information on the status line.) Then press **Enter** twice to quadruple space between the title and the heading of your introductory section.

```
        FACULTY CONSULTING PRACTICES AT LEADING BUSINESS SCHOOLS


                             INTRODUCTION

      In January 1989, a committee of the faculty of the Babcock School was

created and charged with the task of reviewing the policies of the school and

the university with respect to faculty consulting and making a report based
```

Figure 5-10 The First Page

1. 2 Press **(Shift-F6)**, type [**introduction**], press **Caps Lock** and **Enter** to produce a fully-capitalized, first-level heading, shift back to upper-lowercase and move your cursor to the left margin.

1. 3 This is a good place to toggle on Reveal Codes to see what WordPerfect's formatting codes look like. Press **(Alt-F3)** (or **(F11)**) to do so. Press **(Alt-F3)** (or **(F11)**) to toggle Reveal Codes off again when you've finished examining the codes.

```
Edit
     Reveal Codes
```

1. 4 Press **Tab** and begin typing the text of your introductory section.

NOTE: By pressing Tab, you indent the first line of a paragraph. Had you pressed (F4), the indent key, instead, all lines of the paragraph would have been indented.

NOTE: You needn't press Enter every time you come to the end of a line because WordPerfect automatically "wraps around" to the beginning of the next line for you. But do press Enter at the end of a paragraph or at other times when you want to end a line of text prematurely.

NOTE: Two spaces separate sentences, while single spaces follow punctuation marks within sentences—that is, commas, semicolons, and colons.

Typing second-level headings

Liberal use of headings breaks up your text, making it easier to comprehend and more interesting, and provides familiar road signs for the reader wanting to re-read important passages. Review Fig. 5-11 and follow the next five instructions to insert a second-level heading.

governing policies, the amount of time allowed, the degree of control, and limitations placed on the consulting activities of faculty members are considered.

<u>In General, Business Schools Favor Faculty Consulting</u>

Perhaps as many as one-third of the institutions responding to our survey stated in published literature that faculty consulting was desirable and a practice to be encouraged. They also stated that consulting is a

Figure 5-11 Second-Level Headings

1.5 Move the cursor to the end of the last line typed (if it isn't there already) by moving the cursor anywhere in the line and pressing **End**.

1.6 Press **(Shift-F8)**, type [**L**], [**S**], [**3**], and press **Enter**, **(F7)**, **Enter** to switch to triple spacing and move the cursor to the left margin.

Layout
Line S, [3], <R>, <R>, <Enter>

NOTE: Triple space prior to first- and second-level headings. We quadruple-spaced prior to the initial heading shown in Fig. 5-10 because it followed the long document title. If subsequent sections do not start on new pages, be sure to triple space between their first-level headings and the last line of preceding test.

1.7 With your cursor at the left margin, press **(Shift-F8),** type [**L**], [**S**], [**2**] and press **Enter**, **(F7)** to switch back to double spacing since that's the standard for long documents.

Layout
Line S, [2], <R>, <R>

1.8 Press **(F8)** to toggle on the underline feature. Then type the second-level heading, headline style. That is, use initial capitals for all words other than articles, conjunctions, and prepositions.[1]

1.9 At the end of the second level heading, press **(F8)**, **Enter**, and **Tab** to toggle off underlining and move your cursor to the first tab position in the line just below your second-level heading.

1.10 Continue typing your draft.

Typing third-level headings

Third-level headings are *paragraph headings,* underlined phrases or complete sentences that are indented five spaces and begin a new paragraph. Do not change line spacing prior to typing a third-level heading. Review Fig. 5-12 and follow the next two instructions to insert third-level headings.

1.11 With your cursor at the left margin, press **Tab**, **(F8)** to toggle on underlining, and then type the third level headings sentence-style (only the first letter of the first word in the sentence or phrase is capitalized).

1.12 Press **(F8)**, type [.] and press **Space Bar** twice at the end of the heading.

1.13 Continue typing the text of your draft.

Typing long quotations

When you include a quotation longer that three typewritten lines, indent the entire quotation five spaces and set it single spaced. Look at Fig. 5-13 and follow the next five instructions to produce a good result.

```
community which might provide additional benefits for the institution in the

form of contributions, student projects, and placement opportunities.

     Little documentation exists.  One surprising finding of the study was

the paucity of published documentation related to faculty consulting.  And in

cases where documentation was available, most of it was prepared at the
```

Figure 5-12 Third Level Headings

```
they normally address issues such as the amount of consulting permitted and

the approval and reporting procedures.  For example, consider this excerpt

from the Royall School of Management:

          Full-time faculty members are allowed to spend a maximum of one
     day per week (50 days per year) engaged in consulting  activities for
     additional compensation.  All consulting must be approved by the Dean of
     the School of Management and a report of each engagement including name
     of client, dates, and nature of the engagement is to be submitted
     annually. . . .

Frequently, published policy statements also address issues of conflict

of interest and conflict of commitment.  Only the policy document of the
```

Figure 5-13 Long Quotations

1.14 Move your cursor to the left margin one (double-spaced) line below the last line of text preceding the quotation.

1.15 Press **(Shift-F8)**, type [**L**], [**S**], [**1**], and press **Enter**, **(F7)** to set single spacing and return to the Normal Editing screen.

Layout
Line S, [1], <R>, <R>

1.16 Press **(F4)** to indent every line in the quotation five spaces in from the left margin.

NOTE: If the quoted material includes the start of a paragraph (like the quotation in the example), press **Tab** after pressing **(F4)** to indent the first line of the paragraph an additional five spaces.

1.17 Type the quotation but don't press Enter at the end of the quoted passage.

1.18 Instead, press **(Shift-F8)**, type [**L**], [**S**], [**2**], and press **Enter, (F7)**, **Enter** to return to double spacing and jump to the left margin of the next line down.

Layout
Line S, [2], <R>, <R>, <Enter>

Continue typing until your entire first draft is complete.

2. *Import tables and figures.* If your long document includes tables, or figures, or both, we assume you followed our earlier advice and prepared pencil sketches of the layouts of your tables and figures as you wrote your rough draft. Perhaps you also created tables of results in Lotus 1-2-3, Excel, or another spreadsheet package to support your analysis. If you used a statistical package such as SAS, SPSS, or MINITAB, you may have saved your results in an ASCII[2] file that can be retrieved easily into a document (see Section 9-1). We also assume you marked the location of tables and figures in your draft.

   At this point, consult the instructions in Section 6- 2, "Constructing Tables," Section 8- 1, "Working with Graphics," and Section 6- 3, "Importing Figures," for guidance on working tables and figures into your long document.
3. *Check your spelling.* See Section 4- 2, "Spell Checking," to make your *pre-edit* pass through WordPerfect's spell checker. Doing so at this point will save you needless distraction from typos when you edit your first typed draft.
4. *Number pages.* This is a good place to start numbering pages in the text and back matter of your long document. Later, you'll number the front matter, that

is, the table of contents and lists of tables and figures (if the latter are included). See Section 4- 4, "Numbering Pages," for page numbering guidelines.

5. *Block protect headings.* "Block protect" first- and second-level headings and the first two lines of the following text to avoid leaving the headings by themselves at the bottom of a page.[3] To block protect headings and the next two lines of text, take these steps.
   5. 1 Move your cursor to the initial character in the first heading in your long document. (In our management report example, that would be the word, INTRODUCTION, following the report title on page 1.)
   5. 2 Press **(Alt-F4)** (or **(F12)**) to toggle on the block feature and press **Down Arrow** until the cursor is in the second text line below the heading; then press **End**.
   5. 3 Press **(Shift-F8)** and type [Y] to protect the block you defined in step 5. 2.

Edit
Block <Down Arrow>, <End>

Edit
Protect Block

   5. 4 Repeat the procedure in steps 5. 1 to 5. 3 for remaining first- and second-level headings.

6. *Edit your WordPerfect document on-screen.* Proofread and then edit the document.
   6. 1 Review the text to ensure that all necessary punctuation is included.
   6. 2 Carefully examine the text, using Up Arrow and Down Arrow to move a line at a time, or the - and + keys at the right of the numeric keypad to jump to the top and bottom of the screen to scan for errors. To move to the top of your document, press **Home**, **Home**, **Up Arrow**; to move to the bottom, press **Home, Home, Down Arrow**.

   Press either **Right Arrow** or **Left Arrow** to move a character at a time within a line. Press **(Ctrl-Right Arrow)** or **(Ctrl-Left Arrow)** to move a word at a time forward or backward; press **End** to move to the right end of the line; and press **Home**, **Home**, **Left Arrow** to move to the left end of the line before any text.

   NOTE: Pressing Home, Home, Home, Left Arrow moves the cursor in front of any codes at the left end of the line (the codes are visible only when you press (Alt-F3) or (F11) to reveal codes).

6. 3 Turn to Section 4- 1 for editing instructions.

6. 4 When you've finished editing your long document, press **(F7)**. WordPerfect prompts you with,

Save document? (Yes) No

with the cursor flashing under Y.

- Press **Enter** and WordPerfect requests a document name.
- Type a name—TRMPAPER.W51, for example—and press **Enter**. Next, WordPerfect prompts you to exit. If you only want to clear your Normal Editing screen, press **Enter**; if you want to return to DOS, type [**Y**].

File
Exit Y, [*filename*], Y

NOTE: When WordPerfect prompts you for a document name, type [**A:TRMPAPER.W51**] and press **Enter** to save your long document on a floppy disk in drive A instead of the hard drive,

6. 5 If you didn't complete your task in one sitting, recall your long document to the screen. Here's how.

- Assuming WordPerfect is still running, press **(F5)**, **Enter** to see a list of your files. (If WordPerfect isn't running, type [**WP**] and press **Enter** first.)

  NOTE: If you saved your long document on a diskette in drive A, type [**A:**] and press **Enter** after you press **(F5)**.

File
List Files <R>, N, [*filename*], <R>, R

- To recall your long document, press the cursor arrows to highlight its name and type [**R**].

  NOTE: An alternative way to retrieve the long document is to press **(Shift-F10)**, and then, in response to WordPerfect's prompt,

  Document to be retrieved: ,

  type [***document name***] and press **Enter**.

File
Retrieve [*filename*], <R>

7. *Print the first draft.* To view a printer image of your first draft and then print it, see Section 4- 3, "Printing Documents."
8. *Edit the first draft.* Edit your printed draft with a blue or red pen so changes are obvious. (Circle tiny changes such as inserted periods and apostrophes.) Compose additional or substitute material and tie it in to your draft with number or letter symbols that key the new or updated material to specific locations in your draft. When you've marked all necessary changes in your printed draft and written all the additions and changes, run WordPerfect, retrieve your document, and follow the instructions in Section 4- 1, "Editing Text," to revise your material. Repeat the printing, editing, revision cycle as many times as necessary.
9. *Improve word selection with WordPerfect's thesaurus.* At this point, your long document should be quite clean, but you'll undoubtedly detect excessive repetition of some words and insufficient precision in others. Use WordPerfect's thesaurus to help solve those problems. Section 6- 4, "Using the Thesaurus," tells you the steps to follow. When you've finished using the thesaurus, save your long document again and clear your screen.

File
Exit Y, <R>, Y, N

10. *Preparing footnotes or endnotes.* If you plan to incorporate either endnotes or footnotes into your long document, follow these suggestions:
    - 10. 1 Type all source and content notes into a *new* document in the same order to be followed in your long document. We recommend that you use single spacing and then skip a line after every note. Don't number the notes in this *source* document since WordPerfect numbers them automatically in the *destination* document (your long document).
    - 10. 2 Spell check the notes source document, adding often-used proper names, technical terms, and other "new" words to the spell checker's dictionary. (See Section 4- 2, "Spell Checking.")

File
Exit Y, [*filename*], N

    - 10. 3 Press **(F7)**, name the notes document—say, NOTESORS.W51—press **Enter** to save it, and then type [N] to stay active in WordPerfect.
    - 10. 4 Now, before you copy the individual notes into your long document, copy the *notes* source document to a *reference* source document for

subsequent editing and purging of content notes and repeated source notes. This latter document will be your bibliography source document.

- Press **(F5)**, **Enter**, and use the cursor keys to highlight the notes document.
- Type [**C**] and WordPerfect prompts you with,

  Copy this file to: .

  In response, type the name of the reference source document—say, REFSSORS.W51—and press **Enter**.

File
List Files <R>, N, [*filename1*], <R>, C, [*filename2*], <R>, <R>

10. 5 Now, highlight the name of your long document—that is, the report, term paper, or case—and type [**R**] to retrieve it into Doc 1.

N, [*filename*], <R>, R

10. 6 Move your cursor to the position for your first note number placement, press **(Ctrl-F7)**, and type [**F**], [**C**] to create the footnote (or type [**E**], [**C**] to create an endnote). The Endnote/Footnote Editing screen is displayed.

Layout
Footnote
Create

10. 7 Press **(Shift-F3)** to switch to Doc 2 and then retrieve the notes document by taking the following steps:

- Press **(F5)**, **Enter** to list files.
- Highlight the name of the notes document and type [**R**] to retrieve it.

File
List Files <R>, N, [*filename*], <R>, R

NOTE: Retrieving the notes document is a one-time operation.

10. 8 Move your cursor to a point anywhere within the first note and press **(Ctrl-F4)** and type [**P**], [**C**] to *copy* the note as a paragraph to the WordPerfect Move/Copy buffer.

10. 9 Press **(Shift-F3)**, and **Enter** to switch back to the Footnote Editing screen and drop in the text of the note.

Edit
Select
Paragraph C

Edit
Switch Document

Edit
Paste

10.10 Press **(Alt-F3)**, to Reveal Codes and note that there are one or two hard return codes (**[HRt]**s) at the end of the note. Using your cursor arrows, highlight the **[HRt]**s and press **Delete** to delete them. Press **(F7)** to return to the Normal Editing screen.

Edit
Reveal Codes

NOTE: If you don't delete the hard returns, multiple footnotes on the same page will be too widely spaced. If you use endnotes, the list of endnotes will be too widely spaced if you don't remove the extra hard returns.

10.11 Find the next note's position. Then repeat steps 10. 6 through 10.10 with the next note in the notes document.

11. *Hyphenate your text.* Hyphenating the text of your long document will improve its appearance. Follow the instructions in Section 6- 5, "Hyphenation," to do this job.

12. *Prepare and append your list of references.* General guidelines for preparing your bibliography or reference list are in Section 6- 7, "Preparing a Bibliography." The instructions below show you how to modify the copy of your notes document to convert it into a reference list; they are supplemental to the instructions in Section 6- 7.

12. 1 Press **(Shift-F3)**, **(F7)**, and type [N], [N] to switch to Doc 2 and clear the screen.

Edit
Switch Document <(F7)>, N, N

12. 2 Press **(Shift-F10)**, type the name of the references source document—e.g., REFSSORS.W51—and press **Enter**.

File
    Retrieve [*filename*], <R>

12. 3 Set Absolute tabs at every half inch starting at one inch.

- Press **(Shift-F8)** and type [**L**], [**T**], [**T**], [**A**] to reveal the Format: Line menu and set Absolute spacing.
- Press **(Ctrl-End)** to clear existing tabs.
- Type [**0,0.5**], press **Enter**, and then press **(F7)** twice to set tabs every half inch starting at one inch and then return to the Normal Editing screen.

Layout
    Line T, T, A, <(Ctrl-End)>, [1,0.5], <R>, <R>, <R>

12. 4 Delete all the content notes and repeated references to the same source.

- Move your cursor to the first note to be deleted.
- Press **(Ctrl-F4)**, and type [**P**], [**D**] to delete a paragraph.
- Repeat the steps for the other notes to be deleted.

Edit
    Select
        Paragraph D

NOTE: If you delete a note in error, press **(F1)**, and type [**R**] to *undo* the deletion.

12. 5 Press **(F10)**, **Enter**, and type [**Y**] to save the cleaned list (this is just a precautionary save) and then move your cursor to the first line of the first note in the list.

File
    Save <R>, Y

12. 6 Press **Home**, **Home**, **Home**, **Left Arrow**, **(F4)**, **(Shift-Tab)** to move your cursor to the left of all codes and insert a tab and "hanging indent" (see Fig. 5-14).

```
Pfeifer, Phillip E.  1986.  The single period inventory-mix problem with early
     discount pricing.  1986 Proceedings of the decision sciences insititute.
     Atlanta: Decision Sciences Institute: 1121-23.
```

Figure 5-14 Hanging Indent Example

12.7 Edit the text of the note to convert it to bibliographic format. (See Section 6-7 for examples to go by.)

NOTE: Much of the editing involves fairly simple rearrangement of existing elements. For example, the order of names must be changed from the first name, last name order appropriate for footnotes to the last name, first name order required for lists of references. Also the facts of publication for books are placed in parentheses, and page numbers are not provided for books that don't contain collections of articles.

13. *Add Exhibits.* If you plan to include exhibits, now is the time to do so.
    13.1 Press **Home**, **Home**, **Down Arrow**, **(Ctrl-Enter)** to move to the end of the long document and insert a hard page break.
    13.2 Press **(Shift-F8)**, and type [**O**], [**A**], [**1**], [**2**] to advance down to a point two inches from the top edge of the paper.

Layout
Other A, D, [*inches*], <R>, <R>

    13.3 Press **(Shift-F6)**, **Caps Lock**, type [**exhibits**], press **Caps Lock**, and **Enter** twice to insert a title sheet for the exhibits section.
    13.4 Turn to Sections 6-2, 6-3, and 8-1 for guidelines on the preparation of tables and figures.
14. *Add appendices after exhibits.* If you plan to include appendices (for details of research method, production schedules, or data flow diagrams, for example) take the next two steps to insert a title page for them:
    14.1 Press **Home**, **Home**, **Down Arrow**, **(Ctrl-Enter)** to move your cursor to the end of the long document and insert a hard page break.
    14.2 Press **(Shift-F8)**, and type [**O**], [**A**], [**1**], [**2**] to advance down to a point two inches from the top edge of the paper.

Layout
Other A, D, [*inches*], <R>, <R>

14. 3 Press **(Shift-F6)**, **Caps Lock**, type [**appendix**] or [**appendices**], press **Caps Lock**, and **Enter** twice to insert a title page for the appendix.

14. 4 If your appendices are documents, tables, or graphics you plan to construct with WordPerfect, build them separately and copy them to this section using the procedures described above for inserting endnotes and the reference list.

15. *Generate lists of tables and figures.* When your long document contains large numbers of tables, figures, or both, help your reader locate them by generating table or figure lists at the beginning. Refer to the instructions in Section 6- 8, "Listing Tables and Figures," for the instructions required.
16. *Generate the table of contents.* This is the point when you would normally generate your long document's table of contents. Refer to the instructions in Section 6- 9, "Preparing a Table of Contents," for the instructions required.
17. *Construct and insert a title page.* We suggest that you create your title page in Doc 2 and then copy the finished product into position in Doc 1. Refer to Section 6-10, "Preparing a Title Page," for guidelines.
18. *Assign page numbers to the front matter.* (See Section 4- 4, "Numbering Pages.")
19. *Spell check the full document.* (See Section 4- 2, "Spell Checking.")
20. *View and print the final document.* Carefully view your final document, page by page, and then print it. (See Section 4- 3, "Printing Documents" for instructions on viewing and printing documents.)

ENDNOTES

1. Examples of articles are *a, an,* and *the;* examples of conjunctions are *and, but, or;* examples of prepositions are *in, on,* and *above.*
2. ASCII stands for *A*merican *S*tandard *C*ode for *I*nformation *I*nterchange, an important computer standard that relates specific bit patterns [that is 1's and 0's] to particular letters, numbers, punctuation characters, and communication control codes.
3. This "lonesome heading" problem is similar to the problem of widows and orphans referred to earlier in the book.

6

Long Document Support

Long Document Support Modules are instruction sets for writing chores that *supplement* the primary writing effort. They are *supplemental* in the sense that you would use them only when the length, format, and purpose of a primary document demand it. For example, a long term paper with numerous tables and figures might include all of the following components:

- Title page
- Table of contents
- List of tables
- List of figures
- Text
- Tables
- Figures
- Footnotes or endnotes
- List of references

A management report, on the other hand, would include only a subset of these components. Additionally, the arrangement of the components included would vary to some degree from the term paper arrangement.

You should understand that substantial leeway exists for inclusion, exclusion, and placement of the components depending on the length, purpose, and formality of a given document. Also keep in mind that producing the individual components of a long document are semi-independent operations whose scheduling is often quite flexible. For example, the title page may be the very first job finished in the production of a long document— or it may be the last. Similarly, you may prepare tables of results or supporting data as you write the main body of the document, or you may prepare them as a group at the beginning or the end of the job.

This chapter includes ten sets of optional instructions. Their arrangement corresponds to the way most people construct long documents. Individual modules are:

1. References to Other Work
2. Constructing Tables
3. Importing Figures
4. Using the Thesaurus
5. Hyphenation
6. Headers and Footers
7. Preparing a Bibliography
8. Listing Tables and Figures
9. Preparing a Table of Contents
10. Preparing a Title Page

6- 1 REFERENCES TO OTHER WORK

Instructions in this module describe parenthetical references, footnotes, and endnotes and explain how to prepare them. The Overview subsection shows how to construct *parenthetical references* and presents examples of common parenthetical reference formats. Examples of common *footnote and endnote* formats are also provided, and differences between source and content notes and between footnotes and endnotes are then explained. The Procedure subsection presents instructions for inserting parenthetical references in existing text, creating endnotes and footnotes, and generating endnotes at the end of a document.

Overview

Of the three common citation methods, the parenthetical reference is the easiest and most economical to use and is generally acceptable for most research papers. Many course instructors accept any one of the three methods so long as you're consistent in the approach adopted. Check your instructor's requirements ahead of time, however. (See Weidenborner and Caruso at pages 182 to 185 for descriptions of reference systems adopted by several academic disciplines — e.g., chemistry and mathematics.)[1]

(Pappas and Brigham 1979, 143)
(Rothstein and Stone 1967, 183-97)
(Belobaba 1987, 163; Belobaba 1989, 188)
(Kimes 1989, 4-6)
(Boeing Commercial Airplane Company 1982, 9)
(Rothstein 1974)
(Rothstein and Stone 1967, 188)
(Pfeifer 1989, 153)
(Hirshleifer 1984, 201-6)
(Horwitt 1988)
(Alstrup et al. 1989, 14)

Figure 6-1 Parenthetical References

The simplest form of parenthetical reference shows the author's name, a space, the year of publication, and a single page number or range of page numbers. All of the information is enclosed in parentheses. Examples of parenthetical references standing alone are shown in Fig. 6-1; examples of parenthetical references in text are shown in Fig. 6-2.

The usual position for a parenthetical reference is at the end of the last sentence of a paragraph or section containing the text to be cited, immediately preceding the punctuation ending the sentence. Because the full name(s) of the author(s), the title, and some facts of publication are omitted, all parenthetical references must be cited in a reference list at the end of the document. (See Section 6- 7 for an example of a reference list.)

Before discussing footnotes and endnotes, we should point out that notes may be of three types: (1) source notes, (2) content notes, and (3) cross references. *Source notes* cite the original sources of quotes or ideas appearing in a document. Generally, a source note includes the author's name, the title of the referenced work and additional facts of publication. *Content notes* supplement or explain ideas in

The primary difference between today's "yield management" and marginal analysis is that the analytical tools available to support today's marginalist decision making are far more powerful today than they were only a few years ago. This is true largely because of significant advances in information technology and, in particular, the emergence of decision support systems (Bertram 1985).

In the airline industry, the term, "yield management," (Califano 1988, 252) generally refers to two closely related applications of marginal analysis. The first application is overbooking, which is selling tickets in excess of the seat capacity of an aircraft in recognition that some reservations will be canceled and others will result in "no-shows." The second application is capacity control, which is managing the inventory of full fare and discount seats to maximize revenue.

Alternative approaches are: (1) experimentation wherein fares are deliberately and systematically varied and (2) "subjective" demand estimation procedures involving airline "experts" or panels of passengers who are of necessity conjectural in their approaches. Additional engineering-type data are required in order to estimate cost functions (Gilsanen and Petree 1989, 37).

Figure 6-2 Parenthetical References in Text

the text. They're used whenever a particular idea is important enough to include in a document but you think it will disrupt the flow of thought if it's included in text. Footnotes and endnotes, unlike parenthetical references, may be used for source *and* content notes. On the other hand, when you use parenthetical references, the supplemental ideas you'd include in a content footnote are retained in text but treated parenthetically. *Cross references* direct the reader to other parts of the document where additional information may be found.

Footnote and endnote preparation usually requires more work than constructing parenthetical references, but notes are more versatile. When footnotes are included in a document, WordPerfect automatically reduces the number of lines of printed text to accommodate the footnote lines plus some space separating the text from the footnote (or footnotes). WordPerfect begins note numbering at number 1, increasing the note number by 1 with each new note. Note numbers are also adjusted automatically for additions, deletions, and rearrangement of notes.

Footnotes and endnotes are constructed identically, and the placement of *note numbers* in text is also the same for both methods. The only difference between the two styles is that footnotes appear at the bottoms of the pages containing their note numbers and endnotes are collected into a separate section at the end of the document. Generally, footnotes are preferred to endnotes because the latter require frequent trips to the end of a long document. In the case of paper documents, having to flip to the end of the document to consult endnotes can be frustrating. In the case of documents on microfilm, however, endnotes are especially burdensome. Nevertheless, before the development of powerful word processing software, students (and instructors) often opted for the endnote method because footnotes were so difficult to manage in a typewritten manuscript. Because packages such as WordPerfect take care of footnote spacing automatically, that limitation no longer exists. Therefore, we recommend that you use the footnote method.

For instructions on reference format and style, refer to:

Turabian, Kate L., *A Manual for Writers of Term Papers, Theses, and Dissertations* (5th ed.). Chicago: University of Chicago Press, 1987, chaps 9-11.

Walker, Melissa, *Writing Research Papers: A Norton Guide* (2nd ed.). New York and London: W. W. Norton & Company, 1987, chs. 9, 12, 13, appendix A.

Weidenborner, Stephen, and Domenick Caruso, *Writing Research Papers: A Guide to the Process* (2nd ed.) New York: St. Martin's Press, 1986, ch. 8.

Procedure

This subsection includes instructions for incorporating parenthetical references in text and for creating footnotes or endnotes. It also tells how to set up an endnote section and generate endnotes when a long document is printed.

Insert parenthetical references directly into text. Creating a parenthetical reference is simple. Just move your cursor to the most appropriate place in the text or quotation for which a citation is needed. Usually, the best spot is at the end of a sentence or phrase just before a punctuation mark, but logic may suggest another location. Press the space bar, type a left parenthesis, the last name(s) of the author(s) of the work being cited, a space, the publication date, a comma, a page number or numbers and a right parenthesis.

NOTE: If a complete work is being cited, omit page numbers.

Use WordPerfect to add footnotes. Let's assume that you've just finished paraphrasing a concept due to another author. Follow the next three instructions to cite the source of the concept in a footnote.

1. Move your cursor to the space following the punctuation at the end of the last sentence of the passage to which the note refers or to the punctuation at the end of a block quotation.
2. Press **(Ctrl-F7)** and type [**F**], [**C**] to create a new footnote. The Footnote Editing screen is displayed, empty but for the number *1* (if this is your first footnote) in the upper left corner and a message to "Press Exit when done" displayed at the bottom left of the screen.

   NOTE: You may want to change the format settings of your Footnote (Endnote) Editing screen before you begin constructing footnotes. To do so, press **(Shift-F8)** in the Footnote Editing screen and alter the default settings just as you would in text.

3. Type the text of your footnote, taking care to follow the examples shown in Fig. 6-3 and 6-4. Press **(F7)** to return to the Normal Editing screen when you're done.

   Use WordPerfect to add endnotes. Construct endnotes the same way you construct footnotes except that the *endnote* option rather than the *footnote* option is selected after (Ctrl-F7) is pressed. Ensuring that endnotes are *actually printed* requires a few more steps, however.
4. After all endnotes are inserted in the text, press **Home, Home, Down Arrow** to move to the end of the document.
5. Press **(Ctrl-Enter)** to insert a hard page code.
6. Press **(Shift-F6)**, **Caps Lock** and type [**endnotes**]. Press **Caps Lock** again and press **Enter** to create the heading for your endnotes section. (Press **Enter** twice if line format is set for single spacing.)
7. Press **(Ctrl-F7)** and type [**P**], [**Y**] to place all endnotes at this location in the document starting with the number, "1."

```
Layout
        Endnote
                Placement Y
```

ENDNOTES

1. James L. Pappas and Eugene F. Brigham, Managerial Economics, 3d ed. (Hinsdale, Ill.: Dryden Press, 1979), 143.

2. Marvin Rothstein and A. W. Stone, "Passenger Booking Levels," AGIFORS Proceedings 7 (1967): 183-97.

3. Peter P. Belobaba, "Air Travel Demand and Airline Seat Inventory Management" (Ph.D. diss., Massachusetts Institute of Technology, 1987), 163.

4. Sheryl E. Kimes, "Yield Management: A Tool for Capacity-Constrained Service Firms" (Ithaca, N.Y.: Cornell University, School of Hotel Management, 1989), 4-6.

5. Ibid.

6. Ibid., 9.

7. Marvin Rothstein, "Hotel Overbooking as a Markovian Sequential Decision Process," Decision Sciences 5 (Fall 1974): 390.

8. Rothstein and Stone, "Passenger Booking Levels," 188.

9. Marvin Rothstein, "An Airline Overbooking Model," Transportation Science 5 (July 1971): 184.

10. Kimes, "Yield Management," 7.

11. Phillip E. Pfeifer, "The Airline Discount Fare Allocation Problem," Decision Sciences 20, No. 1 (Winter 1989): 153.

12. Jack Hirshleifer, Price Theory and Applications, 3d ed. (Englewood Cliffs, N.J.: Prentice-Hall, 1984).

13. Elizabeth Horwitt, "Carriers Land Profits by Empowering DP Units," Computerworld, 7 March 1988, 73-80.

14. Ibid.

15. Hirshleifer, Price Theory, 203.

16. Robert G. Cross, "Strategic Selling: Yield Management Techniques to Enhance Revenue." Paper presented at the Shearson-Lehman Brothers 1986 Airline Industry Seminar. Key Largo, Florida, February 1986.

17. Phillip E. Pfeifer, "The Single Period Inventory-Mix Problem with Early Discount Pricing," 1986 Proceedings of the Decision Sciences Institute. Atlanta, GA: Decision Sciences Institute, 1986: 1122.

18. Boeing Commercial Airplane Company, Boeing Promotional Fare Management System, Analysis and Research Findings (Seattle: Boeing Commercial Airplane Company, 1982), 34-39.

Figure 6-3 Sample Endnotes

8. Press **(Alt-F5)** and type **[G]**, **[G]**, **[Y]** to generate the endnotes. (Endnotes don't appear in the Normal Editing screen, but they'll show up when the document is printed.)

19. Horwitt, "Carriers Land Profits," 78.

20. Jens Alstrup et al., "Booking Control Increases Profit at Scandinavian Airlines," Interfaces 19, No. 4 (July-August 1989): 14.

21. Horwitt, "Carriers Land Profits," 73-77.

22. Peter P. Belobaba, "Application of a Probabilistic Decision Model to Airline Seat Inventory Control," Operations Research 37, No. 2 (March-April 1989): 183-97.

23. "Enter the Yield Manager," Lloyd's Aviation Economist 2, No. 8 (May 1985): 12-13.

24. Belobaba, "Air Travel Demand," 164.

25. Alstrup et al, "Booking Control," 16.

26. Belobaba, "Application," 188.

Figure 6-4 Sample Endnotes (cont.)

Mark
Generate G, Y

NOTE: Press **(Shift-F7)**, type [**V**], and press **Home**, **Home**, **Down Arrow**, **PgUp** to move to the end of the document and check the printer image of the endnotes.

File
Print V

6- 2 CONSTRUCTING TABLES

This section provides directions for using the WordPerfect "Tables" feature to construct and import statistical tables. Turn here if you have a long document assignment that calls for their inclusion in text or in an exhibit section at the end of the document. The Overview subsection explains the purpose of tables and gives advice on format and construction. Procedure subsections include step-by-step instructions for constructing a sample table from scratch and for importing a table created previously in Lotus 1-2-3.

Overview

The table structure and format principles reflected in these instructions are based on guidelines in Chapter 6 of Turabian's *A Manual for Writers,* 5th ed.

A well-constructed table summarizes information and helps the reader understand relationships not easily comprehended in straight text material. Tables also break up text, making it less monotonous and easier to digest. They are particularly useful for succinctly presenting findings and supporting conclusions and recommendations. Tables certainly can improve the effectiveness of written communications, but they must be consistently and accurately designed and constructed if they're to be easily understood and interpreted at minimal cost.

A table should be inserted following the paragraph where it's first referenced. If it won't fit on the page of first reference, move it to the top of the next page. If you "block protect" your table, WordPerfect will move it to the top of the next page automatically when it won't fit on the current page. Take these steps to block protect all of your tables:

- Press **(Alt-F3)** or **(F11)** to toggle on Reveal Codes.

Edit
    Reveal Codes

- Move your cursor to the top of the table (that's the **[Tbl Def...]** code if you're using the WordPerfect Tables feature).
- Press **(Alt-F4)** or **(F12)** to toggle Block on.
- Press **Down Arrow** until the character just to the right of the **[Tbl Off]** code is highlighted.
- Press **(Shift-F8)** and type [Y] to prevent the block from splitting over a page break.

Edit
    Block <Down Arrow>

Edit
    Protect Block

All tables should be single spaced, centered horizontally and preceded and followed by three blank lines.

Consult Turabian for additional guidance on constructing tables:

Turabian, Kate L., *A Manual for Writers of Term Papers, Theses, and Dissertations* (5th ed.). Chicago: University of Chicago Press, 1987.

Procedures for Creating Tables from Scratch

Constructing a table should *not* be your first WordPerfect project. Indeed, the instructions below assume you're creating or editing a long document in the Normal Editing screen. As a reminder, WordPerfect has two Normal Editing screens, Doc 1, and Doc 2; with Doc 1 as the default. Build your tables in Doc 2, copying them back into your text, into a set of exhibits, or into an appendix (all of which should be in Doc 1). Before you begin constructing tables, think about how the tables are to be numbered in anticipation of producing lists of tables and figures automatically (see Section 6- 8). For term papers, management reports, and written case analyses, it's customary to number tables in consecutive order using arabic numbers. That's the approach used here, but your school or instructor may prefer a different style. If so, modify the instructions that follow.

Tables created using the Tables feature or a Table graphics box are numbered automatically by WordPerfect, but the default table number is an uppercase roman numeral. We have to change that default. Be sure you're in Doc 1 and then follow the instructions below to do so.

- Press **Home**, **Home**, **Home**, **Up Arrow** to move to the top of your document.
- Press **(Alt-F9)** and type [**T**], [**O**] to display the Options: Table Box menu.
- Type [**F**], [**N**] and press **(F7)** to change table numbers to arabic style and return to the Normal Editing screen.

```
Graphics
        Table Box
                Options  F, N, <R>
```

Carefully examine the table in Fig. 6-5. It's a "traditional style" table and we'll refer to it frequently in these instructions.

In this example, we've used a prestige elite, 12-pitch fixed-space font with 12 characters per inch (cpi). That's the standard font used throughout this book. If you use another font, your table may look quite different than the table in Fig. 6-5.

Whenever you construct a table using the WordPerfect "Tables" feature, it's helpful to break the complete task into a set of subtasks, each of which includes one or more closely-related procedures. We do that here. The complete task includes the following set of subtasks:

- Creating the table structure
- Clearing out lines and formatting cells, rows, and columns
- Typing the table contents
- Final formatting

TABLE 1

POPULATION, WAKE COUNTY AND RALEIGH 1960-1980, AND PROJECTED TO 1990 AND 2000

Year	Raleigh		Wake	
	Population	Change %	Population	Change %
1960	93,931	--	169,082	--
1970	121,577	29.4	229,006	35.4
1980	149,771	23.2	300,833	31.4
1990(est)[a]	186,705	24.7	387,175	28.7
2000(est)	226,597	21.4	488,443	26.2

Source: 1960-1980, U.S. Department of Commerce, Bureau of the Census

[a]Raleigh projections were calculated using a least-squares polynomial. Wake County projections were produced by the North Carolina Department of Administration, July, 1981.

Figure 6-5 Population Table

- Adding space below the table, restoring the long document format, and copying the completed table into the long document

Each subtask is described in a separate subsection below.

Create the table structure. The first task is to create the arrangement of rows and columns—i.e., the table structure. In the case of the example table, we create an initial array of five columns (labeled A through E) and five rows (labeled 1 through 5).

1. If Doc 1 is displayed, press **(Shift-F3)** to switch to Doc 2 and then press **(F7)**, and type [**N**], [**N**] to clear the Doc 2 screen.

Edit
    Switch Document <(F7)>, N, N

2. Now we need to take care of some preliminaries such as setting single-spacing and inserting three blank lines in front of the table.

    2. 1 Press **(Shift-F8)**, type [**L**], [**S**], [**1**], and press **Enter, (F7)** to set line spacing to single spacing and return to the Normal Editing screen.

Layout
    Line S, [1], <R>, <R>

NOTE: Right and left margins should be the same as the right and left margins in your long document. Normally, both would be set at 1 inch.

2. 2 Press **Enter** three times to insert three blank single lines.

3. Now select the "Tables" feature and specify your table structure.

3. 1 Press **(Alt-F7)** and type [T] and [C] to create a table.

3. 2 Type [5], press **Enter**, type [5], and press **Enter** again to tell WordPerfect that you want your table to have five columns and five rows.

Layout
Tables
Create [5], <R>, [5], <R>

Clear out extra lines and format columns, rows, and individual cells. When you compare the array of boxes on your screen with the finished table in Fig. 6-5, you probably wonder how you can possibly get from one figure to the other. It's really quite easy. Just follow along on your own PC.

4. Your cursor should be located in the Table Editor and your screen should look like Fig. 6-6. (If you don't see a menu at the bottom of your screen, press **(Alt-F7)** and type [T] and [E] to edit a table.)

Layout
Tables
Edit

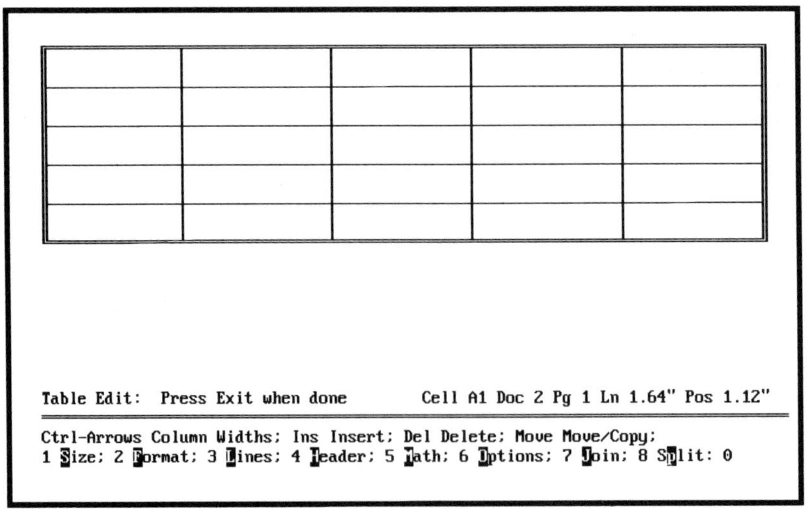

Figure 6-6 The WordPerfect Table Editor

4. 1 Press **Home**, **Home**, **Up Arrow** to move to cell A1 if you're not already there.

NOTE: Look at the status line at the bottom of your screen. It should display "Cell A1 Doc 2 Pg 1 . . ." just above the Table Editor menu.

4. 2 Press **(Alt-F4)** (or **(F12)**), **Home**, **Right Arrow** to block the first row of cells.

NOTE: If you have a mouse, it's *much* quicker to press **(Alt-F4)** (or **(F11)**), move the mouse cursor to the cell that completes the range and press the left mouse button.

4. 3 Type [**F**], [**L**], [**W**], [**1.2**], and press **Enter** to make all five columns 1.2 inches wide to begin with.

NOTE: Click on the letters at the bottom of the Table Editor with your left mouse button, enter numbers from the keyboard and complete operations by pressing the right button. Try it—it's also a *much* quicker way to work.

4. 4 Press **(Alt-F4)** (or **(F12)**), **Home**, **Left Arrow** to block the first row of cells again.
4. 5 Type [**J**], [**Y**] to join the cells.
4. 6 Type [**F**], [**C**], [**J**], [**C**] to format the cell created by the join operation and center the text to be typed into it.

5. Now, let's create a double-high cell at the upper left side of the table for the word, "Year."
   5. 1 Press **Down Arrow** to highlight cell A2.
   5. 2 Press **(Alt-F4)**, **Down Arrow** to block cells A2 and A3.
   5. 3 Type [**J**], [**Y**] to join the cells.
   5. 4 Type [**F**], [**C**], [**J**], [**C**], [**F**], [**C**], [**V**], [**C**] to center the contents of the double-high cell horizontally and vertically.
6. Now we need two double-wide cells for "Raleigh" and "Wake"
   6. 1 Press **Right Arrow** to highlight cell B2.
   6. 2 Press **(Alt-F4)**, **Right Arrow** to block cells B2 and C2.
   6. 3 Type [**J**], [**Y**] to join the cells.
   6. 4 Press **Right Arrow** to highlight cell D2 and then repeat instructions 6. 2 and 6. 3 to join cells D2 and E2.
   6. 5 Press **(Alt-F4)**, **Left Arrow** to highlight the two double-wide cells.

6. 6 Type **[F]**, **[C]**, **[J]**, **[C]** to center the text to be typed into the two cells.

7. Next, format the cells for the column headings, "Population" and "Change."

   7. 1 Press **Down Arrow** to highlight cell B3.

   7. 2 Press **(Alt-F4)**, **Home**, **Right Arrow** to block the cells from B3 to E3.

   7. 3 Type [**F**], [**C**], [**J**], [**C**] to center the column headings.

8. Since cells B4 through E4 will contain only numbers, let's format B4 and D4 for right align (they're whole numbers) and C4 and E4 for decimal align.

   8. 1 Move your cursor to cell B4.

   8. 2 Type [**F**], [**C**], [**J**], [**R**] to format the cell for *r*ight alignment.

   8. 3 Move your cursor to cell C4.

   8. 4 Type [**F**], [**C**], [**J**], [**D**] to format the cell for *d*ecimal alignment.

   8. 5 Move your cursor to cell D4 and repeat instruction 8. 2.

   8. 6 Move your cursor to cell C4 and repeat instruction 8. 4.

9. Finally, we went to join cells A5 to E5 to make one large cell where we'll place the notes for this table.

   9. 1 Move your cursor down and over to cell A5.

   9. 2 Press **(Alt-F4)**, **Home**, **Right Arrow** to block the whole row of cells.

   9. 3 Type [**J**], [**Y**] to combine the five original cells into one long cell.

10. Now it's time to switch to subtask three, typing the table's contents. Before we do so, however, we must return to the Normal Editing screen. We should also save our table structure and format for safety's sake.

    10. 1 Press **(F7)** to leave the Table Editor and return to the Normal Editing screen.

    NOTE: As you may have discovered, you can't type text in the Table Editor. It's used only to define the table's structure and format.

    10. 2 Press **(F10)**, type [***table name***], and press **Enter** to save the table structure. You will soon discover that navigating from cell to cell in the table editor and in the table in the Normal Editing screen may require different sets of keystrokes depending on your destination. Fig. 6-7, "Getting Around in Tables," summarizes the keystroke combinations and sequences used in the Normal Editing screen and in the table editor.

```
File
        Save [filename], <R>
```

Destination	Keystrokes	
	Normal Editing Screen	Table Editor
One row up	Up Arrow	Up Arrow
One row down	Down Arrow	Down Arrow
One character right	Right Arrow	Right Arrow
One character left	Left Arrow	Left Arrow
One cell right	Tab	Tab
One cell left	(Shift-Tab)	(Shift-Tab)
Any cell	No simple way	(Ctrl-Home), cell number ,(e.g., B3), Enter
First cell in row	(Ctrl-Home), Home, Left Arrow	Home, Left Arrow
Last cell in row	(Ctrl-Home), Home, Right Arrow	Home, Right Arrow
First cell in column	(Ctrl-Home), Home, Up Arrow	Home, Up Arrow
Last cell in column	(Ctrl-Home), Home, Down Arrow	Home, Down Arrow
First cell in table	(Ctrl-Home), Home, Home, Up Arrow	Home, Home, Up Arrow
Last cell in table	(Ctrl-Home), Home, Home, Down Arrow	Home, Home, Down Arrow

Figure 6-7 Getting Around in Tables

Type the table contents. You should now be in the Normal Editing screen with the table structure displayed on your screen. At this point, we'll type in all the text and add the footnotes. After we've finished that job, we'll return to the Table Editor to spruce up the table prior to moving it into the document.

11. Press **Up Arrow** to move your cursor to cell A1.
12. Press **Caps Lock**, type **[table]**, press **Space Bar**, type [**table number**], and then press **Enter** twice to skip a line between "TABLE *n*" (1 in this case) and the caption.

NOTE: Tables are numbered in consecutive order beginning with 1 and continuing to the end of the document (including any appendices). Tables in an exhibit section are numbered with roman numerals and labeled, "EXHIBIT I," "EXHIBIT II," etc., however. Thus, if all your tables are exhibits located at the end of your long document, *don't change the numbering style to arabic*. If some tables are in text and others are grouped in an Exhibits section, change the table numbering style back to Roman numerals at the beginning of your exhibits section. Follow the instructions above to do so.

13. Type the table caption, [**population, wake county and raleigh 1960-1980,**]. If the caption is too long to fit on one line—as is the caption in our example—press **Enter** to complete the caption, and type [**and projected to 1990 and 2000**].

    NOTE: Unless the lines are of equal length, split the title so the longer line is on top.

14. Press **Caps Lock** and **Enter**.
15. Move your cursor to cell B2 and type the first spanner head: [**Raleigh**].

NOTE: A "spanner" head labels two or more related columns.

16. Press **Tab** and type [**Wake**].
17. Move to cell B3 and type the first column head: [**Population**].
18. Press **Tab** and type the second column head: [**Change**]. Press **Enter** and type [**%**]. Press **Tab** and follow the same procedures for the last two column heads.
19. Press **Home**, **Home**, **Home**, **Left Arrow** and type [**Year**]. The word, "Year" doesn't appear to be centered vertically in the double-high cell, but when you press **(Shift-F7)** and type [**V**] to view document, you'll see that it indeed is.

File
Print V

20. Move to cell A4, type [**1960**], and press **Enter.** Then type [**1970**] and press **Enter**. Add the other three numbers in the first column.

    NOTE: If you mistakenly pressed Enter following "2000 (est) and inserted an extra blank line, press **Backspace** to remove it.

21. Press **Tab** to move to cell B4, type [**93,931**], and press **Enter**. Then type [**121,577**] and press **Enter**. Add the other three numbers in the second column.
22. Press **Tab** to move to cell C4 and type a pair of hyphens to represent missing values. That's customary when a cell that would normally contain a number is empty. Press **Enter**, type [**29.4**] and press **Enter**. Add the other three numbers in the third column.
23. Fill cell D4 following the instructions in step 21 and cell E4 following the instructions in step 22.
24. Move your cursor into cell A5 and type [**Source**:], press **Space Bar,** and type the source of the data contained in the table: [**1960-1980, U.S. Department**

of Commerce, Bureau of the Census]. Press **Enter** twice.

25. Move your cursor back up into the space immediately following "1990(est)" and press **(Ctrl-F8)** and type [**S**], [**P**] and a lowercase [**a**] to create a superscripted footnote index. Press **Right Arrow** to switch off the superscript attribute.

```
Font
        Superscript
```

NOTE: Table footnote indexes follow immediately the referenced element within the table and should be in alphabetical order starting with the letter *a*, *for each table with notes.* General notes pertaining to a table should be placed after the source note and should begin with the word, "Note(s): ."

WARNING: Unless you want your table footnotes at the bottom of a page—which doesn't make much sense—don't use WordPerfect's Footnote feature to produce them.

26. To create the footnote itself, move your cursor back to the second line below the source note, press **(Ctrl-F8),** type [**S**], [**P**], [**a**], and press **Right Arrow.**

```
Font
        Superscript
```

27. Type the note: [**Raleigh projections were calculated using a least-squares polynomial. Wake County projections were produced by the North Carolina Department of Administration, July, 1981**.].

NOTE: Press **Enter** and follow the same procedure to type in any other table footnotes.

Finish formatting the table in the Table Editor. Now that you can see that the table may just end up looking like the example in Fig. 6-5, we need to toggle on the Table Editor to finish the formatting job. If you're following along, press **(F10), Enter**, and type [**Y**] to save the table in its present form as a precaution.

```
File
        Save <R>, Y
```

28. Toggle on the Table Editor, make the line just below the caption a double line, and remove all outside lines.

28. 1 Press **(Alt-F7)** to toggle on the Table Editor. Your cursor should be in cell A1. If it isn't, move it there now.

Layout Tables Edit

28. 2 Type [**L**], [**B**], [**D**] to make the line under the caption a double line.

28. 3 Block the whole table by pressing **(Alt-F4)**, **Home**, **Home**, **Down Arrow**.

28. 4 Type [**L**], [**O**], [**N**] to remove all outside lines.

NOTE: You'll see small arrows on both sides of the table. They represent half-space lines; you can safely ignore them.

29. Now that we've taken care of all the lines, we have some final housekeeping to do on spacing.

29. 1 Move to cell C4 and press **(Ctrl-Left Arrow)** three times to squeeze up the column. Move to cell E4 and do the same thing. (You can also widen a column by doing the opposite—pressing (Ctrl-Right Arrow).)

29. 2 Finally, type [**O**], [**P**], [**C**] and press **Enter** to center the table on a page.

29. 3 Press **(F7)** or the right mouse button to leave the Table Editor. This is a good spot to save the file again.

Add space below the table, restore the long document format, and copy the completed table into the long document.

30. Press **Home**, **Home**, **Down Arrow** and then press **Enter** three times to insert three blank lines below the table.

31. Now we need to re-establish the original page format, else we may be unpleasantly surprised when we copy this table into the target document.

31. 1 Press **(Shift-F8)**, type [**L**], [**M**], [**1**], press **Enter**, type [**1**] and press **Enter** again to set right and left margins.

31. 2 Type [**S**], [**2**] and press **Enter** to set line spacing to double spacing.

31. 3 Type [**T**], [**T**], [**R**] and press **(Ctrl-End)** to set tab type to "Relative" and clear tab stops.

31. 4 Type [**0,0.5**] and press **Enter**, **(F7)**, **(F7)** to set tabs every half-inch starting at the left margin and then return to the Normal Editing screen.

Layout
Line M, [1], <R>, [1], <R>, <R>, [S], [2], <R>, [T], [T], [R], <(Ctrl-End)>, [0,0.5], <R>, <R>

32. Now lets move the finished table from Doc 2 to a position following its first reference in the text.

    32. 1 Press **Home**, **Home**, **Home**, **Up Arrow** to move to the top left side of the newly created table.

    32. 2 Press **(Alt-F4)** to toggle Block On.

    32. 3 Press **Home**, **Home**, **Down Arrow** to highlight the entire table (including sources, footnotes, and the format change codes).

    32. 4 Press **(Ctrl-F4)** and type [**B**], [**C**] to copy the entire table to the Move/Copy buffer.

    NOTE: You could have moved the table if your last keystroke had been an "M" rather than a "C," but it's always safer to copy a table from Doc 2 to Doc 1. You can always clear Doc 2 later by pressing **(F7)** and typing [**N**], [**Y**], anyway.

    32. 5 Press **(Shift-F3)** to switch back to Doc 1 and reposition the cursor at the beginning of the first line below the paragraph in which the table was first mentioned. Press **Enter** and your table pops into place.

Edit
Select
Paragraph C

Edit
Switch Document

Edit
Paste

NOTE: If the table is too long to fit on the page where it was first referenced, move it to the top of the next page. To do so, move your cursor to the first character in the first line on the next page, and press **Enter**. If you dropped the table in and it flowed over to the next page, follow the next set of steps:

POPULATION, WAKE COUNTY AND RALEIGH 1960-1980,
AND PROJECTED TO 1990 AND 2000

Year	Raleigh		Wake	
	Population	Change %	Population	Change %
1960	93,931	--	169,082	--
1970	121,577	29.4	229,006	35.4
1980	149,771	23.2	300,833	31.4
1990(est)[a]	186,705	24.7	387,175	28.7
2000(est)	226,597	21.4	488,443	26.2

Source: 1960-1980, U.S. Department of Commerce, Bureau of the Census

[a]Raleigh projections were calculated using a least-squares polynomial. Wake County projections were produced by the North Carolina Department of Administration, July, 1981.

Table Edit: Press Exit when done Cell E4 Doc 1 Pg 1 Ln 2.81" Pos 6.75"

Ctrl-Arrows Column Widths; Ins Insert; Del Delete; Move Move/Copy;
1 Size; 2 Format; 3 Lines; 4 Header; 5 Math; 6 Options; 7 Join; 8 Split: 0

Figure 6-8 Finished Population Table

- Toggle on Reveal Codes and highlight the **[Ln Spacing**:1**]** code you inserted before you began building your table.
- Press **(Alt-F4)** to toggle block on.
- Press **Down Arrow** to highlight the table, the three blank lines beneath it, and the format codes.
- Press **Delete** and type [Y] to delete it. (Yes, *delete it!*)
- Move the cursor to the top of the next page and press **(F1)** and type [**R**] to drop the table in at the top of the page.
- Delete any leftover blank lines above the table. (Be careful not to delete any line spacing codes.)

The final result should look like the table in Fig. 6-8.

Procedures for Importing a Lotus Spreadsheet As a Table

You can import a Lotus (or Excel or PlanPerfect) spreadsheet without first converting it to ASCII text. When you do, the import is structured as a WordPerfect table. This WordPerfect capability is very handy, as you will soon see. We divide the complete task of importing a spreadsheet and cleaning up the resulting table into a set of three subtasks. Each subtask is described in a separate subsection below.

- Importing the spreadsheet
- Cleaning out lines and formatting cells
- Adding a table number to the caption and removing extra dollar signs

We don't explain how to add space, restore the long document format, and copy the completed table into the long document since we described those procedures earlier.

Import the spreadsheet. Before you can import a spreadsheet, it must have been constructed previously in Lotus or one of the other spreadsheet packages that WordPerfect supports. You should also be aware that the spreadsheet must be able to fit on a WordPerfect page. If your spreadsheet is larger than a standard 8-1/2 by 11 inch page, try importing it to a landscape-oriented page (11 by 8-1/2 inches), or try importing a range of cells rather than the entire spreadsheet. (Fig. 6-9 shows a spreadsheet that was imported with no difficulty.) A final note prior to instruction steps: be sure you're in Doc 2 with a clear display screen.

33. Press **(Ctrl-F5)** and type [**S**], [**I**] to import a spreadsheet.
34. Then, when you see the Spreadsheet: Import menu, type [**F**], [***spreadsheet name***] ([MARKBUDG.WK1], for example) and type [**P**] to perform the import operation. A table like the one in Fig. 6-10 should pop up on your screen.

File
Text In
Spreadsheet
Import F, [filename], <R>, P

35. As a precaution, press **(F10)**, type [***table name***], and press **Enter** to save the initial table.

A1: [W15] 'Marketing Expenditures by Quarter READY

	A	B	C	D	E	F	G
1	Marketing Expenditures by Quarter						
2		Quarters					
3	Accounts	First	Second	Third	Fourth	Total	
4	Administration	$17,500	$23,250	$19,000	$17,500	$77,250	
5	Advertising	$27,500	$14,000	$23,000	$8,500	$73,000	
6	Trade Shows	$15,500	$23,000	$18,500	$9,500	$66,500	
7	Promotion	$3,500	$8,500	$575	$8,350	$20,925	
8	Literature	$875	$2,500	$9,400	$535	$13,310	
9	Sales Training	$1,250	$1,250	$8,300	$1,250	$12,050	
10	Premiums	$7,150	$1,225	$0	$0	$8,375	
11	Total	$73,275	$73,725	$78,775	$45,635	$271,410	
12							
13							
14							
15							
16							
17							
18							
19							
20							

30-Sep-90 11:47 AM

Figure 6-9 Marketing Budget As a Lotus Spreadsheet

File Edit Search Layout Mark Tools Font Graphics Help (Press F3 for Help)

Marketing Expenditures by Quarter					
	Quarters				
Accounts	First	Second	Third	Fourth	Total
Administration	$17,500	$23,250	$19,000	$17,500	$77,250
Advertising	$27,500	$14,000	$23,000	$8,500	$73,000
Trade Shows	$15,500	$23,000	$18,500	$9,500	$66,500
Promotion	$3,500	$8,500	$575	$8,350	$20,925
Literature	$875	$2,500	$9,400	$535	$13,310
Sales Training	$1,250	$1,250	$8,300	$1,250	$12,050
Premiums	$7,150	$1,225	$0	$0	$8,375
Total	$73,275	$73,725	$78,775	$45,635	$271,410

Doc 2 Pg 1 Ln 1" Pos 1"

Figure 6-10 Marketing Budget As a WordPerfect Table

> File
> Save [filename], <R>

Cleaning and formatting the spreadsheet table. For the purposes of demonstrating how a spreadsheet can be converted to a standard table, we use the example in Fig. 6-9. If you wish to follow along, build a similar spreadsheet and then import it using the instructions above.

36. Let's toggle on the Table Editor and clear out the top row of cells.
    36. 1 Press **(Alt-F7)** and type [T], [E] to toggle on the Table Editor. Your cursor should be in cell A1.

> Layout
> Tables
> Edit

    36. 2 Press **(Alt-F4)**, **Home**, **Right Arrow** to block the first row.
    36. 3 Type [J], [Y] to join all the first-row cells.
37. Next, change the line below the caption to a double line and format the column headings.
    37. 1 Move your cursor to cell A2.

37. 2 Press **(Alt-F4)**, **Home**, **Right Arrow** to block the second row.

37. 3 Type [**L**], [**T**], [**D**] to make the line below the caption a double-line.

37. 4 Press **Home**, **Left Arrow** to move back to cell A2.

37. 5 Press **(Alt-F4)**, **Down Arrow** to block cells A2 and A3.

37. 6 Type [**J**], [**Y**], [**F**], [**C**], [**J**], [**C**], [**F**], [**C**], [**V**], [**C**] to join cells A2 and A3 and center text in the expanded cell horizontally and vertically.

37. 7 Move your cursor to cell B2.

37. 8 Press **(Alt-F4)**, **Home**, **Right Arrow** to block cells B2 to F2.

37. 9 Type [**J**], [**Y**], [**F**], [**C**], [**J**], [**C**] to join the five cells into a single cell and format the single cell for centered text.

37.10 Move your cursor to cell B3.

37.11 Press **(Alt-F4)**, **Home**, **Right Arrow** to block cells B3 to F3.

37.12 Type [**F**], [**C**], [**J**], [**C**] to format the blocked cells for centered text.

38. Next, let's clear out the internal horizontal lines separating the account names in the first column and the dollar figures in each of the other columns.

38. 1 Move your cursor to cell A4.

38. 2 Press **(Alt-F4)**, **(Ctrl-Home)**, type [**A10**] and press **Enter** to block the column from cell A4 to cell A10.

38. 3 Type [**L**], [**I**], [**N**] to remove all the lines separating account names.

38. 4 Move your cursor to cell B4.

38. 5 Repeat instructions 38. 2 and 38. 3.

38. 6 Repeat the procedure for columns 3 through 6.

39. The last things we need to do in the Table Editor is change the bottom double line to a single line, remove the lines at the top, left, and right sides, and center the whole table. We'll take care of the line work by removing *all* outside lines and then restoring the bottom line.

39. 1 Move your cursor to cell A1.

39. 2 Press **(Alt-F4)**, **Home**, **Home**, **Down Arrow** to block the entire table.

39. 3 Type [**L**], [**O**], [**N**] to remove all outside lines.

39. 4 Press **(Alt-F4)**, **Home**, **Left Arrow** to block the last row.

39. 5 Type [**L**], [**B**], [**S**] to restore a *single* line at the bottom of the table.

39. 6 Type [**O**], [**P**], [C] and press **Enter** to center the table.

Add a table number to the caption and remove extra dollar signs. We need to toggle back to the Normal Editing screen, insert a table number in front of the caption we brought over in our spreadsheet and get rid of some of the dollar signs in the table.

File Edit Search Layout Mark Tools Font Graphics Help (Press F3 for Help)

Table 1.—Marketing Expenditures by Quarter

Accounts	Quarters				
	First	Second	Third	Fourth	Total
Administration	$17,500	$23,250	$19,000	$17,500	$77,250
Advertising	27,500	14,000	23,000	8,500	73,000
Trade Shows	15,500	23,000	18,500	9,500	66,500
Promotion	3,500	8,500	575	8,350	20,925
Literature	875	2,500	9,400	535	13,310
Sales Training	1,250	1,250	8,300	1,250	12,050
Premiums	7,150	1,225	0	0	8,375
Total	$73,275	$73,725	$78,775	$45,635	$271,410

C:\EXHIBITS\TABTBL02.W51 Doc 2 Pg 1 Ln 1" Pos 1"

Figure 6-11 Marketing Budget As a WordPerfect Table

40. Toggle back to the Normal Editing screen and save the file.
    40. 1 Press **(F7)** to toggle off the Table Editor.
    40. 2 Press **(F10)**, **Enter**, and type [**Y**] to save the table again.

> File
> Save <R>, Y

41. Insert the table number in the caption and remove the dollar signs.
    41. 1 Move your cursor to the "M" in "Marketing Expenditures by Quarter."
    41. 2 Type [**Table 1.—**].
    41. 3 Press **(Alt-F2)**, type [N], [$], press **(F2)**, **Space Bar**, and **(F2)** again to replace all incidences of the dollar sign with spaces.

> Search
> Replace N, [$], <R>, [Space Bar], <R>

    41. 4 Press **Insert** to toggle on Typeover mode.
    41. 5 Replace all the dollar signs you removed from the fourth and eleventh rows. (Remember to press **Tab** and **(Shift-Tab)** to move laterally from cell to cell.)
    41. 6 Press **Insert** again to toggle Insert mode back on.
42. Press **(F10), Enter**, and type [**Y**] to save your finished table. The final result should look like the table in Fig. 6-11.

```
File
        Save <R>, Y
```

6- 3 IMPORTING FIGURES

This section provides directions for importing graphic figures and illustrations. Turn here when you have a term paper assignment calling for their inclusion or when you plan to include exhibits at the end of a written case analysis. The Overview subsection describes the purpose of figures and illustrations and gives advice on their format; the Procedure subsection includes specific, step-by-step instructions for importing a sample figure.

Overview

Graphs, charts, diagrams, and maps summarize information and help the reader understand relationships not easily comprehended in straight text material. They also break up text, making it less formidable and easier to digest. Figures are especially helpful for presenting findings succinctly and supporting conclusions and recommendations.

When we speak of "figures," we refer to several different types of graphic display, most of which fall into one of the categories listed below.

- Graphs
- Charts
- Diagrams
- Maps
- Illustrations
- Photos

It is not within the scope of this book to explain in detail how figures are produced or to present the philosophy and principles of graphic design. For that level of detail we refer you to several references at the end of this subsection. Nevertheless, some guidance is in order. In the paragraphs below we devote space to explaining what the major figure categories are, indicate how they can be produced, and offer some tips on formatting and construction.

Categories of figures. There are three basic categories of graphs: (1) bars, (2) lines, and (3) pies. Unfortunately, there's no clear distinction between graphs and charts, and many people use the terms synonymously—e.g., bar *graph* and bar *chart.* In this book, we differentiate between the two categories on the basis of the purpose for which the figure is intended. If quantities or trends are being compared over a continuum such as time or distance, then a *graph* is required. Examples are bar graphs and line graphs. If a qualitative, structural, or spatial relationship is being described, then a *chart* is called for. Examples of charts are: (1) pie charts, (2) organization charts, and (3) GANTT charts.

Diagrams also show relationships, processes, and flows. Examples of diagrams are: (1) flow charts and data flow diagrams introduced in information systems courses, (2) PERT and CPM networks introduced in operations management courses, and (3) demand and supply curves introduced in microeconomics courses. Use maps to show how sales territories are organized or where distribution facilities are located. Illustrations are drawings and other types of art work. Examples of illustrations are logos created in a paint program like Windows Paint, an office layout created in a computer-aided design package such as AutoCad, or a rough ad layout created in Harvard Graphics. Another category of figure is a photograph of an individual or object. Photos may be scanned into a file using an inexpensive hand scanner and then inserted into a Graphics Box.

Formatting rules. Listed below are some simple formatting rules that will enhance the appearance of your figures.[2]

Pies

- Always begin the pie at 12:00. That is, the left border of the first "slice" is vertical at 12 o'clock. (Most graphics packages do this automatically.)
- Assign slices clockwise in decreasing order of relative size (simply sort the column or row elements prior to creating the graph).
- Don't have more than eight slices in a pie. When you have more than eight numbers or percentages to be compared, group the smallest values into an "other" category which then becomes the eighth slice.

Lines

- Use single lines to show a trend over time.
- Use multiple lines to make comparisons over time.
- Assign quantity—e.g., dollars, pounds, units—to the vertical axis and time—e.g., months, years—to the horizontal axis.
- Begin the vertical axis at zero.
- Don't show more than four lines on a graph.

Bars

- Use bars to compare related quantities—e.g., sales by region, away-game winning percentages.
- Use simple bars for single-level comparisons—e.g., sales by region.
- Use stacked bars or overlapped bars for multiple level comparisons—e.g., sales *and* advertising by region, percentages of product line sales by consumer type.

So far as placement is concerned, a figure should be inserted following the paragraph where it's first referenced. If a figure won't fit on the page of first reference because the paragraph ends too far down the page, move it to the top of the next page. Figures may be placed on the left, right, or center of the page.

Constructing a figure should *not* be your very first WordPerfect project. Indeed, we assume in the following numbered steps that you are in the process of creating or editing a long document in the Normal Editing screen when you make the decision to import a figure. If this is your first attempt to use the Graphics Box feature, read Section 8- 1, "Working with Graphics," before going further. Examine the sample illustration in Fig. 6-12 carefully; we refer to it frequently in the following instructions, and we'll construct it with the Graphics Box feature of WordPerfect.

Consult the following references for additional guidance on preparing and using graphic images:

Himstreet, William C., and Wayne Murlin Baty, *Business Communications* (8th ed.). Boston: PWS-Kent Publishing Company, 1987.

Turabian, Kate L., *A Manual for Writers of Term Papers, Theses, and Dissertations* (5th ed.). Chicago: University of Chicago Press, 1987.

Procedure

The pie chart shown in Fig. 6-12 was created in Lotus using the spreadsheet shown in Fig. 6-9 in Section 6- 2 and then imported into Harvard Graphics for embellishment.

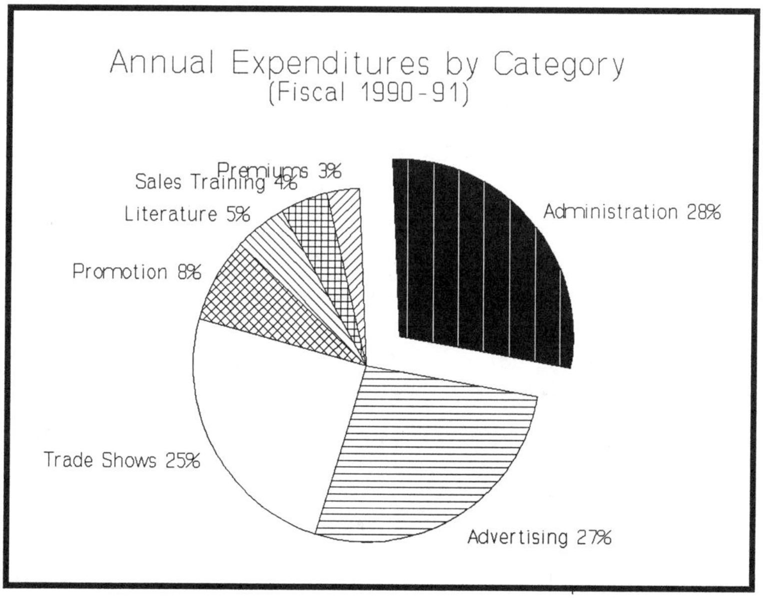

Figure 6-12 Marketing Expenses

Let's assume we've already written and edited the report with which this figure is to be used and don't anticipate making any additional changes requiring major insertions or deletions of text. We also know approximately where the figure should go, and have been writing with reference to a copy of the figure we printed directly from Lotus or Harvard Graphics. Because we don't anticipate any more changes in the text, we've decided to use a page-type box for our imported figure. Because the first reference to the figure is at the top of a page, we'll place the figure at the left center of the same page. The following instructions will accomplish our objectives.

1. Press **(Alt-F9)** and type [**F**], [**C**] to create a Figure Box.
2. Type [**F**], a graphic image filename ([**C:\FIGURES\PIE02**] in this example), and press **Enter**.

```
Graphics
        Figure Box
                Create  F, [C:\FIGURES\PIE02], <R>
```

NOTE: Our pie chart graphic image was imported from Harvard Graphics using HPGL format (Hewlett Packard Graphics Language). This format is recognized by WordPerfect and converted automatically. The image is called "PIE02" and it resides in the "FIGURES" subdirectory on our C drive.

3. Type [**C**] to display the Caption Editing screen, type [**Marketing Expense**]. Since this is a short caption, let's add space between the bottom of the box and the caption and then center the caption.

   3. 1 Press **Home**, **Home**, **Home**, **Up Arrow** to move the cursor to the top of the Caption Editing screen.

   3. 2 Press **(Shift-F8)**, type [**O**], [**A**], [**D**], [**.08**] and press **Enter**, **(F7)** to move the caption down .08" and return to the Caption Editing screen.

```
Layout
        Other  A, D, [.08], <R>, <R>
```

   3. 3 Press **(Shift-F6)**, **(F7)** to center the caption and return to the Definition: Figure menu.

```
Layout
        Align
                Center  <(F7)>
```

NOTE: Click on the letters in the Definition: Figure menu with your left mouse button, enter numbers from the keyboard and complete operations by pressing the right button.

4. Type **[T]**, **[A]** and press **Enter** or the right mouse button to select the page-type option from the "Anchor Type" options menu.
5. Type **[V]**, **[C]** to center the box vertically.
6. Type **[H]**, **[M]**, **[L]** to position the box on the left side of the page. Since we want text to wrap to the right of our box, leave the "Wrapping Text Around Box" field set on "Y."
7. Type **[E]** to check the image in the Graphics Edit screen to make sure it's the one you wanted in this particular Figure Box.
8. Press **(F7)** or the right mouse button twice to return to the Normal Editing screen.

Now let's change the Figure Box options. (Doing so will also change the options for all the Figure Boxes that follow this one.)

NOTE: Be sure you've returned to the Normal Editing screen before you follow the next instructions. Also be sure your cursor is located ahead of the new Figure Box code before you change figure options. Press **(Alt-F3)** to Reveal Codes and find the Figure Box code. It will look like,

[Fig Box:1;PIE01.PIC;[AdvDn:0.08"][Center][Box Num]Marketing Expense]

Perhaps the safest approach to use (but only if you want to change all figure options in a document) is to press **Home**, **Home**, **Home**, **Up Arrow** to move to the top of the document.

9. Press **(Alt-F9)** and type **[F]**, **[O]** to display the Options: Figure menu.

```
Graphics
        Figure Box
                Options
```

NOTE: Click on the letters in the Options: Figure menu with your left mouse button, enter numbers from the keyboard and complete operations by pressing the right button.

10. Type **[B]**, **[D]**, **[D]**, **[D]**, **[D]** to change all four borders to "Double."
11. Type **[O]**, **[.12]**, press **Enter**, type **[.12]**, press **Enter**, type **[.25]**, press **Enter,** type **[.25]**, and **Enter** to change spacing.

NOTE: We like these particular spacing settings. You may prefer something else. Experiment to see what looks best.

12. Type [**C**] to select Caption Number Style and display the existing caption in the editing window at the bottom of the screen.
13. Remove the **[Bold]** codes by moving your cursor just ahead of the codes and pressing **Delete** and just behind the codes and pressing **Delete** again.
14. Now move your cursor to the "F" in "Figure" and press **(F8)**. Press **End** to move your cursor to the end of the word, type [**.—**], press **(F8)** again and then press **Enter** to add a period and two hyphens and underline the caption.

Following appropriate guidelines for the construction of figures, we leave the caption outside and below the Figure Box. Since we'll be using a single level of figure numbers in our report, we also leave the default caption numbering options as is.

15. Press **(F7)** to return to the Normal Editing screen.
16. Press **(Shift-F7)** and type [**V**] to View Document and check the appearance of the Graphics Box.

File
Print V

NOTE: You may need to press PgUp or PgDn to see the figure.

ENDNOTES

1. Stephen Weidenborner and Domenick Caruso, *Writing Research Papers: A Guide to the Process,* 2nd ed. (New York: St. Martin's Press), 1986.
2. Graphics software documentation often advises on style, format, and positioning of elements.

6- 4 USING THE THESAURUS

Instructions in this module show you how to use WordPerfect's built-in thesaurus to improve the precision and liveliness of your writing. The Overview subsection describes the thesaurus and advises you when and how to use it. The Procedure subsection explains the steps required to use this feature.

Overview

A thesaurus is an alphabetized listing of words and their synonyms (words of the same meaning) and antonyms (words of opposite meaning). When used regularly and wisely, a thesaurus can help eliminate those overused words that come most quickly to mind when you prepare the first draft of a long document.

WordPerfect provides a 150,000-word thesaurus that's easy to access and simple to use. Put it to work after you've completed the first draft of a long document. When your first draft is finished, move to the beginning of your document and then review all *essential words*—those key words that give the document its meaning and persuasiveness. As you review each word, ask yourself:

1. Is this word precise enough?
2. Can it be improved?
3. Has it been overused?

If the answer to any of these questions is yes, follow the procedures described below.

Procedure

Move your cursor into the first questionable word.

1. Press **(Alt-F1)**.

Tools
Thesaurus

The Normal Editing screen is replaced with a split screen with two windows. The upper window shows up to four lines of text with the selected word highlighted. The lower window shows one or more columns of words and a menu line at the bottom. (See Fig. 6-13.)

Note that the selected word is at the top of the left-most column in the lower window. Also note that the listed words are grouped by form—e.g., nouns (n), verbs (v), adjectives (a), and antonyms (ant)—and by connotation. Connoted groups of words are numbered. Finally, note that a particular word may have enough synonyms and antonyms to fill all three columns on the screen—or it may have none. In the latter case, the message, "Word not found," is displayed briefly and you're prompted for another word.

Some words in the list are marked with small bullets. They are "headwords," that link to chains of additional synonyms and antonyms. Selecting a headword provides you with additional alternatives for achieving precision in word usage.

2. To select a specific alternative from the words marked with letters, type [**1**], and then type the letter beside your substitute word. The selected list word replaces the highlighted word in the text shown in the top window and the Normal Editing screen reappears.

```
    antonyms (ant)--and by connotation.  Connoted groups of words are

    numbered.  Finally, note that a particular word may have enough synonyms

    and antonyms to fill all three columns on the screen or it may have
particular=(a)
 1 A ·certain              picky
   B ·definite
   C ·specific            particular-(n)
                            5    ·detail
 2 D ·exclusive                  ·fact
   E ·individual                 ·item
   F ·special                    ·specific
   G ·unique
                          particular-(ant)
 3 H ·conscientious         6    ·general
   I  detailed                   ·careless
   J ·meticulous                 ·sloppy
   K ·precise
   L ·thorough

 4 M ·fastidious
   N ·fussy
   O ·persnickety
1 Replace Word; 2 View Doc; 3 Look Up Word; 4 Clear Column: 0
```

Figure 6-13 Thesaurus Screen

3. If the best alternative is not in the lettered column, press the right or left cursor arrow to shift the highlighted letters over to the column containing the best alternative word. Then, type [**1**], and the substitute word's letter code to swap it for the highlighted word in the top window.
4. To display the chain of words linked to a headword, type the headword's letter identifier. The headword selected jumps to the top of the next column to the right with its synonyms listed below.
5. To substitute a word listed under the headword for the highlighted word in your original text, follow the procedure in step 2.
6. When you select a headword, the words to which it is linked may take the place of words that were in the original list of synonyms and antonyms. Words from the original list scroll off the screen. Press **Down Arrow** or **PgDn** to bring them into view again.
7. To switch off the thesaurus and return to the Normal Editing screen, *without* swapping a word from the thesaurus, press **(F1)** or **Enter**.

6- 5 HYPHENATION

Hyphenation refers to the splitting of words at the ends of lines to make the right margin of a document more even and neater in appearance. Before we consider how to use WordPerfect to assist with hyphenation, let's learn what a hyphen is, what the difference is between a hyphen and a dash, and how to split words. We do all that in the Overview subsection. The Procedure subsection presents the instructions needed to hyphenate a document with WordPerfect.

Overview

Let's consider hyphens first. A *hyphen* is the short horizontal line produced when you press the key with two lines of unequal length just to the left of the "=" key. When you press the shift *and* hyphen keys, an "underline," is produced. The underline resembles a hyphen but is typed a little lower on the line.

The hyphen splits *compound* words within a line—the word, "first-rate," in the sentence, "Tony Martinez has done a first-rate job!"—for example. It's also used to break a long word at the end of a line into two groups of related syllables.

In a WordPerfect document, the hyphen can be categorized further as a *hard hyphen,* a *hyphen character,* or a *soft hyphen.* A *hard hyphen* is produced by pressing the hyphen key immediately after typing the first word in a compound like "two-thirds." WordPerfect displays the hyphen on your screen and splits the compound following the hyphen during hyphenation. You are not prompted as to the hyphen's placement.

A *hyphen character,* on the other hand, is produced by pressing the HOME key *before you press the hyphen key.* WordPerfect breaks a compound with a hyphen character at the end of a line when a document is hyphenated but also prompts you for hyphen placement. That is, WordPerfect treats a word containing a hyphen character as one that should *not* be split automatically into groups of syllables. You'd use the hyphen character in situations where you didn't want a compound word split at the end of a line. For example, if you were describing how to use standard calculators to compute bond yields, you'd want to maintain "TI-60," "HP-93," etc., together as complete character strings.

A soft hyphen is generated automatically by WordPerfect in the hyphenation process. The soft hyphen is visible at the end of a line when a single word is broken into two parts. If the hyphenated word is joined following additional editing, however, the hyphen no longer shows up on the screen or in print, but it may be seen by revealing codes. It will appear as a highlighted hyphen.

NOTE: You can insert soft hyphens in long words by pressing the Ctrl and hyphen keys.

A *dash* is shown as two hyphens in a row, e.g., "—"; use a dash to separate parenthetical expressions within sentences. (We did so in the third paragraph in this section.) To produce a dash, press **Home** and type [—]. By pressing Home first, you ensure that WordPerfect keeps the two hyphens of your dash together at the end of a line when it separates the dash and the following text.

Hyphenation Rules. The hyphenation algorithm in WordPerfect usually hyphenates a word at the end of a line correctly. Because the algorithm is not 100 percent accurate, however, choose manual rather than automatic hyphenation and review each WordPerfect hyphenation decision.

NOTE: See Turabian for helpful general hyphenation rules.[1] Also consult *Webster's Ninth New Collegiate* dictionary for exact syllabication of words you might use in the completion of written assignments and other documents.[2] The general rules in Fig. 6-14 are similar to the rules found in Turabian.

Consult the following references for additional guidance on hyphenation:

Rules	Examples
• Don't divide letter combinations pronounced as a single syllable.	an-nounced gassed
• Include the liquid l with ing and ed.	ram-bled whist-ling
• When a consonant is doubled before ing or ed, split the word between consonants.	bet-ting format-ting
• When a word ends with a double consonant, don't split the consonants.	roll-ing fell-ed
• Don't divide the syllables, "able" and "ible.	cap-able compat-ible
• Don't divide suffixes containing eous, ious, ion, ial.	ceous cious tion tial
• Don't make single-letter splits.	u-nison i-terate
• Don't make two-letter splits.	strand-ed en-tail
• Split compound words at the hyphen.	open- one- ended half
• Don't divide proper names unless the correct split is obvious.	Jack-son Ander-son Smith-field Mat-lock
• Don't divide capital letters used as abbreviations for names of countries, states, organizations, or publications.	ALPA AACSB JASA CCITT
• Always hyphenate fractions.	one-half, three-fourths
• Always hyphenate numbers.	fifty-eight, thirty-six
• Don't hyphenate words with the common prefixes, re, un, non, pre, post, over under, sub, super, etc.	reemerge, unlikely uninvolved, prepaid postdate, overstocked

Figure 6-14 Hyphenation Rules

Turabian, Kate L., *A Manual for Writers of Term Papers, Theses, and Dissertations* (5th ed.). Chicago: University of Chicago Press, 1987.

Webster's Ninth New Collegiate Dictionary. Springfield, MA: Merriam-Webster, Inc., 1984.

Procedure

Wait until the final draft stage of your work before hyphenating your document. To avoid unnecessary distraction, hyphenate the finished document all at once as a complete and separate task in the document-building process rather than hyphenating it as you type

Follow the instructions below to use manual hyphenation:

1. Press **Home**, **Home**, **Up Arrow** to move to the top of your document.
2. Press **(Shift-F8)**, and type [**L**] to display the Format: Line menu.
3. Type [**Y**], [**Y**] and press **(F7)** to select hyphenation and return to the Normal Editing screen.

Layout
Line J, L, <R>

4. Press **(PgDn)**, the **plus sign** at the far right of the keyboard, or **Down Arrow** to move through the document.
5. As you move through text, WordPerfect hyphenates most words for you automatically by making reference to its own spelling dictionary which includes information on hyphen positioning. From time to time you may see the message,

   Position hyphen; Press ESC [*displayed word*].

   When you do, press **Left Arrow** or **Right Arrow** to move the cursor to the left or right and then press **Esc**. If you want the entire word to wrap to the next line down, press **(F1)** to cancel hyphenation *for the particular word.*

   NOTE: When you cancel hyphenation for a word by pressing (F1), WordPerfect inserts a [/] "cancel hyphenation" code in front of the word. If you'd like to hyphenate the word at a later time, press **(Alt-F3)** (or **(F11)**) to reveal codes and delete the cancel hyphenation code.

6. Should you decide to toggle off auto or manual hyphenation, press **(Shift-F8)** and type [**L**], [**Y**], [**N**].

ENDNOTES

1. Kate L. Turabian, *A Manual for Writers of Term Papers, Theses, and Dissertations,* 5th ed. (Chicago: University of Chicago Press, 1987), pp. 45-47.
2. *Webster's Ninth New Collegiate Dictionary* (Springfield, MA: Merriam-Webster, Inc., 1984).

6- 6 HEADERS AND FOOTERS

A header is a line or block of text, numbers, a graphic, or any combination of the three standing apart at the *top* of a page. The title and page number at the top of the odd-numbered pages in a textbook is an example of a header. A footer is a line or block of text, numbers, and/or graphics that stands apart at the *bottom* of a page.

Overview

Use headers or footers (or both) to number the pages of a term paper or case analysis. Also use them to add an identifier or the current date at the top of each page in a management report. (See the header example in the multipage business letter in Section 4- 4, "Numbering Pages.") WordPerfect inserts a blank line between your header or footer and the text of your document automatically and adjusts the number of text lines so that header, text, and footer all fit nicely within the top and bottom margins set for your document.

The header or footer is created in a separate Header/Footer Editing screen. When you work in the header/footer editing screen, you can use most of the WordPerfect features you'd use to create a document in the Normal Editing screen: you can set margins or line spacing differently than you've set them in your text. You can also use the date feature to insert the current date automatically.

When you create a header or footer, WordPerfect inserts a code at the top of the current page. (You can see it if you reveal codes.) The code may move away from the top of the page when you insert or delete text, so that the header or footer may not print on the correct page.

Whenever you create a new header or footer, any existing header or footer is discontinued. Thus, you may use several different headers or footers in a long document.

Procedure

The instructions in this subsection are organized into three related sets: (1) creating a header, (2) editing a header, and (3) discontinuing a header. (We omit the procedures for creating, suppressing, and discontinuing footers because they duplicate the header procedures almost exactly.)

Create a Header. Creating a header is easy. Let's see how it's done in the instructions below.

1. Take the following steps to generate a header at the top of your document.
   1. 1 Press **Home**, **Home**, **Home**, **Up Arrow** to move to the top of the document.
   1. 2 Press **(Shift-F8)** and type [**P**] to access the Format: Page menu.
   1. 3 Type [**H**], [**A**], [**P**] to generate the same header on every page. An empty Header/Footer Editing screen is displayed.
2. Create your header on this screen and then press **(F7)** to return to the Format: Page menu.
3. Take the following additional steps to suppress the header on page 1. (Suppression affects only a single page.)
   3. 1 Type [**U**], [**H**], [**Y**] and press **Enter** to suppress the header and return to the Format: Page menu.

      NOTE: Start the header or footer on the first page of the document and then "suppress" it if you don't want it printed on the first page.

   3. 2 Press **(F7)** to return to the Normal Editing screen.

Layout
Page H, A, P, [header], <(F7)>, U, P, Y, <R>, <R>

   3. 3 Press **(Shift-F7)** and type [**V**] to View Document and see how your document looks with the header. Check spacing, page numbers, and the overall look of your document with the header in place.

File
Print V

Edit a Header. Here are the steps necessary for editing a header.

4. Move your cursor to the page where the header code is located and then follow the next two instructions to open the Header Editing screen:
   4. 1 Press **(Shift-F8)** and type [**P**], [**H**], [**A**], [**E**].
   4. 2 Make the appropriate changes and press **(F7)** twice to return to the Normal Editing screen.

Layout
Page H, A, E, [changes], <(F7)>, <R>

Discontinue a Header. You can discontinue a header (or footer) starting on any page of your document by moving to the target page and typing the following keystroke sequence:

5. Press **(Shift-F8)**, type **[P]**, **[H]**, **[A]**, **[D]** and press **(F7)** to return to the Normal Editing screen.

Layout Page H, A, D, <R>

A discontinued header—unlike a suppressed header—doesn't print on any subsequent pages.

6- 7 PREPARING A BIBLIOGRAPHY

The instructions in this module show you how to prepare a bibliography and reference list using WordPerfect's Doc 1 and Doc 2 Normal Editing screens and hanging indent feature.

Overview

The bibliographic style used here is adapted from Kate Turabian's, *A Manual for Writers*, 5th ed. Refer to chapter 10 in the Turabian book for additional information and examples. The examples shown in Fig. 6-15 and 6-16 should provide sufficient formatting guidance for most of the reference material you're likely to use, however.

A bibliography is included at the end of a long document when footnotes or endnotes are used to cite sources. In contrast, a reference list is included when parenthetical references are the chosen form of citation. We describe the bibliography next. Afterward, we point out how the reference list differs from the bibliography.

Constructing a bibliography is a straightforward procedure. If the references are limited, say 25 or fewer, list them alphabetically by author's last name without respect to the type of publication—e.g., book, journal, or monograph. When you have more than 25 references and two or more types of publication are represented, categorize the list by reference type—e.g., books, articles, monographs, and so on. References within categories are then organized in alphabetical order of author's last name.

The *easiest* and safest way to create a bibliography is to write the information on 3 x 5 or 4 x 6 "source" cards, place the cards in alphabetical order, and then type the list directly from the cards. An alternative approach is to draft your reference list on paper, alphabetize it by numbering the individual references so the item

BIBLIOGRAPHY

Alstrup, Jens, Sven-Eric Andersson, Soren Boas, Oli B. G. Madsen, and Rene Victor V. Vidal. "Booking Control Increases Profit at Scandinavian Airlines." *Interfaces* 19, No. 4 (July-August 1989): 10-19.

Belobaba, Peter P. "Air Travel Demand and Airline Seat Inventory Management." Ph.D. diss., Massachusetts Institute of Technology, 1987.

________. "Application of a Probabilistic Decision Model to Airline Seat Inventory Control." *Operations Research* 37, No. 2 (March-April 1989): 183-97.

Boeing Commercial Airplane Company. "Boeing Promotional Fare Management System, Analysis and Research Findings." Seattle: Boeing Commercial Airplane Company, 1982.

Cross, Robert G. "Strategic Selling: Yield Management Techniques to Enhance Revenue." Paper presented at the Shearson-Lehman Brothers 1986 Airline Industry Seminar. Key Largo, Florida, February 1986.

"Enter the Yield Manager," *Lloyd's Aviation Economist* 2, No. 8 (May 1985): 12-13.

Hirshleifer, Jack. *Price Theory and Applications*, 3d ed. Englewood Cliffs, N.J.: Prentice-Hall, Inc., 1984.

Horwitt, Elisabeth. "Carriers Land Profits by Empowering DP Units." *Computerworld*, 7 March 1988, 73-80.

Kimes, Sheryl E. "Yield Management: A Tool for Capacity-Constrained Service Firms." Ithaca, N.Y.: Cornell University, School of Hotel Management, 1989.

Pappas, James L., and Eugene F. Brigham. *Managerial Economics*, 3d ed. Hinsdale, Ill.: The Dryden Press, 1979.

Pfeifer, Phillip E. "The Airline Discount Fare Allocation Problem." *Decision Sciences* 20, No. 1 (Winter 1989): 149-157.

________. "The Single Period Inventory-Mix Problem with Early Discount Pricing." *1986 Proceedings of the Decision Sciences Institute*. Atlanta: Decision Sciences Institute, 1986: 1121-23.

Rothstein, Marvin. "An Airline Overbooking Model." *Transportation Science* 5 (July 1971): 180-92.

________. "Hotel Overbooking as a Markovian Sequential Decision Process." *Decision Sciences* 5 (April 1974): 389-94.

Rothstein, Marvin and A. W. Stone. "Passenger Booking Levels." *AGIFORS Proceedings* 7 (1967): 183-97.

Figure 6-15 Sample Bibliography

numbers match the alphabetical order of the list and then type the items into the bibliography or reference list in numerical order. Another alternative, but one requiring the use of WordPerfect's sort feature, is to type the references into a document in no particular order and then sort them into alphabetical order with the sort feature. As a final note, be sure that the bibliography includes only those sources that have been noted at least once in the text.

REFERENCE LIST

Alstrup, Jens, Sven-Eric Andersson, Soren Boas, Oli B. G. Madsen, and Rene Victor V. Vidal. 1989. Booking control increases profit at scandinavian airlines. Interfaces 19, No. 4 (July-August): 10-19.

Belobaba, Peter P. 1987. Air travel demand and airline seat inventory management. Ph.D. diss., Massachusetts Institute of Technology.

________. 1989. Application of a probabilistic decision model to airline seat inventory control. Operations Research 37, No. 2 (March-April): 183-97.

Boeing Commercial Airplane Company. 1982. Boeing promotional fare management system, analysis and research findings. Seattle: Boeing Commercial Airplane Company.

Cross, Robert G. 1986. Strategic selling: yield management techniques to enhance revenue. Paper presented at the Shearson-Lehman Brothers 1986 Airline Industry Seminar. Key Largo, Florida, February.

Enter the yield manager, 1985. Lloyd's aviation economist 2, No. 8 (May): 12-13.

Hirshleifer, Jack. 1984. Price theory and applications, 3d ed. Englewood Cliffs, N.J.: Prentice-Hall, Inc..

Horwitt, Elisabeth. 1988. Carriers land profits by empowering DP units Computerworld, 7 March, 73-80.

Kimes, Sheryl E. 1989. Yield management: a tool for capacity-constrained service firms. Ithaca, N.Y.: Cornell University, School of Hotel Management.

Pappas, James L., and Eugene F. Brigham. 1979. Managerial economics, 3d ed. Hinsdale, Ill.: The Dryden Press.

Pfeifer, Phillip E. 1989. The airline discount fare allocation problem. Decision Sciences 20, No. 1 (Winter): 149-157.

________. 1986. The single period inventory-mix problem with early discount pricing. 1986 Proceedings of the decision sciences institute. Atlanta: Decision Sciences Institute: 1121-23.

Rothstein, Marvin. 1971. An airline overbooking model. Transportation Science 5 (July): 180-92.

________. 1974. Hotel overbooking as a markovian sequential decision process. Decision Sciences 5 (Fall): 389-94.

Rothstein, Marvin and A. W. Stone. 1967. Passenger booking levels. AGIFORS Proceedings 7: 183-97.

Figure 6-16 Sample Reference List

The reference list is quite similar to the bibliography in purpose and format, but there are some differences between the two. In particular, notice in Fig. 6-16 that the year of publication follows immediately the name of the author; also notice that the title of the publications are capitalized in *sentence-style* rather than *headline-style.* Contrast these examples with the examples in Fig. 6-15 that employs headline-style capitalization.

Consult Turabian for additional guidance on preparing lists of references:

Turabian, Kate L., *A Manual for Writers of Term Papers, Theses, and Dissertations* (5th ed.). Chicago: University of Chicago Press, 1987.

Procedure

To simplify production, construct the components such as the title page and bibliography in WordPerfect's Doc 2 screen and then move them into the Doc 1 screen. We do that here to demonstrate the approach.

In the following instructions we assume that: (1) WordPerfect is running, (2) the Doc 1 Normal Editing screen is displayed on your monitor, and (3) your long document is active in Doc 1.

1. Press **(Shift-F3)** to switch to the Doc 2 screen.
2. Press **(F7)** and type [**N**], [**N**] to clear the Doc 2 Normal Editing screen.

> Edit
> Switch Document <(F7)>, N, N

3. Take the following steps to format your bibliography properly:
   - 3. 1 Press **(Shift-F8)** and type [**L**], [**T**], [**T**], [**A**] to access tab settings on the Format: Line menu, and change the type to "Absolute."
   - 3. 2 Press **(Ctrl-End)** to clear out any existing tabs.
   - 3. 3 Type [**1,0.5**] and press **Enter**, **(F7)** to set tabs every half-inch starting at the left margin and then return to the Format: Line menu. (If tabs are already set at half-inch intervals, ignore step 3. 3.)

> Layout
> Line T, T, A, <(Ctrl-End)>, [1,0.5], <R>, <R>, <R>

   - 3. 4 Type [**S**], [**1**] and press **Enter**, **(F7)** to set line spacing to 1 and return to the Normal Editing screen. (If line spacing is already set to "1", ignore step 3. 4.)

> Layout
> Line S, [1], <R>, <R>

4. Press **(Shift-F6)**, **Caps Lock,** type [**bibliography**], press **Caps Lock** again and then press **Enter** twice. (Alternatively, type [**references**].)
5. Press **(F4)** to indent the first bibliographic entry and then press **(Shift-Tab)** to create a "hanging indent." Type the first entry and press **Enter** twice.

```
Layout
        Align
                Indent
```

```
Layout
        Align
                Margin Release
```

6. Repeat the instructions in step 5 for the remainder of your list of references.
7. Press **(Ctrl-Enter)** at the end of the reference list to insert a hard page code.

Now move the bibliography from Doc 2 to the end of the long document you've been working on in Doc 1. Follow instructions 8 through 10 below to do so.

8. Press **Home**, **Home**, **Home**, **Up Arrow** to move to the top of your bibliography.
9. Press **(Alt-F4)**, **Home**, **Home**, **Down Arrow** to block the complete set of references.
10. Press **(Ctrl-F4)** and type **[B]**, **[C]** to copy the blocked text to the Move/Copy buffer.

    NOTE: You could have *moved* the blocked text rather than copying it, but copying is safer.

11. Press **(Shift-F3)**, **Home**, **Home**, **Down Arrow** to switch back to Doc 1 and move to the end of your long document. (If you haven't already ended your draft in Doc 1 with a hard page break, do so now by pressing **(Ctrl-Enter)**.)
12. Press **Enter** to drop the bibliography in at the end of your long document.

```
Edit
        Copy
```

```
Edit
        Switch Document
```

```
Edit
        Paste
```

6-8 LISTING TABLES AND FIGURES

The instructions in this module tell you how to create a list of tables or figures. The Overview subsection presents a set of formatting guidelines for figure and table lists. The Procedure subsection presents instructions for: (1) creating a dummy page for the list, (2) defining the list, and (3) generating the list.

Overview

If a long document includes many figures, tables, or both, place a formal list or lists of the inclusions following the table of contents at the beginning of the document. A list of tables or figures should conform generally to the format shown in Figs. 6-17 and 6-18. We refer you to Turabian's *A Manual for Writers* for detailed instructions on the construction of lists of tables and illustrations. The rules listed below should serve you well in most situations, however.

LIST OF TABLES

Figure 6-17 Sample List of Tables

LIST OF FIGURES

Figure 6-18 Sample List of Figures

- Numbers used to identify figures and tables are arabic numerals in two separate series. Tables begin with Table 1 and are numbered consecutively to the end of your document. Similarly, figures are numbered consecutively as Fig. 1, Fig. 2, etc.
- Single space within the table and figure captions that comprise the list, but double space between captions.
- Table and figure numbers are aligned on their periods under the heading, "Table" or "Figure."
- Page numbers marking the locations of tables or figures are set flush right under the heading, "Page."
- In most instances, captions within the list are the same as the table or figure captions in text or in an exhibit section. If captions in text are very long, however, they may be shortened after the list has been generated.

- The first and all subsequent runover lines in a long caption are indented three spaces.
- Set the list heading two inches from the top of the page.
- Number list pages with small roman numerals, centered at the bottom of each page. (See Section 4- 4, "Numbering Pages," for detailed instructions.)

When you create your figures or tables using the graphics feature, WordPerfect copies the captions of your figures and tables to lists automatically. The procedures described below assume you've used the graphics feature. If you construct your tables as text in the Table Editor and the Normal Editing screen, follow the approach for making lists outlined in Section 6- 9, "Preparing a Table of Contents."

NOTE: If you construct some of your tables in table graphics boxes and some in the Table Editor, use list 7 for both. When you create tables in table boxes, WordPerfect copies the table captions to list 7 automatically when the list is generated. When you create tables in the Table Editor, be sure to mark your table captions separately but specify that they be included in list 7.

Consult Turabian for additional guidance on preparing lists of tables and figures:

Turabian, Kate L., A Manual for Writers of Term Papers, Theses, and Dissertations (5th ed.). Chicago: University of Chicago Press, 1987.

Procedure

This is important. Prepare lists of tables or figures *only* after you've typed and final edited the text, added all tables and figures, added any appendices, exhibits, or both, and assigned page numbers to the text and back matter.

There are four basic tasks you must complete to prepare a list: (1) take care of the preliminaries such as setting tabs, advancing down to start your heading two inches below the top edge of the page, and creating the heading; (2) define the location of the list; (3) generate the list; and (4) edit the list to ensure correctness of format. Each task is described in turn below.

Take care of the preliminaries. Prior to generating a list, set up a dummy page on which the list will be generated. At this stage of the long document production and packaging process, the dummy page should be at the very beginning of your long document. To set up the dummy page, follow the steps below.

NOTE: If you plan to produce *two* lists—e.g., a list of tables and a list of figures, set up *two* dummy pages.

1. Press **Home**, **Home**, **Home**, **Up Arrow** to move your cursor to the top of the document.
2. Press **(Ctrl-Enter)** to generate a hard page break.

3. Press **(SHIFT-F8)**, type [**L**], [**T**], [**T**], [**R**], and press **(F7)** twice to make sure tab settings are not changed in the text of your long document.

> Layout
> Line T, T, R, <R>, <R>

NOTE: Take this step so that any *new* tab settings you set for your list(s) of tables (or figures) don't change the spacing in later sections of your long document and scramble the format.

4. Press **PgUp** to move up to the dummy page.
5. Press **(Shift-F8)** and type [**L**], [**T**], [**T**], [**A**] to set tabs relative to the left edge of the paper and display the tab set line.
6. Press **(Ctrl-End)** to clear existing tabs.
7. Type [**1,0.25**] and press **Enter** and **(F7)** twice to set tabs starting at the left margin and appearing every quarter inch thereafter and then return to the Normal Editing screen.

> Layout
> Line T, T, A, <(Ctrl-End)>, [1,0.25], <R>, <R>, <R>

8. Press **(Shift-F8)**, type [**O**], [**A**], [**I**], [**2**], press **Enter** and then press **(F7)** to advance the cursor to a point two inches below the top edge of the page.

> Layout
> Other A, I, [2], <R>, <R>

9. Press **Caps Lock**, **(Shift-F6)** and type [**list of tables**] or [**list of figures**]. Then press **Caps Lock** and **Enter** three times to switch the keyboard to lowercase and position the cursor three lines below the heading.

Define the List. The next set of instructions defines the list to be generated on the dummy page or pages you created above.

NOTE: If you didn't prepare your tables or figures with the graphics feature, you must *mark* the entries in your list. (See "Preparing a Table of Contents" for instructions on marking before defining the list. Be sure to mark your entries for a "List" and not for a "TOC," however.)

10. Move your cursor to a point just above the hard page code at the end of your dummy page. (Press **(Alt-F3)** (or **(F11)**) to reveal codes and find the **[HPg]** code.)

10. 1 Press **(Alt-F5)** and type [**D**], [**L**] to define a list.

10. 2 WordPerfect displays the prompt,

List Number (1-10):

If you're generating a list of figures, type [**6**] and press **Enter**; if you're generating a list of tables, type [**7**] and press **Enter**.

10. 3 In response, WordPerfect displays a menu of numbering style options. Since "Flush Right Page Numbers with Leaders" is the desired option, type [**L**] to select it and return to the Normal Editing screen.

```
Mark
        Define
                List [List Number], <R>, L
```

Generate the List. You should be aware that when you generate a list, WordPerfect generates *all* the lists you've defined—e.g., a list of tables *and* the table of contents. Follow the next instruction sequence to generate the list (or lists).

11. Press **(Alt-F5)** and type [**G**], [**G**]. In response, WordPerfect displays the prompt,

Existing tables, lists, and indexes will be replaced. Continue? Yes (No)

Type [**Y**] to generate the list.

```
Mark
        Generate G, Y
```

You will then see the message,

Generation in progress: Pass [n], Page [n]

displayed briefly at the bottom left corner of the screen. Then your list appears.

Edit the list. You can edit the text in the table or figure list just as you'd edit any other text. For example, you can add vertical spacing or shorten the longer captions that were picked up directly from your tables or figures. The original WordPerfect versions of the lists in Figs. 6-17 and 6-18 were both edited heavily to bring them into correspondence with Turabian's guidelines.

WARNING: Don't edit the lists until you're certain that you won't need to regenerate *any* of the reference lists in your document, including lists of figures, lists of tables, or the table of contents. Should you edit a reference list and then find that you need to regenerate, all your editing work will be lost.

WARNING: It's a *very good idea* to edit lists with Reveal Codes toggled on to help you avoid deleting codes by mistake.

6- 9 PREPARING A TABLE OF CONTENTS

The instructions in this section show you how to produce a table of contents automatically. The Overview subsection includes useful formatting rules and construction guidelines. The Procedure subsection presents step-by-step instructions for marking text, creating a heading, defining the table, and generating the list of ordered headings.

Overview

We refer you to Turabian's *A Manual for Writers* for further information and examples, but in the interim we also recommend that you adopt the following rules to make the task easier and more manageable. Your readers will appreciate the simplicity of the resulting table.

- Always center the title, "TABLE OF CONTENTS" or "CONTENTS" and set it in full caps.
- Triple space between the title and the first heading in your table.
- Use two levels of headings. For example, if your document is broken into sections, subsections, and sub-subsections, use only section and subsection headings.
- Double space between headings but single space if a long heading must extend to a second line.
- Indent second level headings three spaces from the first level headings and indent the second line of extended headings three spaces from the first. (We show how this is done below.)
- Position the beginning page number of each element flush right with dot leaders. (We also show how this is done below.)
- When headings extend to a second line, dot leaders and page numbers should align with the continuation line.
- If your document is long enough to be divided into parts, use Roman numerals to identify each part. Chapters and sections are numbered with Arabic numerals.

- Capitalize all major divisions in your text—e.g., CHAPTER, SECTION, ENDNOTES, REFERENCES. Use headline style capitalization for secondary divisions.

Creating the table of contents should be the next to the last stage in the process of packaging a long document. (Be sure to place the table of contents just behind your title page.)

Constructing a list such as the table of contents with WordPerfect involves three tasks. First, search for and *mark* all words or phrases to be included in the list. Second, *define* the list, that is, indicate to WordPerfect where in the document the list is to be generated, and finally, create a heading and then *generate* the list itself. The procedure section below describes the three steps in detail. Your final result should resemble the list in Fig. 6-19.

Consult Turabian for additional guidance on preparing a table of contents:

Turabian, Kate L., *A Manual for Writers of Term Papers, Theses, and Dissertations* (5th ed.). Chicago: University of Chicago Press, 1987.

Procedure

We assume your long document is in the Doc 1 Normal Editing screen. Therefore, press **Home**, **Home**, **Home**, **Up Arrow** to move your cursor to the beginning of your work. Since the *actual generation of the table* is one of the last steps taken, don't be concerned about table headings or placement at this point.

Marking

WordPerfect constructs the table of contents automatically by copying marked chapter, section, and subsection headings directly from the text into the table of contents. If the elements aren't marked ahead of time by you, the author, however, the procedure won't work. To search for and *mark* the headings to be included in your table, follow the instructions below:

1. Press **(F2)** to toggle on the search feature.
2. Enter the text of the first heading to be marked (the search target).

   NOTE: It's usually not necessary to type in the complete heading; just provide a unique string of characters. Perhaps even the first two or three words in a long heading will be sufficient.

3. Press **(F2)** again to start the search. Your cursor should stop in the first element to be included in your table of contents just behind the search string character typed last.

```
Search
        Forward [search string], <R>
```

TABLE OF CONTENTS

Figure 6-19 Sample Table of Contents

4. Move your cursor to the first character and then press **(Alt-F4)** and **Right Arrow** to block the complete element.

   NOTE: When you block the title to be marked, be sure to include any **[Bold]**, **[Und]**, or other attribute codes surrounding your titles if you want the attributes reflected in the table of contents. Press **(Alt-F3)** to toggle on Reveal Codes to see what you're doing.

5. Press **(Alt-F5)**, type [C], [1], and press **Enter** to mark the element for the table of contents and specify it as a level-one element.

> Mark
> Table of Contents [ToC Level:], <R>

Repeat the steps above to search for and mark the next element. Your only concern at this point should to be to indicate that the subheadings in your table are "ToC Level" 2 headings. For example, "FINDINGS" in Fig. 6-19 is at level 1, whereas "In General, Business Schools Favor Faculty Consulting" is at level 2. Repeat the same steps until you reach the end of your document. You are now ready to *define* the table.

Defining

6. Press **Home**, **Home**, **Home**, **Up Arrow** to move back to the beginning of your document. Before you press the actual key sequence that defines the table of contents, *end* the table page with a hard page break and the default tab setting. To do so, take the following steps:
7. Press **(Ctrl-Enter)** to generate a hard page break.
8. Press **(Shift-F8)**, type [**L**], [**T**], [**T**], [**R**] and press **(F7)** twice to set default tabs. Take this step because you may use different tab settings for the table of contents than you used for the text and you won't want the table of contents settings to carry through and scramble the components of the document that follow.

> Layout
> Line T, T, R, <R>, <R>

9. Press **PgUp** to move up to the page where the table of contents will be defined. At this point, set tabs with absolute spacing every half inch starting at one inch and type the heading. Follow the steps below to do so.
   9. 1 Press **(Shift-F8)** and type [**L**], [**T**], [**T**], [**A**] to reveal the Format: Line menu and set "Absolute" spacing.
   9. 2 Press **(Ctrl-End)** to clear existing tabs.
   9. 3 Type [**1,0.5**], press **Enter**, and then press **(F7)** twice to set tabs every half inch starting at one inch and then return to the Normal Editing screen.

> Layout
> Line T, T, A, <(Ctrl-End)>, [1,0.5], <R>, <R>, <R>

10. Press **(Shift-F6)** and **Caps Lock** to center your heading in uppercase.
11. Type [**contents**] or [**table of contents**].
12. Press **Caps Lock** and **Enter** three times to toggle back to lowercase and create some space between the title and the elements of the list.
13. Press **(Alt-F5)** and type [**D**], [**C**] to define a table of contents.
    You should see the Table of Contents Definition menu at this point.
14. Type [**N**], [**2**] to indicate *2* levels of headings and no wrapped format.

    NOTE: If page numbering is already shown as "Flush right with leader," ignore the next step, pressing **(F7)** instead.

15. Type [**P**], [**L**], [**L**], press **Enter**, and press **(F7)** to indicate that page numbers are to be flush right with dot leaders for both levels and return to the Normal Editing screen. Your next (and easiest) task is to generate the table of contents.

```
Mark
        Define
                Table of Contents  N, [2], P, L, L, <R>, <R>
```

Generate

16. Press **(Alt-F5)** and type [G], [G], [Y]. After typing Y, you briefly see the message,

```
Mark
        Generate G, Y
```

Generation in progress: Pass: [n], Page [n],

followed by a display of the newly generated table of contents.

You may wish to edit the table of contents to bring it more in line with the formatting rules set out in the overview section above. More specifically, add spacing between the subheadings and indent the second line of continued headings. You may also wish to number elements, add column headings, etc., so that your table of contents resembles the example in Fig. 6-19.

WARNING: You may regenerate the table of contents by pressing the sequence of keystrokes above. Be forewarned, however, that any editing done on the existing table of contents is lost in the regeneration process.

ENDNOTES

1. In headline style capitalization, all words other than articles, conjunctions, and prepositions are capitalized.

6-10 PREPARING A TITLE PAGE

The instructions in this module show you how to prepare a title page. The Overview subsection provides general guidance on the procedure while the Procedure subsection provides detailed instructions for preparing the title sheet using the advance and date features.

Overview

It's good form to begin most long documents with a title page. If you're uncertain as to whether a title page should be attached to a specific written submission, ask your course instructor's advice. As is true of other components of long documents, you normally have some freedom in the title page format. Although you do have some flexibility, we recommend that you adopt the format in Fig. 6-20—it attempts to incorporate the guidelines and examples of several authorities on written business communications.

After your long document is complete, create the title page in a new "component" document in Doc 2 and then insert it at the beginning of the long document in Doc 1. This approach is in keeping with the principle of modularity applied to the guidelines for preparing other document components. When you follow the instructions in the Procedure section below, you should be able to duplicate the simple title page format in Fig. 6-20.

Procedure

In these instructions we assume that WordPerfect is running and that your Normal Editing screen is clear. If your long document is displayed in Doc 1, press **(Shift-F3)** to switch to Doc 2. If text is displayed in Doc 2, press **(F7)** and type [N], [N] to clear it.

```
Edit
        Switch Document  <(F7)>, N, N
```

Create the title page. Take the following steps to prepare the title page.

NOTE: When you follow the instructions below, the title page appearing on your screen looks much different that the title page in Fig. 6-20. It will probably look more like the example in Fig. 6-21, instead. Although the title page looks like the

RIVERWOOD UNIVERSITY
MCCRARY GRADUATE SCHOOL OF BUSINESS

YIELD MANAGEMENT AND MARGINAL ANALYSIS

MANAGERIAL ECONOMICS (8124)

MARK J. RODGERS
MARCH 16, 1991

Figure 6-20 Printed Title Page

diagram in Fig. 6-21 in the Normal Editing screen, toggling on reveal codes would tell a different story. At the beginning of each line you should see **[AdvToLn:]** codes that show what's really going on. That example was prepared using WordPerfect's Advance feature and the instructions in this set.

```
RIVERWOOD UNIVERSITY
MCCRARY GRADUATE SCHOOL OF BUSINESS
YIELD MANAGEMENT AND MARGINAL ANALYSIS
MANAGERIAL ECONOMICS (8124)
MARK J. RODGERS
MARCH 16, 1991
==========================================================
```

Figure 6-21 On-Screen Title Page

1. Press **(Shift-F8)** and type [**L**] to check line spacing. If line spacing is set to 1 (single spacing), press **(F7)** to return to the Normal Editing screen. If not, type [S], [**1**] and press **Enter** to set single spacing and then press **(F7)** to return to the Normal Editing screen.

> Layout
> Line S, [1], <R>, <R>

2. Press **(Shift-F8)** and type [**O**], [**A**], [**I**], [**2**] to advance to a point two inches down from the top of the page. Press **Enter**, **(F7)** to lock in the distance.

> Layout
> Other A, I, [2], <R>, <R>

3. Press **(Shift-F6)**, **Caps Lock**, type the name of your college or university and press **Enter**.
4. Press **(Shift-F6)**, type the name of your school or department and press **Enter**.
5. Press **(Shift-F8)**, type [**O**], [**A**], [**I**], [**4**] to advance to a point four inches down from the top of the page. Press **Enter**, **(F7)** to lock in the distance.

> Layout
> Other A, I, [4], <R>, <R>

6. Press **(Shift-F6)**, type the title of your paper and press **Enter**.

   NOTE: Your title should be less than ten words long, and try not to begin it with phrases such as "A Report on . . . " or "Recommendations for . . . ." If a long title requires more than one line of text and the two or more lines cannot be of equal length, break the title so the longest line is first, the next longest line second, and so on.

7. Press **(Shift-F8)**, type [**O**], [**A**], [**I**], [**5**], and press **Enter**, **(F7)** to advance to a point five inches from the top of the page.

> Layout
> Other A, I, [5], <R>, <R>

8. Press **(Shift-F6)**, type the name and number of the course for which the document was written and press **Enter**.

9. Press **(Shift-F8)**, type [**O**], [**A**], [**I**], [**8**], and press **Enter**, **(F7)** to advance to a point 8 inches from the top of the page. Press **(Shift-F6)**, type your name in first name, middle initial, last name order and press **Enter**.

Layout
Other A, I, [8], <R>, <R>

10. Press **(Shift-F6)**, **(Shift-F5)** and type [**T**] to generate the date in text form.

Tools
Date Text

NOTE: The month is shown in upper/lowercase. To convert it to full caps, take the following steps:

- Move your cursor to the first letter of the month and press **(Alt-F4)** to toggle block on.
- Press **Right Arrow** to highlight the entire month.
- Press **(Shift-F3)** and type [**U**] to convert to all uppercase.

Edit
Block <End>

Edit
Convert Case
To Upper

11. Press **Caps Lock**, **(Ctrl-Enter)** to toggle your keyboard back to upper/lowercase and end your title page with a hard page code.

Copy the title page to Doc 1. Take the following steps to copy the title page from Doc 2 to the beginning of Doc 1.

12. Press **Home**, **Home**, **Home**, **Up Arrow** to move your cursor to the top of the title page.
13. Press **(Alt-F4)**, **Home**, **Home**, **Down Arrow** to block the entire title page.
14. Press **(Ctrl-F4)** and type [**B**], [**C**] to copy the title page into the Move/Copy buffer.

Edit
Copy

Edit
Switch Document

Edit	
	Paste

15. Press **(Shift-F3)**, **Enter** to switch to Doc 1 and drop the title page in place.

7

Special Applications

This chapter contains instruction sets for creating outlines, using the WordPerfect merge feature, and producing mailing labels. Each instruction set in the chapter has Overview and Procedure subsections, and some of the merge applications are linked to supplemental sets of instructions in Chapter 4. Overview subsections describe the purpose of the application, present examples of standard layouts, and provide hints and tips. Procedure subsections present detailed WordPerfect instructions keyed to the particular document type.

7- 1 PREPARING AN OUTLINE

This module provides general guidelines for the preparation of topical and sentence outlines. Also included are detailed procedures for preparing a traditional outline with WordPerfect's outline feature, manipulating outline elements, and using the paragraph numbering feature. In the remaining pages are an Overview subsection that explains the purpose of outlines and provides general guidelines for creating them and a Procedure subsection that includes detailed construction guidelines.

Overview

An outline is a fragmentary, tree-like document that can be the skeleton or framework for a longer document. Usually, an outline is prepared prior to the writing of a first draft and serves as the blueprint for the first and subsequent drafts. It may be constructed from simple phrases or complete sentences and need not (and perhaps *should not*) be constructed from beginning to end in a linear fashion. Rather, it should be constructed piecemeal, growing branches in some places, shrinking them in other places, and moving the branches from here to there and back again. (Later we refer to the branches in an outline as "families.")

Many writing authorities recommend the construction of an outline as a preliminary to the preparation of a document of any length—even a letter or memo. They *strongly* urge the use of outlines to plan and organize longer documents such as term papers and written case analyses. Course instructors often insist that an outline be prepared prior to the preparation of a paper or report and that it be submitted along with the final draft of the paper or report.

The outline is a plan. Think of the outline as an aid to the construction of a document rather than another bothersome requirement to be written *after* the basic writing assignment is complete. If you view the outline in this positive light, your term paper, report, or case analysis will be written more easily and your final draft will be of higher quality. By conceptualizing the outline as a plan to guide the writing of your draft, you improve the organization and content of your final document from the very start of your project. An outline lets you see your project as a whole and avoid the danger of losing yourself in details.

Outlines need not be fixed and unchangeable. Although it's always wise to prepare an outline to guide your writing project, it need not be immutable and, like other types of plans, may be modified as your work progresses. How you prepare and use an outline depends largely upon your own personal style. You may even work more effectively if you write your outline *after* your rough draft is complete because the process of writing the first draft may help you organize your thoughts as you work. Constructing the outline after you write the first draft enables you to move text around, delete material and add new material in a more organized way. The second draft will be that much better as a result.

Topical and sentence outlines. There are two basic outline types: topical outlines and sentence outlines. The *topical outline* is the more common of the two and is also the more easily constructed and modified. It is comprised of a set of numbered, indented phrases arranged chronologically or according to some other order and is the form most of us use when we plan the organization of a document. The *sentence outline* is also numbered and indented but is comprised of complete sentences rather than short phrases.

Generally, a sentence outline takes longer to write than a topical outline, but it has a significant additional benefit: It can be constructed with the topic sentences of the paragraphs that will make up the final document. If a sentence outline is prepared with care, your long document is almost written; all that remains of the writing project is to expand upon the ideas introduced in the topic sentences. (As a matter of form, don't include topical outline elements in a sentence outline, and vice versa.)

Creating the outline. To create the outline, jot your ideas down on paper or index cards just as they occur to you without worrying much about organization.

When all the initial ideas are written down, number them in whatever order seems most appropriate. We recommend that you adopt the traditional outline numbering system shown in Fig. 7-1. Although WordPerfect lets you create an outline with up to eight levels, avoid confusion by limiting yourself to three or four—unless you plan to write a very long document.

The next step is to type your rough outline directly into WordPerfect using the Outline feature. By using WordPerfect, you can easily move individual topics around in the Document Editing screen, cutting and pasting here and there in order to improve the organization. You can also insert new items into an existing outline.

The WordPerfect Outline feature provides several numbering options in addition to the traditional style shown in Fig. 7-1. (Other styles supported are paragraph, legal, and bullet.) Because the traditional style is universally accepted in both undergraduate and graduate schools of business, we have adopted it for these instructions. If you're interested in learning about or using any of the other systems, consult the WordPerfect reference manual.

Procedure

In this subsection we first provide instructions for setting appropriate tabs; then we show how to construct an outline. Next, we show how to delete and move sets of outline elements. Finally, we provide instructions for automatically numbering paragraphs.

Tab settings. The tab settings in the format line can affect the appearance of an outline significantly. If you set your tabs according to the instructions below, your outline elements should be attractively arranged.

1. Press **(F7)** and type [**N**], [**N**] to clear your screen.

Element	Level
I. Chairman of the Board	1
A. President and Chief Operating Officer	2
1. Vice-President — Operations	3
a. Senior Director — Manufacturing	4
(1) Director — Peripherals	5
(a) Plant Manager — Flint	6
i) Department Manager	7
a) Supervisor	8

Figure 7-1 Traditional Outline Numbering Style

File
Exit N, N

2. Press **(Shift-F8)** and type [**L**], [**T**], [**T**], [**R**] to select tabs from the Format: Line format menu.
3. Press **(Ctrl-End)** to clear existing tabs.
4. Type [**0,0.333**] and press **Enter** to set tabs at every third of an inch starting at the left margin.

Layout
Line T, T, R, <(Ctrl-End)>, [0,0.5], <R>, <R>

5. Press **(F7)** twice to return to the Document Editing screen.

Outline construction. To produce a traditional outline, follow the next eight instructions.

1. Move the cursor to the location on your Document Editing screen one line above the spot where you wish to start the outline. (Normally, you'd begin your outline at the left-hand margin.)
2. Press **(Shift-F5)** and type [**O**], [**O**] to activate the outline feature.

Tools
Outline
On

Note the word "Outline" at the bottom left corner of your display screen.

3. Press **Enter** to start generating outline numbers.
4. If you'd like to start with a number at a level lower than level 1 (Roman numerals), press the tab key one or more times after the level 1 number appears. (One tab for capital letters, two tabs for Arabic numerals, etc. Press **(Shift-Tab)** if you go too far.)

NOTE: WordPerfect automatically generates outline numbers at all levels; *do not attempt to insert your own numbers along with the numbers generated automatically by WordPerfect.*

5. After the first outline number has been generated, press **Home**, **Tab**, **Space Bar** or **(F4)** and begin typing phrases or sentences. Press **Enter** at the end of the first element.

NOTE: The Home, Tab key sequence is called a "hard tab." Use it if an indent or spaces won't do.

NOTE: If you press Enter again immediately after the outline number appears on your screen, you push the number down one line. Do so whenever you need to add vertical space in your document. Press **Backspace** three times and **Enter** again if you add an extra line by mistake.

6. Press **Tab** to move to the next lower level (capital letters to Arabic numbers, for example). Observe that the cursor jumps to the next tab position and an outline number at the next lower level is generated. Use this approach to generate the capital letter, A (at the second level), after a Roman numeral (at the first level) or the number 1 (at the third level) after a capital letter. Press **Space Bar** or **(F4)** and type the next element.

   NOTE: If you move your cursor too far to the right (too far down in terms of levels) so that you generate a fourth or fifth level outline number when you intended to generate a third level number, press **(Shift-Tab)** to move it back. To delete an outline number entirely, press **Backspace** and erase it. (These fixes also work for an existing outline, but be sure your cursor is on the outline number to be repositioned or deleted. Press **(Alt-F3)** or **(F11)** to Reveal Codes as a precaution.)

7. Continue to press **Enter** and **Tab** to generate and position numbers and then type elements until your outline is complete.
8. When your outline is complete, press **(Shift-F5)** and type [**O**], [**F**] to toggle off the outline feature.

```
Tools
        Outline
                Off
```

NOTE: This final step is important if you intend to type normal text following your outline. If the outline is in a document all by itself, however, don't toggle off the outline feature; it toggles off automatically when you save your document.

Deleting and moving families of elements. Branches in an outline are called "families." Higher level elements in a family are called "parents," while lower level elements are called "children." Elements on the same level are referred to as "siblings." WordPerfect includes options that let you delete, move, and copy entire families of elements. In the instructions below, we show you how to delete and move families. Copying a family is a straightforward extension of moving a family.

Deleting a family

1. Move your cursor to the highest level element in the family to be deleted (the dBASE family labeled I.A in the example shown in Fig. 7-2, for example).
2. Press **(Shift-F5)**, type [**O**], [**D**], [**Y**]. The family disappears and remaining outline numbers readjust automatically. (See Fig. 7-3.)

```
Tools
        Outline
                Delete Family
```

NOTE: If you delete a family by mistake, press **(F1)** and type [**R**] to recover the lost material.

```
Edit
        Undelete  R
```

```
File Edit Search Layout Mark Tools Font Graphics Help        (Press F3 for Help)
                          Microcomputer Software

I.     Database Managers
       A.   dBASE
            1.   dBASE III+
            2.   dBASE IV (1.0)
            3.   dBASE IV (1.1)
       B.   Fox Pro
       C.   Paradox
II.    Graphics
       A.   DrawPerfect
       B.   Freelance
       C.   Harvard Graphics
III.   Spreadsheets
       A.   Lotus 1-2-3
            1.   Release 1.01
            2.   Release 2.01
            3.   Release 2.2
            4.   Release 3.0
       B.   Microsoft Excel
       C.   PlanPerfect

C:\JUNK\SMPLOUT1.W51                               Doc 1 Pg 1 Ln 1" Pos 1"
```

Figure 7-2 Outline Example

```
File Edit Search Layout Mark Tools Font Graphics Help          (Press F3 for Help)
                         Microcomputer Software

I.     Database Managers
       A.     Fox Pro
       B.     Paradox
II.    Graphics
       A.     DrawPerfect
       B.     Freelance
       C.     Harvard Graphics
III.   Spreadsheets
       A.     Lotus 1-2-3
              1.     Release 1.01
              2.     Release 2.01
              3.     Release 2.2
              4.     Release 3.0
       B.     Microsoft Excel
       C.     PlanPerfect




Outline                                        Doc 1 Pg 1 Ln 1.5" Pos 1"
```

Figure 7-3 Outline Example—Family Deleted

Moving a family

1. Move your cursor to the highest level element in the family to be moved (the dBASE family labeled I.A in the example shown in Fig. 7-2, for example).
2. Press **(Shift-F5)**, type **[O]**, **[M]** and press cursor arrows to move the family (see Fig. 7-4).

```
Tools
        Outline
                Move Family
```

   2.1 Press **Up Arrow** to move the family *up* in the outline.
   2.2 Press **Down Arrow** to move the family *down* in the outline (see Fig. 7-5).
   2.3 Press **Left Arrow** to *promote* the family so that all members are at *higher* levels.
   2.4 Press **Right Arrow** to *demote* the family so that all members are at *lower* levels (see Fig. 7-6).
3. Press **Enter** to complete the move.

Paragraph numbering. Occasionally, you may wish to number the paragraphs in a long document. For example, you might want to number the alterna

```
File Edit Search Layout Mark Tools Font Graphics Help        (Press F3 for Help)
================================================================================
                           Microcomputer Software

I.     Database Managers
       A.     dBASE
              1.     dBASE III+
              2.     dBASE IV (1.0)
              3.     dBASE IV (1.1)
       B.     Fox Pro
       C.     Paradox
II.    Graphics
       A.     DrawPerfect
       B.     Freelance
       C.     Harvard Graphics
III.   Spreadsheets
       A.     Lotus 1-2-3
              1.     Release 1.01
              2.     Release 2.01
              3.     Release 2.2
              4.     Release 3.0
       B.     Microsoft Excel
       C.     PlanPerfect

Press Arrows to Move Family; Enter when done.
```

Figure 7-4 Outline Example—Move Start

```
File Edit Search Layout Mark Tools Font [Graphics] Help      (Press F3 for Help)
================================================================================
I.     Database Managers
       A.     Fox Pro
       B.     Paradox
       C.     dBASE
              1.     dBASE III+
              2.     dBASE IV (1.0)
              3.     dBASE IV (1.1)
II.    Graphics
       A.     DrawPerfect
       B.     Freelance
       C.     Harvard Graphics
III.   Spreadsheets
       A.     Lotus 1-2-3
              1.     Release 1.01
              2.     Release 2.01
              3.     Release 2.2
              4.     Release 3.0
       B.     Microsoft Excel
       C.     PlanPerfect


Press Arrows to Move Family; Enter when done.
```

Figure 7-5 Outline Example—Move Down

```
File Edit Search Layout Mark Tools Font [Graphics] Help        (Press F3 for Help)

I.      Database Managers
        A.      Fox Pro
        B.      Paradox
                1.      dBASE
                        a.      dBASE III+
                        b.      dBASE IV (1.0)
                        c.      dBASE IV (1.1)
II.     Graphics
        A.      DrawPerfect
        B.      Freelance
        C.      Harvard Graphics
III.    Spreadsheets
        A.      Lotus 1-2-3
                1.      Release 1.01
                2.      Release 2.01
                3.      Release 2.2
                4.      Release 3.0
        B.      Microsoft Excel
        C.      PlanPerfect


Press Arrows to Move Family; Enter when done.
```

Figure 7-6 Outline Example—Move Demote

tives in a written case analysis you're preparing for a policy course. To number paragraphs automatically, follow these instructions.

1. Press **(Shift-F5)** and type [**P**] to select paragraph numbering.
2. In response to the prompt,

   Paragraph Level (Press Enter for Automatic): ,

   type [**3**] and press **Enter** to select level 3, arabic numbers. After you type 3, the number 1 is generated on your screen at the location of the cursor.

Tools
    Paragraph Number [3] <R>

NOTE: You may prefer another numbering arrangement—e.g. level 2 for capital letters, level 4 for lowercase letters, etc. If so, press [**2**] or [**4**] instead of pressing [1].

NOTE: If you press Enter instead of typing a level number, WordPerfect automatically selects the level number corresponding to the tab stop where your cursor is located. For example, if your cursor is at the left margin, WordPerfect assigns a level 1 number; it it's at the first tab, WordPerfect assigns a level 2 number, and so forth.

3. Press **Tab** or **Space Bar** once or twice (or press **(F4)** if you wish to have indented paragraphs) and type the paragraph after the number appears.

   NOTE: In contrast to the situation when the Outline feature is toggled on, pressing the Tab key does not change the level of a paragraph number.

4. When you're ready to begin the next paragraph, press **(Shift-F5)** and type [**P**], [**3**] to generate the second paragraph number. Notice that the number increases automatically.

```
Tools
        Paragraph Number [3] <R>
```

As you type the text of a draft, you may want to insert new paragraphs in text already created. If you do, move your cursor to the spot where the new material will go, press **(Shift-F5)** and type [**P**] and a level number to generate a paragraph number. Then add the new text. Notice that the new paragraph number is already in the proper sequence. That is, the paragraph numbers following the newly inserted material are adjusted upward automatically.

The paragraph numbering feature is cumbersome because it requires that you press (Shift-F5) type [P], and press Enter every time a new paragraph number is generated. However, this particular key sequence is easily captured in a simple macro (see sec. 8- 2 for more complete instructions on creating macros). Build the macro if you'll use paragraph numbering frequently.

- Press **(Ctrl-F10)** to toggle on the macro feature.
- Press **(Alt-N)** in response to the WordPerfect prompt,

  Define Macro: .

- Type a descriptive phrase such as, "Auto paragraph numbering" and press **Enter** in response to the WordPerfect prompt,

  Description: .

- With the message, "Macro Def" flashing in the lower left corner of your Normal Editing screen, press **(Shift-F5)** and type [**P**], [3], and press **Enter, (F4)** to toggle on the paragraph numbering feature at level 3 and indent the text of the paragraph to follow.
- Press **(Ctrl-F10),** to toggle off the macro feature and save the new macro as ALTN.WPM.

```
Tools
    Macro
        Define [macro name] <R> [description] <R>
```

```
Tools
    Paragraph Number [3] <R>
```

```
Tools
    Macro
        D
```

Now you can generate paragraph numbers automatically by pressing and holding the Alt key and pressing N.

ENDNOTES

1. A topic sentence is the lead sentence in a paragraph and expresses the paragraph's main idea. The other sentences in the paragraph develop, elaborate upon, or interpret the main idea.

7- 2 MERGE APPLICATIONS

Knowing how to produce merge letters and envelopes will be a big help when it's time for you to look for a job. Merge know-how can also save lots of time and effort if you're responsible for sending out notices to members of a club or fraternal organization. The instructions in this section show you how to use WordPerfect's merge feature to help complete these sorts of tasks. The module includes an Overview subsection that explains how the merge feature works and provides some general guidelines for using it productively and a Procedure subsection that presents detailed instructions.

Overview

When you use the merge feature, blocks of unchanging text in a *primary file* are repeatedly combined with elements of variable text (called "fields") in a *secondary file* to produce a *merged file*. An example of a primary file might be the text in a placement letter. An example of a secondary file might be the names, titles, company names, and addresses to be typed on the placement letters you'll send out four to five months before graduation.

The purpose of the merge feature is to avoid retyping text that doesn't change from one document to the next. Placement and solicitation letters typify the merge application. Other examples of merged files are lists of names, addresses and telephone numbers; labels and envelopes; and forms.

Merge operations in WordPerfect are controlled by codes in the primary file that match the order of some or all of the variable fields in the secondary file. Most codes are inserted by pressing the key combination (Shift-F9) and typing a letter matching a menu option displayed at the bottom of your screen. Several menu options insert a code directly; others are displayed and then picked from a pop-out window that appears when you type [M] (for "More"). The single exception to this method is the {END FIELD} code that can be generated by pressing (F9).

Procedure

In this subsection, we describe four different merge applications:

- A simple merge of primary and secondary files
- Merge printing envelopes
- Merging text from the keyboard
- Creating simple lists

First, however, we explain some basic principles of the merge feature.

Basic principles of merging and the simple merge operation. The first step in the simple merge operation is to decide *what* variable information is to be included in the secondary file and *how* to arrange it. Answers to the "what" and "how" questions depend upon the nature of the merge application you have in mind. For example, if your application is a placement letter mailing, you will surely want to include the fields below. The complete set of fields is called a "record."

1. Personal title (Mr., Ms., Dr., etc.)
2. First name (John)
3. Last name (Smith)
4. Job title (Personnel Director, Manager of Human Resource Development)
5. Company name (Eastman Kodak, Inc.)
6. Company address (may be two or more lines)
7. City (Rochester)
8. State (NY)
9. Zip code (14650)

You should also include a phone number field if telephone follow-up is part of your job search strategy. On the other hand, if your merge application is providing support for club membership activities, the next set of fields—at a minimum—would be appropriate:

1. Name (Stephen F. Jones)
2. Preferred name (Steve)
3. Address (316 Polo Road)
4. City (Winston-Salem)
5. State (NC)
6. Zip code (27106)
7. Phone number (761-0737)

You must also decide how to arrange the names. For example, do you want: (1) the complete name in a single field; (2) the first name and middle initial in one field and last name in another field; or (3) the first name in one field, the last name in a second field, and the middle initial in a third. Other structural issues you must deal with are: (1) how to accommodate occasionally missing information—e.g., company name, (2) how to represent multiple line addresses, and (3) when and how to abbreviate information.

Constructing your secondary file with care and imagination is important because it may be usable for several merge applications. If you include complete information pertaining to a group of subjects, one subset of the information can be used for one merge application—say, a newsletter—and a different subset can be used for a second merge application—say, a phone solicitation calling list. Think about all the potential applications of the information in your secondary file. By doing so ahead of time, you avoid expending unnecessary additional effort later.

After you've specified the structure and contents of your secondary file, you're ready for the second step of the simple merge operation—creating the secondary file. Switch on your PC and run WordPerfect by typing [**WP**] and pressing **Enter**. (If WordPerfect is running already, Press **(F7)** and type [**N**], [**N**] to clear your Document Editing screen.)

```
File
        Exit  N, N
```

1. Type the information for the first field (it might be a personal title like Mr. or Ms.) and press **(F9)**. Notice that {END FIELD} pops in at the end of the line, and your cursor drops down to the next line.
2. Type the second field (it might be first name), and press **(F9)**. Continue typing the fields one after another, until all are entered.
3. After you type the last field (zip code, for example), press **(Shift-F9)** and type [**E**]. The merge code, {END RECORD}, and a hard page break are added.

```
Mr.{END FIELD}
Louis{END FIELD}
Avalos{END FIELD}
Personnel Director{END FIELD}
Triangle-G Company{END FIELD}
2525 DuPont Drive{END FIELD}
Irvine{END FIELD}
CA{END FIELD}
92715{END FIELD}
{END RECORD}
==========================
Ms.{END FIELD}
Randi{END FIELD}
Azevedo{END FIELD}
Director, Human Resources{END FIELD}
Chicken Every Day, Inc.{END FIELD}
70 W. Hedding, Suite 108{END FIELD}
San Jose{END FIELD}
CA{END FIELD}
95110{END FIELD}
{END RECORD}
==========================
Ms.{END FIELD}
Paula{END FIELD}
Baker{END FIELD}
President{END FIELD}
Pizza Time, U.S.A.{END FIELD}
8th & S. Court House Road{END FIELD}
Arlington{END FIELD}
VA{END FIELD}
22204{END FIELD}
{END RECORD}
==========================
Mr.{END FIELD}
Li{END FIELD}
Fang{END FIELD}
Personnel Director{END FIELD}
Beijing Express{END FIELD}
Glenhardie Center, Suite 7
3443 Mount Auburn Street{END FIELD}
Wayne{END FIELD}
PA{END FIELD}
19087{END FIELD}
{END RECORD}
==========================
```

Figure 7-7 Secondary File

```
Tools
        Merge Codes
                End Record
```

Now, repeat steps 1, 2, and 3 for the other records in your data set. A sample of secondary file records is shown in Fig. 7-7.

4. Press **(F7),** type [**Y**] and in response to the WordPerfect prompt,

Document to be saved: ,

type a document name—SECDOC01.W51, for example—press **Enter,** and type [**N**] to save the secondary file and clear your screen.

File	
	Exit Y, [filename], <R>, N

WARNING: Each record must contain exactly the same number of fields, and field contents must be consistent from record to record. For example, if there are nine fields in the first record, there must be *exactly* nine fields in all other records. If company name is in the fifth field in record 1, it must be in the fifth field in all subsequent records.

NOTE: A given field may be blank in one or more records. For example, when company name is a field in a secondary file, some records in your source list may not show a company name because someone on the list may be self-employed. In such cases, press **(F9)** when the cursor is at the very beginning of the empty line.

NOTE: Individual fields can vary in length and even include hard returns. For example, a street address might be a single line in some records and a double line in others (see the fourth record in Fig. 7-7, for example).

The third step in the simple merge operation is to create the *primary file*, usually a simple document such as a letter. Before you type the primary file, however, decide which fields in your secondary file will be included and exactly where to place them. Perhaps the easiest way to do so is to type the complete primary file, including margins, tabs, other format specifications, as well as the punctuation required for variable fields. (An example is the colon at the end of the salutation line.) When you've typed the text of the primary file, move your cursor to the target location of the first field and follow the next three instructions. (A placement letter primary file is shown in Fig. 7-8.)

5. Press **(Shift-F9)** and type [**F**]. WordPerfect displays the prompt,

   Enter Field: ,

   at the bottom of the screen.
6. In response, type the number of the field *in your secondary file* that belongs at this particular location. For example, if the first field to be inserted in the primary file is the personal title—e.g., Mr. Mrs., Ms., Dr.—and personal titles are in field 1 of your secondary file, type [**1**]. If personal title is field 3 in the secondary file, type [**3**] instead. After typing the field number, press **Enter**.

14 Del Monte Drive
Winston-Salem, NC 27103
{DATE}

{FIELD}1~ {FIELD}2~ {FIELD}3~
{FIELD}4~
{FIELD}5~
{FIELD}6~
{FIELD}7~, {FIELD}8~ {FIELD}9~

Dear {FIELD}1~ {FIELD}3~:

Marketing fast food franchises in a highly competitive industry presents a significant challenge. It takes knowledgeable and aggressive personnel to penetrate the market and maintain a company's edge.

When you add marketing staff, you will need individuals who are comfortable in the restaurant industry, who know your product, and who have a proven record of achievement. I have ample experience in food service operations, excellent interpersonal skills, and a history of accomplishment. Several years ago, I developed a planning system for a chain of restaurants that enabled the business to double in size while exceeding sales growth and profit objectives. More recently, I managed a large, full-service restaurant. During my tenure there, sales revenue increased by twenty-five percent; employee turnover was reduced by fifty percent and food costs were cut by ten percent.

At this point in my career, I would like to turn my attention toward the marketing side of the food service business. After studying your annual report, franchise literature, and organization structure, I believe I can add strength to your franchise marketing team.

I look forward to discussing employment opportunities with you personally. Since it is difficult to reach me by telephone, I shall call you on Wednesday, January 16, to see when an appointment can be arranged.

Thank you for your time and consideration.

Sincerely yours,

Mark J. Rodgers

Figure 7-8 Sample Placement Letter

Tools
Merge Codes
Field [field number] <R>

7. Move your cursor to the target location of the second field in your primary file, press **(Shift-F9)**, type [**F**], the code number of the secondary file field that goes with the second field in the primary file, and press **Enter**.

NOTE: Don't forget spacing and punctuation.

NOTE: The same field can be used more than once. For example, if your primary file is a letter, the addressee's first name can be used in the inside address, in the salutation, and even in the body of the letter itself (if you'd like to be extra friendly). A good way to keep track of the numbers and contents of secondary file fields as you work on your primary file is to retrieve the secondary file into Doc 2 and then refer to it as needed by pressing (Shift-F3), to switch from Doc 1 to Doc 2 (and back again when you have the information you need). Here's how.

- Press **(Shift-F3)**, to switch to Doc 2.
- Press **(F7)** and type [**N**], [**N**] to clear the Doc 2 normal editing screen.

Edit
Switch Document <(F7)>, N, N

- Press **(Shift-F10)**, type [***name of secondary file***], and press **Enter** to retrieve the secondary file into Doc 2.

File
Retrieve [filename], <R>

- Press **(Shift-F3)** to switch back to Doc 1.

Edit
Switch Document

NOTE: You can edit field codes. This capability is especially useful if you type the wrong field code. If that happens, delete the wrong number and insert the right one.

As you insert field codes into the primary file, be sure to include appropriate spacing, punctuation, and attributes. (You might think of field codes as stand-ins for the information to be included in the final printed document.) For example, if you wish to emphasize a particular field with underlining or boldface in the final document, underline or boldface the field code itself. More specifically, if a particular field code is a stand-in for company name, and you want company name to be set in boldface,

- Move your cursor to the left brace ({) in the company name field code,
- Press **(Alt-F4)** to toggle "block" on and then press **Right Arrow** until all characters in the code are highlighted.
- Press **(F6)** to bold it.

NOTE: If a particular field can be blank (recall the company name example used earlier), insert a question mark in front of the tilde at the end of the the field code—{FIELD}5?~, for example. Doing so ensures that a blank line is not produced in your final document when the corresponding field is blank in the secondary file.

NOTE: Since your primary file may well be sent to hundreds of addressees, make doubly sure it's error free. Use the spell checker, and review the file carefully for errors in style, grammar, and misused words before beginning the final step in the merge process.

NOTE: You may have been wondering about the purpose of the {DATE} standing on a line by itself at the end of the address in the example in Fig. 7-8. It is a date code that produces the date automatically. To insert the code,

- Press the cursor arrows and **Tab** to move your cursor to the last line of the return address.
- Press **(Shift-F9)**, type [**M**] to open the merge codes pop out window, type [**D**] and press **Enter**.

```
Tools
        Merge Codes
                More {DATE} <Enter>
```

The fourth step in the simple merge operation is merging the primary and secondary files to create the merged file itself. Follow the instructions below to complete this last step:

8. Save your primary file by pressing **(F7)**, typing [**Y**], and typing a document name—PRIDOC01.W51, for example—in response to the prompt,

   Document to be saved: .

   Then press **Enter** and type [**N**].

```
File
        Exit Y, [filename], <R>, N
```

9. Press **(Ctrl-F9)** to select sort and merge.
10. Type [**M**] to select merge.
11. In response to the prompt,

    Primary file: ,

type the name of the *primary file* and press **Enter**.

12. In response to the prompt,

Secondary file: ,

type the name of the *secondary file* and press **Enter** again.

```
Tools
        Merge  [primary file] <R> [secondary file] <R>
```

The variable information in the secondary file combines with the text in the primary file to produce a "merged file" that appears in the Document Editing screen with a hard page code at the end of each combined document.

NOTE: When the primary and secondary files are being merged, the message, * Merging * appears at the bottom left corner of your screen. If your secondary file has many records, the process may be lengthy. Be patient.

When the merge process is complete, the merged file is ready to be printed. A merged file can take up lots of disk space; we advise you not to save it after printing. You can easily rebuild it by following instructions 9-12. Turn to Section 4- 3, "Printing Documents," for printing instructions.

Merge printing envelopes. If you produce merge *letters,* you'll probably want to generate merge *envelopes,* too. They're also produced more efficiently with the merge feature.

NOTE: In the instructions below, we assume you won't be printing your return address on the envelope. If that's not the case, refer to the instructions in Section 4-5 and adjust the procedure described below.

1. If you use standard #10, 9-½" by 4" envelopes, select the primary envelope document for printing by following these instructions:

```
File
        Exit  N, N
```

1. 1 Press **(F7)**, [**N**], [**N**] to clear the Document Editing screen.

1. 2 Type [**L**], [**M**] [**4.25**], press **Enter**, type [**0**], and press **Enter, (F7)** to select line format options and set left and right margins for envelopes and return to the Document Editing screen.

NOTE: If an envelope form is not listed on the Format: Paper Size/Type menu, turn to Section 4- 5 for instructions on defining document sizes and types.

1. 3 Type [**M**], [**1.75**], press **Enter**, type [**0**], and press **Enter** twice to set top and bottom margins at 1.75 and 0 inches and return to the Format menu.

1. 4 Press **(Shift-F8)** and type [**P**], [**S**], [**N**], [**envelope**] (or highlight the "envelope" option using your cursor arrows), press **Enter** and type [**S**], to select the "envelope form" and return to the Format: Page menu.

2. Create the primary *envelope* file by pressing **(Shift-F9)**, typing [**F**], and then typing a merge code for personal title. Follow the same procedure for first name, last name, job title, company, address, city state, and zipcode that match the merge codes in your letter. See Fig. 7-9.
3. Press **(F7),** type [**Y**], and type a document name—PRIDOC02.W51, for example—in response to the prompt,

   Document to be saved: .

   Press **Enter**, and type [**N**] to save the envelope as a new primary file and clear your screen.

File
Exit Y, [filename], <R>, N

4. Generate an envelope merged file by following steps 9 through 12 above. The only thing you'd do differently would be to substitute the name of your *envelope* document for your *letter* document in step 11.
5. Press **(Shift-F7)** and type [**V**], to view your envelopes. (Turn to Section 4- 5, "Creating, Editing, and Printing Envelopes," if you need additional help.)
6. Assuming all is satisfactory, press **(F1)** and type [**F**] to return to the Print menu and begin printing envelopes.

```
{FIELD}1~ {FIELD}2~ {FIELD}3~
{FIELD}4?~
{FIELD}5?~
{FIELD}6~
{FIELD}7~, {FIELD}8~ {FIELD}9~
```

Figure 7-9 Envelope Codes

```
File
        Print  V, <(F1)>, F
```

Merging text from the keyboard. In the simple merge used to produce merge letters and envelopes, a *secondary file* was combined with a *primary file* to produce a *merged file.* Use the simple merge to advantage when a form letter or other document must be sent to large numbers of addressees. You can also use the merge feature to automate the production of memos (and other documents) to avoid having to type the heading, date; and to, from, and subject lines each time you prepare a memo. In this case, WordPerfect produces the unchanging text, and you type the variable text as needed. Follow the next set of instructions to set up this "memo generator."[1]

1. Press **(F7)** and type [**N**], [**N**] to clear your screen.

```
File
        Exit  N, N
```

Then type the word [**MEMORANDUM**] centered, in boldface, and in full caps and press **Enter** three times to skip two lines.

NOTE: Press **(Shift-F6)** to center text and **(F6)** to toggle the boldface attribute.

2. Type the word, [**DATE:**], press **Tab** once or twice, press **(Shift-F9)** to display the merge codes main menu, and then type [**M**] to display the pop-out supplemental menu.
3. Type [**D**] and press **Enter** to place a {DATE} code at the top left side of your memo after the word, "DATE:." Press **Enter** again.

```
Tools
        Merge Codes
                More  {DATE} <Enter>
```

NOTE: {DATE} generates the current date.

4. Type [**TO:**], press **Tab** once or twice, press **(Shift-F9)**, and type [**M**] to display the merge codes pop-out menu once more.
5. Type [**K**] and press **Enter** to place the code {KEYBOARD} after the tab on the TO: line. Press **Enter** again.

```
Tools
        Merge Codes
                More {KEYBOARD} <Enter>
```

NOTE: {KEYBOARD} is like a stop light to WordPerfect; it causes the program to stop and wait for you to enter text from the keyboard.

6. Type the word, [**FROM:**], press **Tab**, type [***your own name***], and press **Enter**.
7. Type the word, [**SUBJECT**:], press **Tab** and **(Shift-F9)**, and type [**M**], [**K**] and press **Enter** to place another {KEYBOARD} code on the SUBJECT: line.
8. Press **Enter** three times to move the cursor to the left margin of the memo.
9. Press **(F7)**, type [**Y**], and type a document name—PRIDOC03.W51, for example—in response to the prompt,

   Document to be saved: .

   Press **Enter**, and type [**N**] to save the memo and clear your screen.

```
File
        Exit  Y, [filename], <R>, N
```

10. Press **(Ctrl-F9)** and type [**M**] to select merge.
11. In response to the prompt,

    Primary file: ,

    type [**PRIDOC03.W51**] and press **Enter**.
12. In response to the prompt,

    Secondary file: ,

    just press **Enter.** The merge process begins.

```
Tools
        Merge  [primary file] <R> [secondary file] <R>
```

Line by line, WordPerfect displays the memo just as you typed it, complete with the current date, *until it reaches the {KEYBOARD} code you entered on the TO: line.* There, the process stops with the cursor blinking. Type the name of the person for whom the memo is intended and press **(F9)**. This is the green light for WordPerfect to proceed.

WARNING: Be sure to press (F9) here and after every other keyboard entry until you reach the text area of the memo. *Don't press Enter.* If you happen to press Enter instead of (F9) after typing variable information, press Backspace to erase the hard return and then press (F9).

WordPerfect next types the complete FROM: line and follows with the SUBJECT: line to the point where you placed your second {KEYBOARD}. There, WordPerfect stops for input again. In response, type the subject of the memo and press **(F9)**. WordPerfect takes over again, skipping two lines and moving the cursor to the left edge of your screen. Now type the text of the memo.

That's all there is to it. Similar procedures can be used to produce headings for letters or to fill in and print club or fraternity membership forms automatically.

You can enhance the automation of the memo generating process by including prompts in the primary file. We describe this process by example, using the "interactive" memo just created. If you created an interactive memo for yourself, clear the normal editing screen by pressing **(F7)** and typing [N], [N] and then retrieve it by pressing **(Shift-F10)** and typing the memo's name.

```
File
        Exit  N, N
```

```
File
        Retrieve  [filename], <R>
```

To make the required changes, follow the next set of instructions.

13. Move your cursor to the left brace of the first {KEYBOARD} code.
14. Press **(Shift-F9)**, type [**M**], type [**prom**], and press **Enter**. Then type [**Type name of addressee**], and press **Enter** again.

```
Tools
        Merge Codes
                More  {PROMPT} <Enter>
```

15. Move your cursor to the left brace of the second {KEYBOARD} code and repeat the same procedure but type [**Type subject**] instead.
16. Finally, press **Home**, **Home**, **Down Arrow** to move your cursor to the point where the body of the memo will be typed. Repeat the procedure above a third time but type [**Type memo text**] and press **Enter**.
17. Insert another {KEYBOARD} code after the prompt.
18. Save your modified memo.

When you run merge with this primary file, the messages "Type name of addressee," "Type subject," and "Type memo text" appear in turn at the bottom left corner of your screen. This feature is especially helpful if someone else will be using your automatic memo generator.

Creating simple lists. The merge feature can also be used to create simple lists such as names and addresses or names, phone numbers, and account numbers. To create a simple list, clear your screen and take the steps listed next.

1. Move the cursor to the target location of the *first* field in your list, press **(Shift-F9)**, type [**F**] and the secondary file code number corresponding to the *first* field in your list, and press **Enter** to generate the first variable for your list.

Tools
    Merge Codes
        Field [field number] <R>

2. Move the cursor to the location of the *second* field, press **(Shift-F9)**, type [**F**] and the secondary file code number for the *second* field in your simple list, and press **Enter** to generate the second variable for your list. (Note that the second field in our example is enclosed in parentheses.)
3. Follow the same steps for all other fields to be included in your list.
4. At the end of the field list, press **Enter** twice to skip a line between sets of linked information.

Tools
    Merge Codes
        Next Record

5. Press **(Shift-F9)** and type [**N**] to insert the {NEXT RECORD} code.
6. Press **(Shift-F9)**, type [**M**], [**nest p**], and press **Enter** twice to insert the {NEST PRIMARY} code.

> Tools
> Merge Codes
> More {NEST PRIMARY} <Enter>

The {NEXT RECORD} code tells WordPerfect to skip to the *next record in the secondary file*; the {NEST PRIMARY} code says "use *the same primary file* again."

A list generator primary file is shown in Fig. 7-10. The generator uses the club membership fields from the second example above to produce a list that displays full name, preferred name (in parentheses), and phone number on one line with the address on the lines below.

7. Press **Home**, **Home**, **Up Arrow** to move to the top of the document and press **(Alt-F4)** (or **(F12)**) to switch block on.
8. Press **Home, Home**, **Down Arrow** to highlight all field codes and the hard return at the beginning of the skipped line, and then press **(Shift-F8)** and type [**Y**] to toggle on the Block Protect feature.

   NOTE: Take the last two steps only if your list is likely to be longer than a single page. Block protecting the fields prevents splitting blocks of information at page breaks.

9. Save the list generating primary file as PRIDOC04.W51 and clear the screen.

> File
> Exit Y, [filename], <R>, N

10. Press **(Ctrl-F9)** and type [**M**] to select merge.
11. In response to the WordPerfect prompt,

    Primary file: ,

    type [**PRIDOC04.W51**] and press **Enter**.

```
{FIELD}1~ ({FIELD}2~)    {FIELD}7~
{FIELD}3~
{FIELD}4~, {FIELD}5~ {FIELD}6~

{NEXT RECORD}{NEST PRIMARY}
```

Figure 7-10 List Generator

```
Richard E. Aikernes  (Dick)    765-2252
3450 Neely Drive
Winston-Salem, NC 27106

Garvey L. Bean  (Garvey)       765-1489
2356 Faculty Drive
Winston-Salem, NC 27106

Thomas J. Bruebaker  (Tom)     784-4086
3127 Old Greensboro Road
Winston-Salem, NC 27105
```

Figure 7-11 Membership List

12. In response to the WordPerfect prompt,

    Secondary file: ,

    type the name of a matching secondary file and press **Enter** again.

Tools
Merge [primary file] <R> [secondary file] <R>

The list is generated automatically as you watch the screen. Fig. 7-11 shows the first three names on the list.

13. Press **(Shift-F7)** and type [**V**] to view the list.
14. Press **(F1)** and type [**F**] to print the list.

File
Print V, <(F1)>, F

NOTE: Don't bother saving the resulting merged file list because changes in variable information should be made in the *secondary file,* not in a saved list.

NOTE: With only minor changes, the steps used here to generate a simple list can be used to produce mailing labels. Instructions for doing so are in Section 7- 3.

ENDNOTES

1. Review the instructions in Section 3- 1 if you need help setting up a basic memorandum.

7- 3 PREPARING MAILING LABELS

Knowing how to create mailing labels can be useful in courses like Marketing Research (for identifying and addressing self-administered questionnaires), for field projects, or for internships. Knowing how to create mailing labels may also come in handy if you're an officer of a club or other organization that mails literature to its members from time to time. You can also use labels to identify books, magazines, and other belongings.

Instructions in this module show you how to create and print mailing labels with WordPerfect's merge feature. The Overview subsection explains the purpose of mailing labels and provides general guidelines for creating them; the Procedure subsection includes detailed instructions for performing six operations required to prepare and print "one-up" strips of labels on a dot matrix printer and sheet labels on a Hewlett-Packard LaserJet.

Overview

Mailing labels are self-stick tags that are pulled off a backing sheet and affixed to envelopes or cards. They're almost always printed on a dot matrix or laser printer. The same steps taken to create and print mailing labels may also be followed to prepare continuous-form 3 by 5 cards for notes or references or "Rolodex" cards for organization membership lists. Continuous form index card and Rolodex card stock, as well as label stock, are readily available through stationery stores, forms mail order houses, computer stores, and book stores.

Six operations are required to prepare mailing labels:

1. Create a *secondary file* of names and addresses.
2. Define a *label size and type* (a one-time only operation for each printer you plan to use for labels).
3. Create a *primary file* for the field codes of the address elements.
4. Combine the primary and secondary files to produce a *merged file.*
5. Select a printer and view a printer image of the labels.
6. Print the labels.

A secondary file in WordPerfect is analogous to a "database" in dBASE or RBase in that it contains a group of related, fixed-length *records,* each of which is composed of one or more data elements called *fields.* Unlike the usual database record, however, all secondary file fields end with {END FIELD} and all records end with {END RECORD} and a hard page code [**HPg**].

Relational database management systems such as dBASE typically have a tabular data layout: fields are displayed in columns and records are displayed in rows. The data layout of secondary files is different—the fields and records are in a single column. All fields of the first record are in one group; all the fields of the second record are in the next group, and so on. One notable similarity between record groups is that the *order* of the fields is identical. Thus, if first name is the second field in record one, it is also the second field in all other records.

Procedure

The separate subsections that follow describe each of the six operations required to prepare and print mailing labels. The instructions provided will enable you to produce labels with a personal title and a full name on the first line, a street address on the second, and city, state, and a 5-character zip code on the third. Extending these instructions to other applications is straightforward, but we advise you to consult Section 7- 2, "Merge Applications," if you plan to use multiple-line fields (street address, for example) or fields that may be blank in some records (company name, for example).

Creating a secondary file. The secondary file (the "database document") used in this example includes the following seven fields:

Field	Contents
1	Personal Title (Mr., Ms., Dr.)
2	First name (Benton)
3	Last name (Acton)
4	Street address (or P.O. Box) (Harris Boulevard)
5	City (Arlington)
6	State (VA)
7	Zip Code (22209)

NOTE: Ignore suffixes (Jr., II, Esq., etc.) or reserve another field for them.

To create the secondary file (the name and address document), follow these instructions:

1. Assuming WordPerfect is running, press **(F7)** and type [**N**], [**N**] to clear your Document Editing screen.

```
File
     Exit N, N
```

2. Construct the first record.
   2. 1 Type the title of the first person in the list—e.g., Mr., Ms., Dr.—and press **(F9)**.
   2. 2 Type the first name and press **(F9)**.

2. 3 Type the last name and press **(F9)**.

NOTE: By placing first name and last name in two separate fields, you can use individual components of the name in the salutation (Mr. Benton Acton, Dear Benton:, Dear Mr. Acton:) or in the body of your letter or memo ("Since this is a one-time only offer, Benton, I wanted to be sure . . . ").

2. 4 Type the street address and press **(F9)**.
2. 5 Type the city name and press **(F9)**.
2. 6 Type the initials of the state (in full caps) and press **(F9)**.
2. 7 Type the zip code, press **(Shift-F9)**, and type [**E**] to end the record and generate a hard page break (a double line beneath the city, state, and zip code line).

```
Tools
        Merge Codes
                End Record
```

Repeat the instructions under step 2 for each individual in your name and address database. Fig. 7-12 shows two records in a secondary file.

3. Press **(F7)**, type [**Y**] and type a document name—SECDOC02.W51, for example—in response to the WordPerfect prompt,

    Document to be saved: .

    Press **Enter** and type [**N**] to save the secondary file and clear your screen.

```
Mr.{END FIELD}
Benton{END FIELD}
Acton{END FIELD}
1400 Harris Boulevard{END FIELD}
Arlington{END FIELD}
VA{END FIELD}
22209{END RECORD}
===========================
Mr.{END FIELD}
Charles{END FIELD}
Allen{END FIELD}
1055 Claremont Street{END FIELD}
Denver{END FIELD}
CO{END FIELD}
80220{END RECORD}
===========================
```

Figure 7-12 Secondary File for Labels

```
File
        Exit  Y, [filename], <R>, N
```

Defining a label size and type. WordPerfect must be told that the dimensions of a label are not the same as the dimensions of the standard 8-½" by 11" text page. Otherwise, it tries to print your labels as if it were printing a normal text page—not a good result. Tell WordPerfect about the changed situation by defining a label size and type. You can see if you've sent the right message when you View Doc below. If you have sent the right message, the form in View Doc looks like a label or a sheet of labels. If not, the form displayed will have a different shape. (An 8-½" by 11" text page containing a single record is most likely.)

Defining a label size and type is a one-time operation for each printer. Once you've defined a specific label size and type—a 4" x 2", "one-up" label for example—that option continues to be listed in your paper size and type list. You only need to select the option to use it.

1. An important first step is selecting the printer you'll be using for your labels from the options available on the Print: Select Printer menu. Follow the next three instructions to do that.
   1. 1 Press **(Shift-F7)** and type [**S**] to display the Print: Select Printer menu.
   1. 2 Use cursor arrows or your mouse to highlight the name of the printer you plan to use to print your labels.
   1. 3 Type [**S**] and press **(F7)** to select the printer and return to the Normal Editing screen.

```
File
        Print  S, [N], [printer name], <R>, S, <R>
```

NOTE: If the printer you'd like to use isn't listed on the Print: Select Printer menu, you need to add it. See Section 9- 5, "Defining and Selecting Printers" to see how that's done.

2. Press **(Shift-F8)** and type [**P**], [**S**] to display the Format: Paper Size/Type menu.

   NOTE: If the labels you plan to use are already listed among the options displayed, press **(F7)** and go to the third operation—creating a primary file.

3. Type [**A**], [**L**] to add labels and display the Format: Edit Paper Definition menu.

4. Type [**A**], [**Y**] to display the Format: Labels menu. Because you might be using either a dot matrix or laser printer to print your labels, let's do it both ways. Required parameters are shown in Table 7-1 below.

Layout
Page S, A, L, A, Y

NOTE: You must type several parameters into the Format: Labels menu. We show the parameters for one-up 3-½" x 1" labels (dot matrix printer) and three-up 2-⅝" x 1" labels below (laser printer). If you have different size labels, use a ruler to obtain your own measurements.

5. Type in the label parameters that differ from those shown in the menu on your display screen. (It's not necessary to re-enter the ones that are already correct.) Press **Enter** after each entry.
6. *Dot matrix printers only.* When the Format: Labels menu is complete, press **Enter** again to return to the Format: Edit Paper Definition menu and take the following steps:
   6. 1 Type [**S**], [**O**] to select the "Other" size.
   6. 2 Type the label's width and height—e.g., 3.5" and 1".

TABLE 7-1. FORMAT: LABELS MENU PARAMETERS FOR ONE-UP LABELS (DOT MATRIX) AND THREE-UP LABELS (LASER)

Parameters	One-Up	Three-Up
Label Size		
Width	3.500	2.625
Height	1.000	1.000
Number		
Columns	1	3
Rows	1	10
Top Left Corner		
Top	0	0.500
Left	0	0.188
Distance Between		
Columns	0	0.125
Rows	0	0
Label Margins		
Left	0.500	0.013
Right	0	0.123
Top	0	0
Bottom	0	0

7. Press **(F7)** to return to the Format: Paper Size/Type menu after you've entered all the label parameters. You'll notice that your labels have been added to the list of options.

   NOTE: Different sized labels have different dimensions in the Labels column on the far right.

8. Press **(F7)** twice to return to the Normal Editing screen.

   NOTE: One of the macros that WordPerfect Corporation includes in the software package is called LABELS.WPM. If you plan to use standard Avery or 3M labels, run this macro to generate your label paper size/type definition automatically. Instructions for doing so are at the end of the module.

Create the Primary file. The next operation required is to create the primary file.

1. Press **(Shift-F8)** and type [**P**] to display the Format: Page menu.
2. Type [**M**], [**0**], press **Enter**, type [**0**], press **Enter**, type [**C**], [**Y**] and press **(F7)** to set the top and bottom margins at 0 and 0, vertically center the text on your label, and return to the Normal Editing screen.

Layout
    Page M, [0], <R>, [0], <R>, C, Y, <R>

3. Press **(Shift-F9)**, type [**F**], [**1**], press **Enter**, **Space Bar**, **(Shift-F9)**, type [**F**], [**2**], press **Enter, Space Bar, (Shift-F9)**, type [**F**], [**3**], and press **Enter** twice to generate the first line (which includes the personal title, and first and last names together with proper spacing).

Tools
    Merge Codes
        Field [field number] <R>

4. Press **(Shift-F9)**, type [**F**], [**4**], and press **Enter** twice to generate the street address.
5. Press **(Shift-F9)**, type [**F**], [**5**], press **Enter**, type [**,**], press **Space Bar**, **(Shift-F9)**, type [**F**], [**6**], press **Enter**, **Space Bar**, **(Shift-F9)**, type [**F**], [**7**], and press **Enter** for the city, state, and zip code line. The resulting label primary file is shown in Fig. 7-13.

```
{FIELD}1~ {FIELD}2~ {FIELD}3~
{FIELD}4~
{FIELD}5~, {FIELD}6~ {FIELD}7~
```

Figure 7-13 Label Codes

6. Press **(F7)**, type [**Y**] and type a document name—PRIDOC05.W51, for example—in response to the WordPerfect prompt,

   Document to be saved: .

   Press **Enter**, and type [**N**] to save the primary file and clear your screen.

File
Exit Y, [filename], <R>, N

Merging primary and secondary files. Now, follow instructions 1, 2, and 3 to create a merged file.

1. Press **(CTRl-F9)** and type [**M**] to select the merge feature. WordPerfect prompts with,

   Primary file: .

2. Type the name of the primary file—e.g., PRIDOC05.W51—and press **Enter.** WordPerfect prompts with,

   Secondary file: .

3. Type the name of the secondary file and press **Enter**. After a few seconds, you should see the merged file displayed on the Normal Editing screen (see Fig. 7-14).

Tools
Merge [primary file] <R> [secondary file] <R>

NOTE: If you see extra lines and spaces in your merged file, they probably occurred because you formatted your primary or secondary file incorrectly. For example, you may have pressed Enter following the last field code in your primary file. You may also observe missing commas or improper spacing in the city, state, zip code line. If you spot problems, retrieve your primary or secondary file and

```
File Edit Search Layout Mark Tools Font Graphics Help        (Press F3 for Help)
================================================================================
Mr. Robert Zbeard
456 Elmwood Street
Malden, MC 02177
================================================================================
Ms. Gladys Smith
888 Sprooswood Trail
High Point, NC 27003
================================================================================
Mr. Emory Emmery
P.O. Box 8845
Chattabox, TN 37732
================================================================================
Mr. Silversmith Bismarck
9212 Princess Drive
Salem, VA 23136
================================================================================
Mr. Benton Acton
1400 Key Boulevard
Arlington, VA 22209
================================================================================
Mr. Charles Allen
1055 Claremont Street
                                                  Doc 1 Pg 1 Ln 1" Pos 1"
```

Figure 7-14 Merged File

make the necessary changes. If you make corrections in your primary or secondary files, press **(F7)** and type [N], **[N]** to clear your screen and then repeat steps 1, 2, and 3.

Selecting a printer, viewing labels, and printing. Follow the next set of instructions to: (1) select a printer, (2) view your finished labels to ensure that form and arrangement are satisfactory, and (3) print the finished product. At this point, the merged file should be displayed on your screen.

1. *Dot matrix only.* Insert a strip of labels in your printer and align it so that the position of the first line of the initial label to be printed is directly under the print head.
2. Press **Home**, **Home**, **Home**, **Up Arrow** to move to the top of the merged file.
3. Press **(Shift-F8)**, type **[P]**, **[S]** to display the Format: Paper Size/Type menu.
4. Highlight the new label definition with your cursor arrows or mouse and type [S] to select it. Press **(F7)** to return to the Normal Editing screen.

> Layout
>   Page S, N, [Labels], <R>, S, <R>

5. Press **(Shift-F7)** and type [**V**] to see a printer image of your labels. The View Document screen should display the labels in the proper relationship to the dimensions you entered (single labels in the case of the one-up labels, an entire sheet in the case of the three-up labels).
6. Press **(F1)** and type [**F**] to print the labels.

```
File
        Print  V, <(F1)>, F
```

Using the LABELS macro. Instructions for using the LABELS macro to create paper size/type definitions for standard labels are given below.

1. Press **(Shift-F7)** and type [**S**] to display the Print: Select Printer menu.
2. Use the cursor arrows or mouse to highlight the printer you plan to use and type [**S**] to select it.
3. Select one of the following options:
   - Continuous (for tractor-feed or paper tray)
   - Bin number (if you'll use an alternate bin)
   - Manual (for manual feed of label sheets)
4. Press **(Alt-F10)**, type [**labels**] and press **Enter** to run the labels macro.
5. Highlight the label size and type you plan to use and press **Enter**.
6. Press **(F7)** to return to the Normal Editing Screen. That's all there is to it.

8

Advanced Features

This chapter includes instruction sets for operations that support the production of all types of other documents but do not in and of themselves produce documents except in a narrow, technical sense. Learning how to use some of the modules will help you save a great deal of time later on if you become a frequent WordPerfect user. Examples of major time savers are Creating and Using Macros and Sorting Lines and Paragraphs. Learning how to use the features included here will help you improve the appearance of your documents and enhance their quality. Examples of quality enhancers are Working with Graphics, Working with Equations, Drawing Lines and Boxes, and Formatting Text in Columns.

Since these features are tools of extensive power and versatility, we urge you to learn how to use them and then to apply them at every opportunity. You will find out quickly that they ease the burden of document creation and add to the attractiveness of your finished products.

8- 1 WORKING WITH GRAPHICS

This section provides general guidelines for inserting graphic boxes in long documents. Also included are instructions for importing a graph from Lotus 1-2-3 and changing the characteristics of the graphics box created to hold it. Turn here if you have an assignment that can be enhanced by adding computer graphics images or if you need to put together a newsletter for a club or other organization. The Overview subsection describes the purpose of graphics boxes and lines and gives advice on their format and construction. The Procedure subsection includes step-by-step instructions for creating graphics boxes and modifying their characteristics.

Overview

Some writing assignments almost mandate the inclusion of charts, illustrations, or other graphical material because difficult concepts are explained more effectively or voluminous information is better summarized with graphics than it is with straight text. Most course instructors have always understood the communication value of graphics but have not usually required the inclusion of graphical exhibits in written assignments. They realized that business students did not have the materials, equipment, or knowledge to produce acceptable graphics within the usual term paper or written case time frame. With rapid advances taking place in the display and storage capabilities of personal computers, however, that situation has changed. In coming years, instructors will expect frequent inclusion of graphics in written assignments. They know that graphic images are now much easier to produce and incorporate into text material, and they also know that graphics are being used more heavily in the business environment.

What is the graphics feature. WordPerfect can display graphic images or text in window-like boxes called "Graphics Boxes" that are inserted into existing text. The resulting graphic images can be printed by any printer capable of producing graphics.

Purpose. Graphics boxes improve the appearance of documents by letting you take advantage of the large number of graphics packages available in the market. With the graphics feature, you move images into text electronically, avoiding the time-consuming cutting and pasting of the past. Graphics boxes are especially useful for inserting graphs and illustrations into long documents, but they can also be used to improve the communications effectiveness of memos and letters. One caution though: lots of work is still required and a substantial amount of experimentation is recommended. Think twice before you try the graphics feature — especially if you're facing a deadline on a term paper or written case.

Graphics Boxes. There are three primary graphics capabilities in WordPerfect: boxes, equations, and lines. Substantial space is devoted to graphics boxes in this section, but we only *describe* the graphics lines capability here. We refer you to the WordPerfect workbook and reference manual for the detailed procedures required to create lines. Equations are covered in Section 8- 6.

Four types of graphics boxes are available: (1) Figure Boxes, (2) Table Boxes, (3) Text Boxes, and (4) User-defined Boxes. All four are identical in purpose and features. The only differences between them are the box labels you see in the Document Editing screen (the four box types are labeled at the top left as, "FIG *n*," "TAB *n*," "TXT *n*," or "USR *n*," where '*n*' represents the graphics box number) and the figure lists that can be produced automatically for each box type. Other *apparent* dissimilarities in borders, inside and outside spacing, captions, and box numbering systems are easily modified default values. By making changes in the Options: Figure menu (to be discussed below), the printed Figure Box can be made to appear identical to the printed Table, Text, or User-defined Box.

What can you show in a graphics box. One type of graphic you can show in a graphics box is one of WordPerfect's own images. They have the extension, .WPG and were created by Marketing Graphics Incorporated (MGI). They are eye-catching but probably not applicable to your day-to-day documents, and substantial effort is required to create, position, and identify the graphics boxes needed to contain them. It's worthwhile to experiment with .WPG images in order to learn more about the graphics capability, however. If you don't have any Lotus or Harvard Graphics images to experiment with, use the WordPerfect images when you follow the instructions below.

Another type of file you can show in a graphics box is a list, table, or small block of text. Here again, however, we don't think it's worth the effort of learning how to display text in a graphics box. The formatting required for an acceptable result is time-consuming and tricky for the novice, and quite a significant time investment is required to become reasonably proficient. If you want to set text off in a separate box, the Tables feature described in Section 6- 2 is easier to use and gives equally satisfactory results for most applications.

The primary value of graphics boxes to the business student is the ability to meld graphs and illustrations into text, thereby eliminating the need to cut and paste them in place or include them at the end of a document as exhibits. If you're familiar with Lotus 1-2-3, Harvard Graphics, or other graphics software packages, you can use WordPerfect's graphics box feature to insert the images created in other software packages directly into your WordPerfect documents. No more need to cut and paste Lotus graphs into your written assignments.

We should point out that the examples in this book were constructed with Lotus 1-2-3 and Harvard Graphics images because both packages are often accessible to students working in university computer labs.

Horizontal and vertical lines. As we indicated earlier, WordPerfect also has a powerful line graphics capability that can improve the appearance and readability of documents produced on a graphics printer. With this feature, horizontal and vertical lines of variable length and thickness can be positioned anywhere in a document. Line graphics can even be used to produce grey-scaled banners for headlines, side bars, and call-outs.[1]

It's more work to produce graphics lines than to produce lines using the Line Draw feature described in Section 8- 5, "Drawing Lines and Boxes," but graphics lines are essential if you use proportionally spaced fonts or a printer that doesn't support the IBM line-draw character set. Graphics lines are also effective for desktop publishing applications, but we don't advise their use in standard documents unless you have an artistic bent and some extra time on your hands.

An overall assessment. Graphics boxes (and graphics lines) are essential for desktop publishing applications but probably require too much additional work for the average correspondence or long documents a student writes. If you're responsible for a newsletter or similar publication, however, graphics boxes add distinctiveness and eye appeal and are surely worth the extra effort required to include them. If you work heavily with Lotus, presentation graphics packages such as Harvard Graphics, or statistical software with graphical output capabilities, learning about WordPerfect graphic capabilities may be a very good investment.

A final observation we should make about graphics is that images acceptable to the WordPerfect graphics feature are of two basic types: (1) object-oriented images (also called "vector graphics") and (2) bit-mapped images. Object-oriented images correspond to the line drawings in a technical journal or magazine; they can be re-sized, re-shaped, and rotated easily and with no distortion. Lotus 1-2-3, Harvard Graphics and AutoCad (among other software packages) produce object-oriented images. (WordPerfect's .WPG files are also object-oriented images.) Bit-mapped images cannot be enlarged without significant distortion, and cannot be rotated or mirrored in WordPerfect.[2] "Paint" programs (such as Dr. Halo, PC Paintbrush, Windows Paint, and MacPaint) generate bit-mapped images.

Consult the following references for additional guidance on preparing and using graphic images:

Himstreet, William C., and Wayne Murlin Baty, *Business Communications* (8th ed.). Boston: PWS-Kent Publishing Company, 1987.

Turabian, Kate L., *A Manual for Writers of Term Papers, Theses, and Dissertations* (5th ed.). Chicago: University of Chicago Press, 1987

Procedure

In this procedural description, we import a Lotus bar graph created using some of the numbers in the spreadsheet in Fig. 8-1.

Incorporating a WordPerfect graphic in a document is two step procedure. First, you create an *empty* figure, table, text, or user-defined box. Second, you fill the box with a graphic image, text, or a table. In addition, you often change the size of the box, its position on the page, its caption, and some appearance attributes such as the border surrounding the box. These changes can be made before or after you fill the box, however.

After you've created the box, its *outline* is observable in the Document Editing screen, but you must toggle on View Document to see the *actual contents* of the box. Press **(Shift-F7)** and type **[V]** in the Document Editing screen to use the View Document feature to see the results of your graphic experimentation. You save lots of time and printer paper when you do.

Marketing Expenditures by Quarter

Accounts	First	Quarters Second	Third	Fourth	Total
Administration	$17,500	$23,250	$19,000	$17,500	$77,250
Advertising	$27,500	$14,000	$23,000	$8,500	$73,000
Trade Shows	$15,500	$23,000	$18,500	$9,500	$66,500
Promotion	$3,500	$8,500	$575	$8,350	$20,925
Literature	$875	$2,500	$9,400	$535	$13,310
Sales Training	$1,250	$1,250	$8,300	$1,250	$12,050
Premiums	$7,150	$1,225	$0	$0	$8,375
Total	$73,275	$73,725	$78,775	$45,635	$271,410

Figure 8-1 Quarterly and Total Marketing Expenditures by Category

File
Print V

NOTE: If your PC doesn't have a graphics adapter, object-oriented images are roughly outlined by dots in the View Document screen; bit-mapped images do not appear at all. Even if your PC doesn't have a graphics card, images should still print correctly so long as your printer supports graphics.

Creating and Modifying a figure box. For purposes of illustration, we use a Lotus 1-2-3 image here. Try experimenting with the .WPG clip-art graphic files included on the FONTS/GRAPHICS disk in your original software package before you attempt to import graphics from another package.

The procedures described here are quite complex. We urge you to follow along on your own PC. We assume in the instructions that you're doing so. Before you begin, pick out a document two or three pages long that you can play with and make sure some of the WordPerfect graphic images have been installed on your system and that you've told WordPerfect where they're to be found. (If you're not sure if WordPerfect knows where the graphic images are located, see Section 9- 3 for setup instructions.)

For the sake of realism, let's start off with a two- or three-page document displayed on the Normal Editing screen.

Press **(Alt-F9)** and type [F], [C] to create a figure box.

Graphics
Figure
Create

The Definition: Figure menu shown in Fig. 8-2 replaces the normal Editing screen. Note that the menu lists nine options. We explain the purpose of the options shown in the context of importing and working with our Lotus graph. Each option is treated under a separate heading below. Follow along with a Lotus or WordPerfect graphic image.

Filename

Type [**F**], [***filename***], and press **Enter**.

Note that the filename shown in Fig. 8-2 is BAR01.PIC. The string, ".PIC," is the extension for a Lotus 1-2-3 graph (versions 1A, 2.0, and 2.2). WordPerfect accepts graphics files with a .PIC extension automatically. WordPerfect also accepts several other graphics formats directly (see Fig. 8-3). In doing so, WordPerfect examines the file format and then converts it automatically to .WPG format.[3]

NOTE: You can use WordPerfect's GRAPHCNV.EXE program to convert many graphics formats to .WPG formats before you use the graphics box feature. Refer to the WordPerfect reference manual for instructions.

The file named can be either a text file or graphics file. Text can also be typed directly into the graphics box with the Edit option discussed below. (Text can be imported or typed directly into any graphics box type, not just a Text Box.)

You can delete a filename, leaving an empty box in your document or substitute a new filename by clearing the existing name from the filename field. To clear the field, type [F] to select the Filename option and press **(Ctrl-End)**. When you clear the filename field, WordPerfect displays the prompt,

Enter filename:.

```
Definition: Figure

     1 - Filename                 BAR01.PIC

     2 - Contents                 Graphic

     3 - Caption

     4 - Anchor Type              Paragraph

     5 - Vertical Position        0"

     6 - Horizontal Position      Right

     7 - Size                     3.25" wide x 2.44" (high)

     8 - Wrap Text Around Box     Yes

     9 - Edit
```

Figure 8-2 "Definition: Figure" menu

CGM	Computer Graphics Metafile
DHP	Dr. Halo PIC Format
EPS	Encapsulated PostScript
HPGL	Hewlett-Packard Graphics Language
IMG	GEM Paint Format
MSP	Microsoft Windows Paint Format
PCX	PC Paintbrush Format
PIC	Lotus 1-2-3 PIC Format
PNTG	Macintosh Paint Format
PPIC	PC Paint Plus Format
TIFF	Tagged Image File Format

Figure 8-3 Graphics Formats Supported by WordPerfect

In response, type a new filename (but only if you wish to replace the contents of the box). WordPerfect then responds with:

Replace contents with [*filename*]? No (Yes).

Type [**Y**] in response to go ahead with the replacement.

Occasionally, you may create a graph and not recall its filename. If that happens, use the List Files feature in the Filename field of the Definition: Figure menu:

- Type [**F**], press **(F5)**, **Enter** and press the cursor keys to select the Filename option, use List Files, and highlight a graphic file to be inserted in the graphics box.
- Type [**R**] to import the file.

NOTE: If you specified a special directory for your graphic files when you installed WordPerfect, the files in that directory should be displayed. If your target file isn't shown in the list, highlight "Parent" or the name of a subdirectory, press **Enter,** and then review the resulting list. You may need to repeat this procedure several times to trace through the directory structure to your target file.

Contents

The contents field shows the current contents of the box or the word, "Empty." When you type [**O**], the menu,

Contents: 1 Graphic; 2 Graphic on Disk; 3 Text; 4 Equation: 0

is displayed. Type the letter designating an option other than the one displayed to substitute a new image type.

NOTE: If your document contains many graphic images, it may become too large to store on a floppy disk. Use the Graphic on Disk option with images stored on one floppy and documents stored on another if you plan to include many images in a particular document.

Caption

A caption (also referred to as a "legend") won't be displayed with the graphics box unless you select the Caption option. When you select the option, a new editing screen is displayed. You can append text to the default caption shown or backspace to delete the default and then create your own. Follow the instructions below to type a caption. We assume the Definition: Figure menu is displayed on your screen.

1. Type [C] to select the Caption option and then type a caption following the default text shown (usually "Figure n," where n is the figure number).
2. Press **Home, Home, Left Arrow** to move to the first letter of the caption.
3. Press **(Shift-F6)** to center it if the caption is shorter than the width of the box.

```
Layout
        Align
                Center
```

Then add some space to separate the caption from the lower border of the box by using the WordPerfect Advance feature. Adding a little space improves the appearance of your graphics. Follow these instructions to advance the caption down .08 inches.

4. Press **Home, Home, Home, Up Arrow** to move the cursor ahead of all codes.
5. Press **(Shift-F8)**, type [**O**], [**A**], [**D**], [**.08**], press **Enter** and then press **(F7)** twice to advance the caption down .08 inches and return to the Definition: Figure menu.

```
Layout
        Other  A, D, [.08], <R>, <R>, <(F7)>
```

We could return to the Normal Editing screen to check our handiwork at this point, but let's wait until we've made a few additional changes first.

Anchor Type

There are three "Anchor Type" options: paragraph, page, and character.[4] Notice that "Paragraph" is displayed in the "Anchor Type" field. The paragraph box is locked to a specific paragraph and remains with surrounding text. Therefore, it may move vertically on a page or even from page to page after a session of heavy editing. Position the box by moving the cursor to the line where you'd like the top of the box to appear. (If there's insufficient space for the box at the bottom of the page, it moves to the top of the next page automatically.) If a paragraph type graphics box is appropriate, ignore the Anchor Type option.

Unlike a paragraph box that's locked to a specific paragraph and stays with the paragraph no matter where it's located in your document, page type boxes are locked to an exact position on a specific page. If a page box is preferable to a paragraph box, type [**T**], [**A**] to change graphics box type to "page." The prompt,

Number of pages to skip: 0,

is displayed at the bottom left corner of the screen. If you want the graphics box to stay on the current page, press **Enter**. If you want the box to appear later in the document, type the number of pages to be skipped and then press **Enter**. (If you switched to the page box, type [**T**], [**P**] to toggle back to the paragraph box.)

Vertical Position

A paragraph box *code* is placed at the beginning of a paragraph with an offset distance showing the position of the cursor measured in inches from the first line of the paragraph. Thus, if the cursor is in the second or subsequent lines in the paragraph when the graphics box feature is selected, a non-zero offset distance is displayed in the Vertical Position field on the Definition: Figure menu. (If the cursor is in the first line of the paragraph, the offset distance is zero inches.) To move a box up or down in a paragraph, type in a new offset distance. WordPerfect attempts to keep a box on the same page even if the Vertical Position field is greater than zero. If it can't do so, the box moves to the top of the next page.

Page boxes remain at a fixed position on a page even if surrounding text is changed after insertions or deletions. Use the Vertical Position option to place the box at the top, center, or bottom of the page. Place the box at a specified distance from the top of the page with the Set Position option. (The Full Page option fills the entire page.)

Horizontal Position

The default horizontal position for either a paragraph or page box is on the right side of the page so that the right border of the box lines up with the right margin. You can switch the horizontal position of a paragraph box to the left or center of the page or you can span the entire page by selecting the "Full" option. When you specify a page box with the "Margin" option selected, the box can also be positioned at the right, left, or center of a page.

NOTE: It's not usually advisable to select "Center" for either a paragraph or page box because text wraps on only one side of the box. One way to circumvent this problem is to make the box as wide as the page. To do so, select the "Full" option.

Page boxes may also be placed between columns in a column-formatted document. We describe that procedure at the end of this section.

Size

The Default graphics box size is 3.25" by 3.25" but the actual size is dependent on the relative dimensions of the image displayed. Once the image has been specified, width and height are automatically linked together in a fixed ratio. If one or both are changed so that the automatic relationship is modified, the effect is to add space in the longer dimension.

Wrapping Text Around Box

The default value is "Yes." If this option is changed to "No," the graphic image is ignored and text is typed right over the graphic. Not a result you'd normally want to see.

Edit

A graphics image may be edited, but it's usually not necessary. There are some exceptions to the general rule, however. One exception is enlarging an image so it can be "cropped."[5] Another exception is to mirror a graphic image so it faces the binding of a document. A third is to rotate text 90 degrees so it can be printed in landscape mode.

Here's how to edit a graphic image (assuming the Definition:Figure menu is displayed and you have a graphic in your figure box),

1. Type [**E**] to enter graphics editing mode.

Once the graphics editing screen is displayed, you have several options available. (See Fig. 8- 4.)

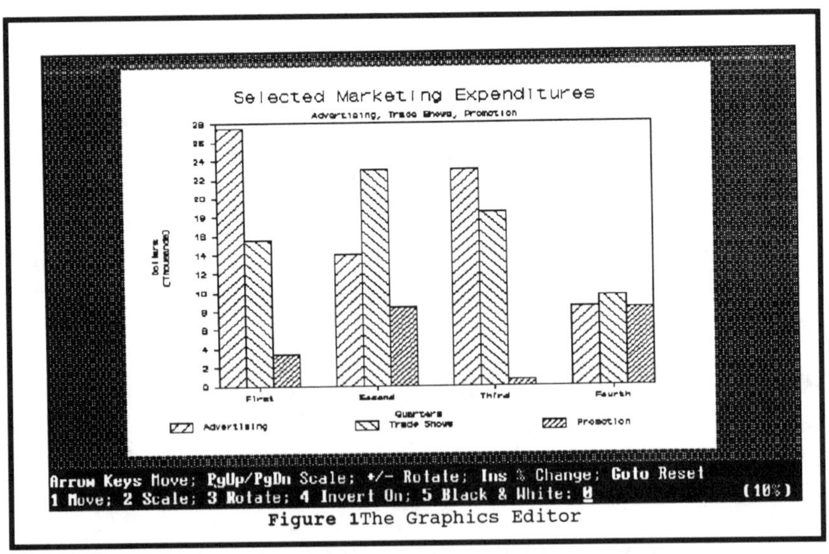

Figure 8-4 The Graphics Editor

2. Press **Insert** to change the percentage of anticipated change in image movement or scaling; the percentage change cycles through four options (1%, 5%, 10%, and 25%).
3. Press the arrow keys to move the image up, down, right, or left by the percentage shown in the lower right corner of the graphic editing screen.
4. Press the **PgUp** or **PgDn** keys to scale the image up and down.

If the image is object-oriented or if the box contains text and the printer you've selected has a landscape-printing capability, the image can also be rotated by pressing the + (clockwise rotation) or - (counter-clockwise rotation) keys on the numeric key pad. You can also rotate or mirror the image with the keystrokes at the bottom of the screen. A bit-mapped image can't be rotated or mirrored, but it can be reversed. One final option is to convert a color image to black and white. Type [**B**] in the graphics editor to do so. Press **(F7)** to return to the Definition: Figure menu.

Changing Figure Options. Figure box borders, inside and outside spacing, caption format, caption number style, and caption location can be modified easily. The approach is identical for the three other graphics box types. Instructions for doing so are given next.

Changing borders

The default border for a figure box is a single line. Table and text boxes have thick rules at top and bottom and no side borders, while user-defined boxes have no borders at all. In this example, we change the border of our Lotus graph from single-line to double-line. With the Normal Editing screen displayed on your monitor, follow these instructions to display the Options: Figure menu. (It should look like Fig. 8- 5.) In these instructions we make all our changes in the Options: Figure menu. After all the changes are made, we return to the Normal Editing screen to view the document.

1. Press **Home**, **Home**, **Home**, **Up Arrow** to move to the top of the document.
2. Press **(Alt-F9)** and type [**F**], [**O**] to select figure box options.
3. Type [**B**] to change borders.

```
Graphics
        Figure
                Options B
```

4. Select a border style for each side of the box from the list at the bottom of the Options: Figure menu by typing the letter corresponding to your choice and pressing **Enter**.

```
Options: Figure

     1 - Border Style
              Left                          Single
              Right                         Single
              Top                           Single
              Bottom                        Single
     2 - Outside Border Space
              Left                          0.167"
              Right                         0.167"
              Top                           0.167"
              Bottom                        0.167"
     3 - Inside Border Space
              Left                          0"
              Right                         0"
              Top                           0"
              Bottom                        0"
     4 - First Level Numbering Method       Numbers
     5 - Second Level Numbering Method      Off
     6 - Caption Number Style               [BOLD]Figure 1[bold]
     7 - Position of Caption                Below box, Outside borders
     8 - Minimum Offset from Paragraph      0"
     9 - Gray Shading (% of black)          0%

Selection: 0
```

Figure 8-5 Options: Figure Menu

Changing outside spacing.

Outside spacing is the spacing between surrounding text and the border of the box. Default outside spacing for a figure box is 0.167" on all sides. In this example, we assign 0.25" to the top and bottom and 0.12" to each side. Follow these instructions to do the same thing. If you have a mouse, move the mouse cursor to the lettered option and press the left button. Pressing the right button has the same effect as pressing the Enter key.

1. Type [**O**] to select Outside Border Space.
2. Type [**.12**], press **Enter**, type [**.12**], press **Enter**, type [**.25**], press **Enter**, type [**.25**] and press **Enter** to assign the new spacing.

Changing inside spacing

Inside spacing is the space between the graphic image *inside* the box and the border. Inside spacing may be changed from the 0.0" default values displayed in the Definition: Figure menu by following a path similar to the path traced above.

Changing figure numbers

The default figure number is a single-level Arabic number that is automatically incremented by one step with each additional figure box inserted in a document. Figure numbers may be modified in two ways. First, they can be changed from single-level numbering to dual-level numbering. For example, Figure 1, Figure 2, can be changed to Figure 1-1, Figure 1-2, etc. Second, single-level and dual-level numbers can be expressed as Arabic numerals, letters, or Roman numerals in any combination. For example, Figure 1 could be changed to Figure A or Figure I. Similarly, Fig. 1-1 could be changed to Fig. 1-a or Figure I.1.

The default *style* of the figure number, that is "Figure 1" in bold, can be similarly altered by abbreviating it, setting it in italics, underlining it, or setting it in a font larger or smaller than the font of surrounding text. For example, the default Figure 1 could be changed to Fig. 1, *Figure* 1-1, EXHIBIT I, or even Table 1 - a. Follow these instructions to change numbering,

1. Type [**F**], ***[number code]*** to select the first level number.
2. Type [**S**], ***[number code]*** to select the second level number.

   NOTE: Choose this option only if your long document requires two-level numbering.

   Follow these additional instructions to change caption number style.

3. Type [**C**] to select Caption Number Style and display the default caption in an editing window at the bottom of the screen.
4. Make your modifications. For example, shorten "Figure" to "Fig" and add a period and two hyphens following the number. Change the attribute from boldface to underline.
   4. 1 Press **Home**, **Home, Left Arrow** and press **Delete** to delete the **[Bold]** code on the left hand side.
   4. 2 Press **(Ctrl-F8)**, type [**A**], [**I**], press **Enter** to set the caption in italics.

Changing the position of the caption

The default position of figure box, text box, and user-defined box captions is below the box and outside the border. (The default position of the table box caption is *above* the box and outside the border.) Select this option to move the caption above the box, inside the border, or both.

Now that you've changed several figure options, take the following steps to check your work.

1. Press **(F7)** to return to the Normal Editing screen.
2. If your figure box isn't on the current page, follow the next four instructions:
   2. 1 Press **(F2)** to toggle on the search feature.
   2. 2 Press **(Alt-F9)** and type [**F**], [**F**] to search for a figure box.
   2. 3 Press **Up Arrow** if you want to search backward.
   2. 4 Press **(F2)** to start the search.

```
Search
        Forward  <(Alt-F9)>, [F], [F], <R>, <R>
```

2. 5 Press **(Shift-F7)** and type [**V**] to see your results in View Document.

```
File
        Print  V
```

Changing box numbers. If you want to identify each graphics box by chapter or section, change the figure box numbers. Here's how to do that (assuming the Normal Editing screen is displayed on your screen).

1. Move your cursor to the vicinity of the box in the Normal Editing screen.
2. Press **(Alt-F3)** to Reveal Codes.
3. Highlight the code of the figure whose level-one number will be increased.

   NOTE: The change code *must precede* the first box whose number is to be changed.

4. Press **(Alt-F9)** and type [**F**], [**N**] to select the "New Number" option.

```
Graphics
        Figure
                New Number
```

5. Enter the new numbers, separated by a hyphen (even if the original numbers were separated by some other character — e.g., a period).

   NOTE: The new number must be in the same format — e.g., arabic, letter, roman — as the number to be changed, else it will be ignored.

Deleting a graphics box. A graphics box is easily purged from a document. Just delete its code. Toggle on Reveal Codes to see the code (a figure box code would look like, **[Figure:1;CLOCK.WPG;]**) highlight it, and then press **Delete**.

Inserting a Page Box in a two-column document. Don't attempt to follow the instructions below unless you have a two-column document handy. Follow the guidelines in Section 8- 4 to convert one of your existing documents to two-column format if knowing this procedure might be helpful.

To place a page box between the columns in a two-column document, be sure your cursor is positioned following a **[Col On]** code, and follow the instructions below:

NOTE: You should be in the Normal Editing screen and "Col" should be displayed at the left end of the status line.

1. Press **(Alt-F9)** and type [**F**], [**C**].
2. Type [**T**], [**A**] and press **Enter** to change the box type to "Page" and keep it on the current page.
3. Type [**C**] to display the Caption Editing screen.

```
Graphics
      Figure
            Create  [T], [A], <R>, [C]
```

   Modify the default caption or delete the default caption and create a caption of your own. Press **(F7)** when you're through editing the caption.

4. Type [**F**], [***filename***] and press **Enter** to insert a graphic or text file into your graphics box.
5. Type [**V**] and select the box position by typing [**T**] (top), [**C**] (center), or [**B**] (bottom). Alternatively, select "Set Position" and specify a distance from the top of the page in response to WordPerfect's prompt.
6. Type [**H**], [**C**] to set the horizontal position and select the "Columns" option. WordPerfect prompts with,

   Enter column(s): 1 .

7. In response, type [**1-2**] and press **Enter**.

   NOTE: If you're working with more than 2 columns, the procedure is identical except that you'd type [**F**] (for full) to stretch the box across all the columns specified.

8. Type [**C**] and press **(F7)** to center the graphic between the two columns and return to the Normal Editing screen.
9. Press **(Shift-F7)** and type [**V**] to see what the box looks like.

```
File
      Print  V
```

ENDNOTES

1. A "side bar" is like a content footnote that has been moved up into the body of the text itself; you might think of the side bar as a *written* aside. It usually contains text tangentially related to the primary subject of a document. A "call-out," (or "pull-quote") on the other hand, is a quote from surrounding text set in a larger font and bordered at top and bottom by thick rules.
2. As the name implies, "mirroring" refers to the process of producing a mirror image of a graphics file. Obviously, mirroring text doesn't make much sense, but mirroring other graphics so that they all "look" to the binding is a useful practice well known to graphic designers.
3. WordPerfect Corporation continues to enhance its graphic conversion utility so that the list shown in Figure 8-3 may understate the number of formats WordPerfect can convert.
4. The character box is useful for desktop publishing applications—incorporating a logo in a header, for example—but of not much use for inserting figures, tables, and blocks of text into long documents.
5. Cropping is a graphics term referring to the practice of cutting away sections of a photograph to remove extraneous elements, thereby highlighting a primary element. For example, in a group photo of the Three Stooges, Curly and Larry could be cropped out to focus exclusively on Moe.

8- 2 CREATING AND USING MACROS

This section describes WordPerfect's powerful macro feature. The Overview subsection explains what a macro is and how macros can be used to save time and effort. The Procedure subsection includes the instructions needed to record keystrokes, run a macro, and repeat, chain, and nest macros to increase their usefulness.

Overview

A macro is a recording of a sequence of keystrokes stored on disk that can be used over and over again. The macro feature is like the paper roll that "programs" a player piano to hammer out a familiar tune without human involvement. Because the macro principle is so powerful and so appealing to users, many other software applications — Lotus 1-2-3, Microsoft Excel, and Sidekick, for example — also incorporate the capability. (In some applications the macro capability is called "scripting.")

Experienced WordPerfect users create macros to reduce the tedium of repetitive tasks such as creating memo headings, numbering pages, saving and printing documents, and appending closings to letters. When you create a macro, your keystrokes are saved in a program that can then be run by pressing a simple combination of the Alt key and a letter key, or by pressing the (Alt-F10) key combination, typing a macro name and pressing Enter. As a general rule, use Alt-key macros for frequent tasks, such as transposing words and deleting sentences. Use named macros for infrequent tasks such as converting footnotes to endnotes.

Procedure

You must record a set of keystrokes in a macro file before you can actually use the macro. We describe the recording process next. Afterward, we describe macro execution. Then we present the steps required to "chain" and "nest" macros so a macro can call itself again or call another macro.

Recording the Macro. Before you begin recording the keystrokes to be captured, be sure you've saved any work you can't do without. Then, make a dry run through the procedure you wish to capture by jotting the sequence of keys to be pressed on a piece of paper. After you've listed the sequence, take the following steps:

1. Press **(Ctrl-F10)** to start macro definition.
2. WordPerfect displays the prompt,

   Define macro: .

   In response, press and hold **(Alt)** and type a letter key to designate an "Alt-Key" macro. For a named macro, type a macro name of one to eight letters or numbers and press **Enter**.

   NOTE: It's a good idea to assign a meaningful mnemonic code or name to your macros to help you remember their intended purpose. For example, assign Alt-N (that is, press and hold Alt and then press n) to a page numbering macro or the name MEMOHEAD to a macro that creates a standard memo heading.

3. In response to the prompt,

   Description: ,

   enter a short description of the macro as a reminder of its function and press **Enter**. The description can be up to 39 characters long.

```
Tools
        Macro
                Define  [macro name] <R> [description] <R>
```

4. To record keystrokes, press the sequence of keystrokes to be captured in the macro. WordPerfect's "Macro Def" prompt blinks at the bottom left of your

screen. Normally, you'll see the blinking "Macro Def" message during the entire recording process. Some macros may include keystrokes that cause WordPerfect to display menus or prompts at the bottom left corner of the screen where "Macro Def" would normally be blinking. When that happens, "Macro Def" is overwritten but keystroke recording continues.

5. Press **(Ctrl-F10)** again at the end of the recording sequence to save the macro and switch off keystroke capturing.

```
Tools
        Macro
                Define
```

NOTE: WordPerfect assigns the extension, ".WPM" to all macros. Thus, the Alt-N and MEMOHEAD macros referred to above would be assigned the filenames, ALTN.WPM and MEMOHEAD.WPM.

Follow along and create the two macros described next. The first macro underlines the word where the cursor is located. The second transposes two consecutive words.

Underliner

- Move your cursor to the target word.
- Press **(Ctrl-F10)** to toggle on the macro feature.
- Press **Alt**, type [U], and press **Enter** in response to the prompt,

Define macro: .

- Type [**Word underliner**] (or some other description) and press **Enter** in response to the prompt,

Description: .

```
Tools
        Macro
                Define  [macro name] <R> [description] <R>
```

- Press **(Ctrl-Right Arrow)** to jump to the next word.
- Press **(Ctrl-Left Arrow)** to jump back to the *beginning* of the target word.
- Press **(Alt-F4)** (or **(F12)**) to toggle the block feature.
- Press **Space Bar** to provide a target for the block feature.

- Press **Left Arrow** so that the space following the target word isn't underlined.
- Press **(F8)** to underline the target word.
- Press **(Ctrl-F10)** to toggle off the macro feature.

Tools		
	Macro	
		Define

Transposer

- Move your cursor to the first of the two target words.
- Press **(Ctrl-F10)** to toggle on the macro feature.
- Press **Alt**, type [T], and press **Enter** in response to the prompt,

Define macro: .

- Type [**Word transposer**] (or some other description) and press **Enter** in response to the prompt,

Description: .

- Press **(Ctrl-Backspace)** to delete the first word.
- Press **(Ctrl-Right Arrow)** to move past the second word.
- Press **(F1)** and type [**R**] to "undo" the earlier deletion.
- Press **(Ctrl-F10)** to toggle off the macro feature.

6. On occasion you'll press the wrong keys as you create a macro and want to back away from the procedure and start over. If that happens, press **(Ctrl-F10)** to "complete" the macro as it were. Then take the following steps:

   6. 1 Press **(Ctrl-F10)** and type the original macro name. WordPerfect displays the macro name and responds with the following prompt:

   Already exists: 1 Replace; 2 Edit; 3 Description: 0,

   6. 2 Type [**R**], [**Y**] in response and start over.

Executing the Macro. When you're ready to execute the macro, move your cursor to the exact location in the document where the captured keystroke sequence is to begin.

Press **(Alt-F10)**. WordPerfect prompts for the name of the macro. In response, type the macro name (in upper or lowercase) and press **Enter**.

Tools		
	Macro	
		Execute [macro name], <R>

If you've used an Alt-key/letter combination to name the macro, running the macro is even easier: press and hold **Alt** and then type the letter key you've assigned. *Don't press (Alt-F10) to run an Alt-key macro.*

Repeating, Chaining, and Nesting Macros. At times, you may want a macro *to repeat itself.* For example, assume you've created and stored a macro that produces a line between the left and right margins of a page when you press (Alt-L). Now, you'd like to run that macro five times in a row to create some written response space in a marketing research questionnaire you're designing. Take these steps to get the desired result:

- Press **Esc** and type [**5**] to repeat the next keystroke five times.
- Press **(Alt-L)** to run the line drawing macro. Presto! Five lines appear.

At other times you may want to have one macro call another (this action is called "chaining"). To do so, build the *calling* macro as you would normally do, except that the very last keystrokes entered in the recording process should be (Alt-F10) followed by the name you've assigned (or will assign) to the macro to be *called.* If the called macro is an Alt-key macro, type its name as "Alt" followed by its associated letter key. For example, type AltN for the name of an Alt-key macro that numbers pages. When you've identified the macro to be called, press **(Ctrl-F10)** to end the recording process.

At still other times, you may want one macro to call another but with a return to the *calling* macro to perform some additional steps after the *called* macro has done its work. This process is called "*nesting*," and the steps for creating the *calling* macro are similar to those above. The major differences are: (1) the call occurs before the end of the *calling* macro, (2) the *called* macro *must have been created prior to* the creation of the *calling* macro, (3) the *called* macro must be an Alt-key macro, and (4) the call to the Alt-key macro *must be made* by pressing Alt and typing a key.

8- 3 SORTING LINES AND PARAGRAPHS

The guidelines in this module tell you how to use WordPerfect as a sorting tool. The Overview subsection explains the difference between alphanumeric and numeric sorts and the concept of a collation sequence. The Procedure subsection presents sorting instructions for lists, paragraphs, and secondary merge files.

Overview

From time to time, coursework or extracurricular activities may require you to sort lines of text, references in a bibliography, or secondary merge files. Use WordPerfect's sort feature to do these jobs quickly with minimum fuss. WordPerfect sorts *lines of text* such as lists of names, office numbers, and phone numbers; *paragraphs* such as bibliographic references; and *secondary merge files* such as a list of personnel officers. If you're thinking about importing a spreadsheet into WordPerfect and then sorting the resulting table, do the required sorting in the spreadsheet package prior to importing. It's usually faster.

WordPerfect sorts in ascending or descending order. It can place an unordered list in A to Z order (ascending) or Z to A order (descending); it can sort *alphanumerically* (text) or *numerically* (numbers). In this regard, it's useful to know the *collation sequence* of the alphanumeric and numeric sorting processes: If the sort is alphanumeric and *ascending,* special characters such as *, @ come first in the sorted list, followed by numbers in their natural order, then uppercase and lowercase letters in order, that is, Able, abet, Carole, carol, etc. If the sort is alphanumeric and *descending,* the order is reversed.

The table in Fig. 8-6 shows three lists of the same items. The first column in the list is in no particular order; the next column is the same list sorted in ascending order. Column three is the same list sorted in descending order.

The collation sequence for a numeric sort is similar to that for an alphanumeric sort except that letters *precede* numbers in the list sorted in ascending order. When lists are inherently *qualitative*—e.g., names, cities, and phone or social security numbers—sort them *alphanumerically.* When lists are inherently *quantitative*—e.g., account balances, monthly sales, or household beer consumption—sort them numerically.

Procedure

In the following paragraphs, we describe the line sort in detail. Afterward, we explain procedures for sorting paragraphs and secondary merge files by contrasting them to the line sort.

No order	Ascending	Descending
Charlie	...(blank)	Zoo keeper
436	@GO	golfball
...(blank)	1aB	Charlie
@GO	436	Backgammon
Backgammon	armchair	armchair
golfball	Backgammon	436
Zoo keeper	Charlie	1aB
armchair	golfball	@GO
1aB	Zoo keeper	...(blank)

Figure 8-6 Unordered and Ordered Alphanumeric Lists

WARNING: Save the *original version* of your file before sorting it. The result of a sort operation may not turn out as you had expected and WordPerfect has no "un-sort" feature—yet.

If you haven't saved the file before, press **(F10)** and type a filename in response to the prompt,

Document to be saved: .

File
Exit Y, [filename], <R>, N

Sort by Line. Follow the steps below to sort a simple list of individuals or objects displayed on your monitor.

1. Move your cursor into the first line to be sorted and press **Home**, **Home**, **Left Arrow**.
2. Press **(Alt-F4)** (or **(F12)**) to toggle on the block feature.
3. Press **Down Arrow**, type **[+]**, or press **PgDn** to highlight the complete list.

Edit
Block <Down Arrow>

NOTE: If there are no headings, or other text in your list whose position *should not* change, you need not define the list by blocking it prior to following the remaining steps in the procedure.

4. Press **(Ctrl-F9)** and type [S] to select the sort feature. In response, WordPerfect prompts,

   Input file to sort: (screen)

5. Press **Enter** to signal that the *list to be sorted* is on the Normal Editing screen. WordPerfect then prompts,

   Output file for sort: (screen)

6. Press **Enter** to signal that the *sorted list* is to be displayed on the Normal Editing screen. At that point, the Normal Editing screen is replaced by a dual-windowed display similar to the one in Fig. 8-7. In the top window are the first ten lines of the list to be sorted. In the bottom window are two menus: (1) the Sort by Line menu and (2) the Sort menu.

```
Baker, Robert          Reynolda   308   5402  Code 16    Politics
Katz, Barbara          Physics    211   5771  Code 05    Physics
Baumgarten, Goebels    Tribble    403   5889  Code 66    Philosophy
Beck, Robert M.        Salem      C122  3289  Code 18    Psychology
Ewing, David P.        Babcock    204   5238  Code 16    Accountancy
Allen, Herbert         Babcock    101   5803  Code 47    Mathematics
Stewart, Charles       Winston    228   5104  Code A4    Biology
Soloman, Terry         Scales     A73   5180  Code 05    Fine Arts
Smith, Alice M.        Reynolda   229   5413  Code 16    Politics
Bednarek, Charles      Leighton   005   3466  Code 80    Athletics
                                                    Doc 2 Pg 1 Ln 1" Pos 1"
[                      ▲          ▲     ▲     ▲          ▲               ▲     ]
------------------------------ Sort by Line ------------------------------

Key Typ Field Word           Key Typ Field Word           Key Typ Field Word
 1   a    1     1             2                            3
 4                            5                            6
 7                            8                            9
Select

Action                       Order                        Type
Sort                         Ascending                    Line sort

1 Perform Action; 2 View; 3 Keys; 4 Select; 5 Action; 6 Order; 7 Type: 0
```

Figure 8-7 Sort Screen

7. Type [**K**] to select sort keys. Your cursor jumps to the first of nine groups of key settings in the Sort by Line menu. We describe how field entries are made for the first key. If you wish to sort your list using one or more additional keys, move your cursor to a new set.

   NOTE: Multiple sort keys would be used if your objective were to sort customers *within* city and cities *within* state. In that case, three keys would be required. *State* is the first key; *city* is the second, and *customer name* is the third.

Tools
Sort <R>, <R>, T, L, K

8. Your cursor should be under the small letter *a* located beneath the *Typ* heading (the *a* stands for "*a*lphanumeric"). If the sort is to be alphabetic, ignore this variable and press Right Arrow to move the cursor under the *Field* heading. (To perform a *numeric* sort, replace the a by typing [**N**].)
9. Your cursor should now be under the *Field* heading, and the value shown there should be *1*, meaning that field 1 will be the first sort key. If the first field, say, name in the list in Fig. 8-8, is to be your sort key, press Right Arrow to move to the next variable in the set, *Word*. If, instead, you'd like office lo-

```
Baker, Robert  [Tab]Reynolda 308  [Tab]5402  [Tab]Code 16  [Tab]Politics
Katz, Barbara  [Tab]Physics 211   [Tab]5771  [Tab]Code 05  [Tab]Physics

      Etc.

Allen, Herbert  [Tab]Babcock 101  [Tab]5803  [Tab]Code 47  [Tab]Mathematics
```

Figure 8-8 Directory Segment

cation to be your sort key, change *1* to *2* and then press **Right Arrow.** Had you wanted the 5th field in a list to be your sort key, you would have changed the *1* to a *5*.

NOTE: In a WordPerfect list, fields are defined only by tabs, indents, or location at the left margin. For example, note in Fig. 8-8 that the names are flush left and that office location, phone extension, code number, and department are preceded by tabs. Tabs can be any of the following: **[Tab]**, **[Dec Tab]**, **[Rgt Tab]**, or **[Cntr Tab]**.

WARNING: Since WordPerfect defines sort fields to the right of the left margin with tabs or indents, it's important to have only one tab separating each column from its adjacent column.

10. Your cursor should now be under the *Word* heading, and the value shown there should also be *1*, meaning that the list will be sorted on the *first* word in the field. Most of the time you'd sort a list on the first word in the field, but there may be occasions when sorting on the second, third, or even last word may be more appropriate. If you want to sort on the second or third word in the field, change the *1* to a *2* or *3*. If you wanted to sort a list on the *last* word in a field *and* the field contains different numbers of words from one record in the list to the next (consider cities, states, and zip codes in an address field), change the 1 to a -1. For example, had you wanted to sort the list above using code number as the key, you could have done so by defining the key variables below:

    1 a 4 -1

    Alternatively, you could have defined them as

    1 a 4 2

NOTE: If you're typing a list of names in natural order, be sure to type a hard space between the components of compound last names that contain particles. For example, press **Home, Space Bar** to insert a hard space between the two parts of the last names in the following list.

Petra Von Festenberg
Willem Van Metre
Francesca Da Rimini
Kiri Te Kanawa

11. Press **Right Arrow** to define secondary, tertiary, and so on keys if you need to sort your list on more than one key.
12. Press **(F7)** to move your cursor to the Sort By Line menu.
13. Type [**P**] to "Perform the Action" of sorting the list.
14. At the completion of the sort process, the original list is replaced by the sorted list, rearranged according to the entries you made in the Sort by Line menu.

Sort by Paragraph. For the paragraph sort, paragraphs are defined as collections of words, numbers, etc. separated by two hard returns. The individual paragraphs may have only a single line, or they may have many lines. Thus, a collection of single-spaced, standard text paragraphs separated by blank lines would qualify. So would a list of single-spaced bibliographic references separated by blank lines.

NOTE: All paragraphs must end with two hard returns, including the last paragraph in the file.

To sort by paragraph, retrieve a file of paragraphs and then follow steps 4 through 6 above as you would for a line sort. Then take these steps:

1. Type [**T**], [**P**], [**K**] to change the sort *type* to *paragraph*. Your cursor is moved into the Sort By Paragraph menu.

```
Tools
      Sort <R>, <R>, T, P, K
```

2. Press **Right Arrow** to move your cursor under the *Field* heading.

   You will normally sort your paragraphs on a number or a name that's flush left. (Consider a list of references, for example.) If so, leave the value of *Field* unchanged at 1. On the other hand, if your paragraphs are indented, change the value of *Field* to 2. With an indent and a tab, change *Field* to 3, and so on.
3. Press **Right Arrow** to move your cursor under the "Line" heading.

   If the sort key is in the first *line* of each paragraph, leave the default value of 1 unchanged. If the key is in the second line, change the value to 2, and so on. If the key is in the *last* line, and your paragraphs have variable numbers of lines, change the value to *-1*.

4. Press **Right Arrow** to move your cursor under the *Word* heading.

   If the sort key is the first *word* in the line containing the key, let the default value of 1 stand. In the case of numbered paragraphs, the first "word" is the paragraph number. Following the principles established earlier, change the value of the word field to 2, 3, -1, etc., depending upon whether the second, third, last, or some other word is to be the key.

   NOTE: You may have more than one key in a paragraph sort just as you may use multiple keys in a line sort.

5. Press **(F7)** and type [**P**] to exit the Sort by Paragraph menu and perform the sort.

Sort Secondary Merge Files. Sorting secondary merge files is similar to sorting paragraphs. To sort secondary merge files, follow step 4 through 6 in the Sort by Line instructions. Then do the following:

Type [**T**], [**M**], [**K**] to change the sort *type* to *merge file* and move your cursor into the Sort by Secondary Merge File menu.

From this point on, sorting entries in a merge file is similar to sorting paragraphs. Identify the field containing the sort key as well as line within field and *word* position within line. You should also be aware that a *field* in a secondary merge file is defined by the {END FIELD} code at its end. Thus, a Secondary Merge file *field* might include the words in only a single line (if that line ends with {END FIELD}, or the words in a double line such as an address line where the *first physical line* in the field contains the street address and a hard return code and the *second physical line* contains the city, state, and zip code and ends with an {END FIELD} code.

8- 4 FORMATTING TEXT IN COLUMNS

This section advises on situations when multiple column formats may be more appropriate than full-page formats and describes newspaper style and paragraph style columns with block protect on and block protect off. The Procedure subsection includes instructions for defining paragraph and newspaper style columns, toggling columns on and off, and moving from column to column.

Overview

Most students are familiar with a single-column layout because that's what they use for letters, papers, and other written material produced on a typewriter or word processor. They're also used to *reading* multiple-column layouts in newspapers, magazines, travel itineraries, and advertising brochures. Most students are *not* accustomed to producing these formats, however.

The standard, full-page, single-column format is suitable for virtually all of the long documents you'll write for class assignments and the correspondence you'll write for placement or club and organization work. From time to time, however, a multiple-column format may be a better choice. For example, a resume can be formatted as a two-column document. (We show you how to do that in Section 3- 3.) But there are other documents that are also more easily prepared using a column format. Think about case analysis exhibits that show two or more categories of information, dialogues, and written procedures (Figs. 8-9 and 8-10 below are illustrative). Many clubs and organizations publish newsletters to keep their memberships informed about recent happenings, changes in leadership, and coming events. If you're the editor of a club newsletter, you should be aware that a newsletter looks better and is more readable when formatted in two or three columns, newspaper style.

WordPerfect supports three varieties of multi-column formats: (1) newspaper style, (2) paragraph style *without* block protect, and (3) paragraph style *with* block protect.

In newspaper style format, not surprisingly, text fills the first column on a page and then cascades over into the second column. When the second column is

NAME	EDUCATION	RESPONSIBILITIES
Brown, George	A.B., Dartmouth M.B.A., Wharton	Project Manager, On-Line Inventory Information System.
Hendries, Jill	B.S., Georgia Tech M.SC., Carnegie Mellon Ph.D., Brown	Design, development, and implementation of new financial systems. Training new system users. Promotion of new systems to management.

Figure 8-9 Staff Profiles

Bill Plunkett	V-P, Sales	I don't care, Jeffries, I specifically instructed you to check with the folks in distribution before you gave out a ship date.
Bert Jeffries	Sales Rep., Atlanta Region	Bill, I've tracked orders and ship dates for years now, and I've found that there's almost always a three-week gap between the two. I felt very safe in quoting that date. I'm sorry.

Figure 8-10 Training Script

filled, text cascades over into the third column, and so on. As soon as all columns on a page are filled, additional text flows into the first column on a new page. When you type several additional sentences in the middle of an existing text column, you can see the new material push the existing text from column to column. Similarly, when you delete a few sentences, the following text flows backward, cascading over column boundaries in reverse.

Paragraph style columns look like the text in Figs. 8-9 and 8-10. Fig. 8-9 has three columns: Name, Education, and Responsibilities, and the three categories of information must be maintained in the same relative position for each individual listed in the exhibit. (We refer collectively to all categories of related information as an "entry." For example, Jill Hendries' name, educational accomplishments, and job responsibilities, taken collectively, is a single *entry*.) If information were to be added in the responsibilities column for George Brown, all the information for Jill Hendries would be pushed down across the three columns.

In paragraph style *without* block protect, text in the longest column extending past a soft page code may be broken so that some of the text in the longest column stands by itself at the top of a new page. In paragraph style *with* block protect, on the other hand, if text in the longest column would extend past a soft page break, the page is broken prematurely and *all* adjacent columns in an entry are moved to the top of the next page.

Two basic procedures are required when you create any one of the three column formats. First, you *define* the column format by telling WordPerfect the style you plan to use, the number of columns, and column spacing. Then, you switch on the column definition specified. Only after you've defined the appropriate column style, numbers of columns, and spacing and switched columns on can you format text into columns. After you have defined columns, however, you can switch column format on and off as needed.

Procedure

In this subsection we describe the steps required to: (1) define *parallel columns with block protect on,* (2) switch columns on and off, (3) create and edit text, and (4) navigate from one column to the next. Then we describe the steps needed to define and use *newspaper style columns.* The procedures for defining parallel columns with block protect *off* and working within that style are almost identical to the procedures for parallel columns with block protect *on.* Therefore, we don't describe the block protect off procedures here.

Parallel Columns with Block Protect On. After you've planned what your column format will look like (and preparing a pencil sketch complete with measurements to plan your work is a *very* good idea), here's how to proceed with paragraph style with block protect on.

1. Move your cursor to the page and line where you want the column format to begin. Then press **Home**, **Home**, **Left Arrow** to begin the definition ahead of any text.
2. Press **(Alt-F7)** and type [**C**], [**D**] to choose columns and select column definition. The Normal Editing screen is replaced by the Text Column Definition screen shown in Fig. 8-11.
3. Type [**T**], [**B**] to select parallel columns with block protect *on*.

   NOTE: Type [**P**] instead of [**B**] to define parallel columns with block protect *off.*

4. Type [**N**] and the number of columns you plan to use and then press **Enter**. (We selected "3" as the number of columns for Figs. 8-9 and 8-10 shown above). After the number of columns has been entered, notice that left and right default margin settings are automatically created by WordPerfect.
5. Type [**D**] to see that the distance between columns is 0.5" (also a default) and then press **Enter**. A half-inch space between columns produces results with good eye appeal.
6. If columns of equal width are acceptable, press **Enter** to return to the Normal Editing screen and the Columns/Tables/Math menu. If columns of unequal width are more appropriate—and that's usually the case with parallel columns—type [**M**] to change margins. Then, eyeball the dimensions in your pencil sketch and type over the default margin settings displayed in the Text

```
Text Column Definition

     1 - Type                                        Newspaper

     2 - Number of Columns                           2

     3 - Distance Between Columns

     4 - Margins

     Column     Left      Right      Column     Left      Right
      1:        1"        4"         13:
      2:        4.5"      7.5"       14:
      3:                             15:
      4:                             16:
      5:                             17:
      6:                             18:
      7:                             19:
      8:                             20:
      9:                             21:
     10:                             22:
     11:                             23:
     12:                             24:

Selection: 0
```

Figure 8-11 Text Column Definition Screen

Column Definition screen, pressing **Enter** after each new entry. Press Enter one more time to display the Normal Editing screen.

7. Type **[O]** to toggle columns on. Notice that "Col 1" is added to the left end of your status line. That's the signal that column mode is toggled on.

Layout
    Columns
        Define T, B, N, [3], <R>, M, [1], <Enter>, [2.25], <Enter>, [2.75], [4.25], <Enter> [4.75], <Enter>, [7.5], <Enter>, <R>, O

8. Type and edit text just as you would in a full-screen format. Creating and editing text works the same way in parallel columns as it does in a single-column format, but your work area is more narrow.
9. Press **(Ctrl-Enter)** to jump to the next column after completing the column *1* information for the first entry. (Remember that an entry is all the related information in the row that stretches across the page.) Type all the information in that column. Be sure to press **Enter** to end lines not meant to wrap to the next line down — e.g., the degree information in Column 2 of Fig. 8-9.
10. Press **(Ctrl-Enter)** to jump to the third column when the information in column 2 is complete.
11. After you've typed all the information in the last column for the first entry, press **(Ctrl-Enter)** to jump back to the left margin. Type the column *1* information pertaining to the next entry. (Notice that WordPerfect inserts a blank line between entries.)
12. Continue typing the other entries in your exhibit or table, column by column.
13. When you edit your exhibit, you'll need to switch from entry to entry and column to column.
    - 13. 1 Press **Up Arrow** to move up in the same column.
    - 13. 2 Press **Down Arrow** to move down.
    - 13. 3 Press **(Ctrl-Home), Right Arrow** to move to the right across columns within the same entry.
    - 13. 4 Press **(Ctrl-Home), Left Arrow** to move to the left.
    - 13. 5 Press **(Ctrl-Home), Home, Right Arrow** to move to the right-most column.
    - 13. 6 Press **(Ctrl-Home), Home, Left Arrow** to move to the left-most column.

NOTE: If you have a mouse attached to your PC, moving from column to column is as easy as moving the mouse cursor to the target column and pressing the left button.

WARNING: It's a *very good idea* to edit column-format documents with Reveal Codes toggled on even if the screen looks a bit messy when you do it. Editing in Reveal Codes helps you avoid deleting hard page codes (**[HPg]**), block protect on and off codes (**[Block Pro:On]**, **[Block Pro:Off]**), and column on and off codes (**[Col on]**, **[Col off]**) by mistake. You can't see the codes without toggling Reveal Codes on, deleting them will almost certainly scramble your text, leaving you frustrated and angry.

14. Press **(Alt-F7)** and type [C], [F] when you've typed all the entries in your exhibit and want to toggle back to a full-page format. You can toggle columns back on again any time.

```
Layout
        Columns
                Off
```

NOTE: Switch columns off at the end of the last entry in an exhibit. Don't press **(Ctrl-Enter)** to jump to the left margin before you toggle columns off.

15. After completing your exhibit, you may notice that the layout can be improved if spacing within or between columns is changed. To change spacing, move your cursor to the first line of your exhibit and take the following steps,
    15. 1 Press **Home**, **Home**, **Left Arrow** to position your cursor to the left of all text.
    15. 2 Press **(Alt-F3)**, to toggle on Reveal Codes and press **Left Arrow** until the **[Block Pro:On]** code is highlighted. (The **[Col Def]** code should be the next code to the left.)
    15. 3 Press **(Alt-F7)** and type [C], [D] to define columns.

```
Layout
        Columns
                Define
```

The Text Column Definition screen with existing settings displaces the Normal Editing screen. Change the space and margin settings on the screen to create your new layout and press **(F7)** twice to see the effect on your exhibit. Repeat the procedure until you're satisfied with the results.

NOTE: When you reveal codes, you may see two or more column definition codes in a row. Only the right-most code is in effect. You can delete the others to reduce clutter and make your file a teeny bit smaller. Do so *very* carefully.

Newspaper style columns. To define newspaper columns, start off with steps 1 and 2 above. Then follow the instructions below.

1. Since the WordPerfect default column type is "Newspaper," leave that option alone. (Do change it if another option is displayed, however.)
2. If more than two columns are needed, type [**N**], enter the number of columns to be defined, and then press **Enter**. If two columns will do the job, skip this option.
3. Type [**D**] and press **Enter** to see that the distance between columns is 0.5 inches. That's acceptable for two-column formats. For three-column formats, change the spacing to 0.35 inches.
4. Type [**M**] if you want to change the default column margin settings. (The default settings produce columns of equal width.) Otherwise, skip this option and press **Enter** to return to the Normal Editing screen and the Columns/Tables/Math menu.
5. Type [**O**] to switch columns on.

```
Layout
        Columns
                Define  <R>, O
```

Typing and editing text in newspaper style columns is basically the same as typing and editing a full-page format document. Aside from occasionally having to switch from one column to another, the only difference is that the column format is a more constrained environment. When you need to switch from one column to another, follow the instructions given above for parallel columns.

A final note. If your columns are more ragged than you'd like, move to the top of your first column and toggle on hyphenation. (See Section 6- 5.) Press **(Ctrl-F3)** and type [**R**] to rewrite the screen after you've done so. You may also be asked to help with the hyphenation. If your columns are still too ragged, try making the hyphenation zones smaller and assess the effect. Here's how:

- Press **(Shift-F8)** and type [**L**] to select line formats.
- Type [**Z**] to change the hyphenation zones.
- Change default values by typing new numbers and pressing **Enter**.
- Type [**Y**], [**Y**] to toggle hyphenation on.
- Press **(F7)** to return to the Normal Editing screen.

```
Layout
        Line  Z, [6], <R>, [2], <R>, Y, Y, <R>
```

8- 5 *DRAWING LINES AND BOXES*

This module includes guidelines for drawing lines and boxes that are visible in the Normal Editing screen and don't require use of the WordPerfect graphics feature. The Overview subsection tells how the Line Draw feature can improve a document's appearance and points out some of its strengths and limitations. The Procedure subsection includes instructions for drawing lines and boxes, copying boxes, typing text inside an existing box, and using the advance feature to draw a box around proportionally spaced text.

Overview

When you prepare long documents (and perhaps shorter ones as well) including lines and boxes in the text can increase communication effectiveness. For example, you can draw vertical or horizontal lines to set off a heading, divide sections of text, or insert response lines in a self-administered questionnaire. Boxes can emphasize particular points by setting them off by themselves. Boxes can also be used to create organization charts and flow charts.

Some advantages of Line Draw. The WordPerfect graphics feature is an excellent way to incorporate lines and text boxes in a document (see Section 8- 1, "Working with Graphics" and Section 6- 3, "Importing Figures"), and the Tables feature is great for boxes (see Section 6- 2). The older Line Draw feature may be still be preferable under certain conditions, however.[1] First, the Line Draw feature is easier *to learn to use* than graphics and easier to use on an irregular basis because fewer steps are required to produce satisfactory results. Therefore, Line Draw may be more appropriate for the casual user. Second, Line Draw results are directly observable in the Normal Editing screen. The more mysterious lines created with the graphics feature are *not* directly observable in the Normal Editing screen. You must press (Shift-F7) and type [V] to View Document so that you can see the lines. You must also press (Alt-F3) or (F11) to see the codes that define individual graphics lines. Third, in several respects, the Line Draw feature is more flexible than tables or graphics. For example, it's fairly simple to copy boxes made with the Line Draw feature. Achieving a similar result using the Tables and Graphics features is more cumbersome.

Some limitations of Line Draw. Also be aware of some limitations of the Line Draw feature. First, lines can't be drawn around indented, aligned, or justified text. Second, Line Draw is destructive in the sense that drawing a line over existing text replaces the text with line characters, character for character. Similarly, typing characters over a line created in Line Draw breaks the line. Both effects result because Line Draw *figures* are constructed from Line Draw *characters*. Third, you can't draw past the right margin. If you try, the figure you thought you were creating will be distorted. Fourth, your printer must support line drawing characters.

On the last point, create a series of boxes and lines and then examine them with View Document (press **(Shift-F7)** and type **[V]**) to see if your printer does support line drawing characters. If not, try substituting the characters -, |, + for horizontal and vertical single line and corner characters. Substitute the equals sign (=) for double lines. The final limitation of Line Draw is that it only works properly when you use fixed-space fonts such as Courier and Prestige Elite.

Procedure

In this section we provide instructions for completing five drawing tasks:

- Drawing a single-line box or line
- Drawing a double-line box
- Typing text in a box
- Copying a box
- Using the Advance feature to post-draw a box over existing text

Drawing a line. Make sure the Normal Editing screen is displayed, then follow these instructions. (Fig. 8-12 shows the results of the next three operations.)

1. Use the arrow keys, the space bar, the tab key, or the indent key, (F4), to move the cursor to the starting point of your line.
2. Press **(Ctrl-F3)** and type [**L**], [**1**] to switch on the Line Draw feature and select the "single-line" option. The *single-line* option is the WordPerfect default. When it's in effect, the number 1 is displayed at the right of the menu, and you don't need to type 1.

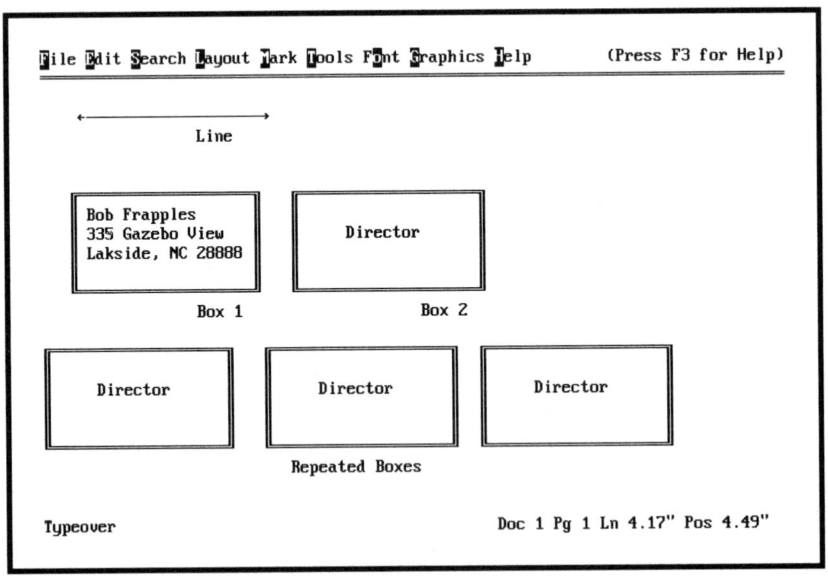

Figure 8-12 Line Draw Results

```
Tools
        Line Draw
```

3. Press **Right Arrow** a few times and see a single line being drawn on the Normal Editing screen.
4. Type [**5**] and press **Left Arrow** a few times and erase part of the line you just drew.
5. Press **(F7)** to exit the Line Draw feature.

Drawing a box. To draw a double-line box, follow the next set of instructions.

1. Move the cursor to the starting point for the upper left corner of the box.
2. Press **(Ctrl-F3)** and type [**L**], [**2**] to select a double-line option.

```
Tools
        Line Draw  2
```

3. Press **Right Arrow** 20 times to draw the top of the box.
4. Press **Esc**, type [**5**], and press **Down Arrow** to draw the right side of the box.
5. Press **Esc**, type [**20**], and press **Left Arrow** to draw a third line 20 characters in length.
6. Finally, press **Esc**, type [**5**], and press **Up Arrow** to draw the left side and complete the box.
7. Press **(F7)** to toggle off Line Draw.

Typing inside a box. The box you've just drawn contains 72 space characters. Use the cursor keys to move your cursor to the upper left corner inside the box. Then follow the next instructions.

1. Press **Insert** to switch to "typeover" mode (this is important). Type some text in the box — your name and address, for example — being careful to stay inside the borders. When you've typed enough text in the box to get a sense of the process, use the Left Arrow key and the Space Bar to delete all the text you typed.

   Now, let's use an old typist's trick to center text in the box.
2. Move the cursor to the horizontal center of the box.
3. Press **Left Arrow** once for each *two* letters in the title to be centered. For example, to center the word, "Director," press **Left Arrow** once for "Di", once for "re", etc. Press **Left Arrow** four times to center the whole word.

4. Now, type the word, Director, and see that it's centered inside the box.

   NOTE: As you've probably observed, the Backspace key is destructive when you're in Insert mode: when you press it, the right border of the box moves left. Recover by pressing the **Space Bar** to push the right border back out again.

Copying a box. Producing attractive organization charts and other figures with a series of repeated boxes can be accomplished by copying a box you've already created. Follow the steps in the example below to do that.

1. Move your cursor to the upper left corner of the box created earlier. (If you deleted that box, create another one.)
2. Press **(Alt-F4)** to switch block on.

```
Edit
        Block
```

3. Move your cursor down to the lower right corner of the box.
4. Press **(Ctrl-F4)** and type [**R**], [**C**] to copy a rectangle.
5. Move your cursor to the point on the Normal Editing screen where a new box is to be placed and press **Enter**.

```
Edit
        Select
                Rectangle  C, <Enter>
```

To pop the same box into other locations on the Normal Editing screen, repeat the next instruction once for each box.

6. Move your cursor to a new target spot, press **(Ctrl-F4)** and type [**R**], [**R**].

```
Edit
        Paste  R
```

The instructions above *copy* a box. Similar steps can be used to *move* a box from one location to another. Just select the *move* option instead of the *copy* option after you press (Ctrl-F4) and type [C] in instruction 4 above.

Another way to repeatedly draw single-line boxes is to create a macro that draws them for you. This technique is outlined next.

- Press **(Ctrl-F10)** to define a macro.
- Type [**Box**] and press **Enter** to name the macro.
- Type a description — e.g., [**Autobox — 20X4**] — and press **Enter** to describe the macro.

```
Tools
        Macro
                Define  [box] <R> [Autobox—20x4] <R>
```

- With "Macro Def" blinking in the lower left corner, press **(Ctrl-F3)** type [**L**], [**1**], press **Esc**, type [**20**], press **Right Arrow**, **Esc**, type [**4**], press **Down Arrow**, **Esc**, type [**20**], press **Left Arrow**, **Esc**, type [**4**], and press **Up Arrow**, **(F7)**, **(Ctrl-F10)**.

```
Tools
        Macro
                Define
```

To draw a box using the macro,

- Move your cursor to the target location of the upper left corner of the box.
- Press **(Alt-F10)** to activate a macro.
- In response to the prompt,

  Macro:

  type [**box**] and press **Enter**.

```
Tools
        Macro
                Execute  [macro name], <R>
```

Using the Advance feature to post-draw a box. Next we show how to use the Advance feature to draw a box around pre-existing text. Use this trick to get around the limitations of proportionally spaced text mentioned at the outset.

1. Jot the line and position numbers at the lower right side of your display screen on a piece of paper.
2. Press **Enter** twice.
3. Press **Space Bar** three times and type [**BOX TEXT EXAMPLE**].

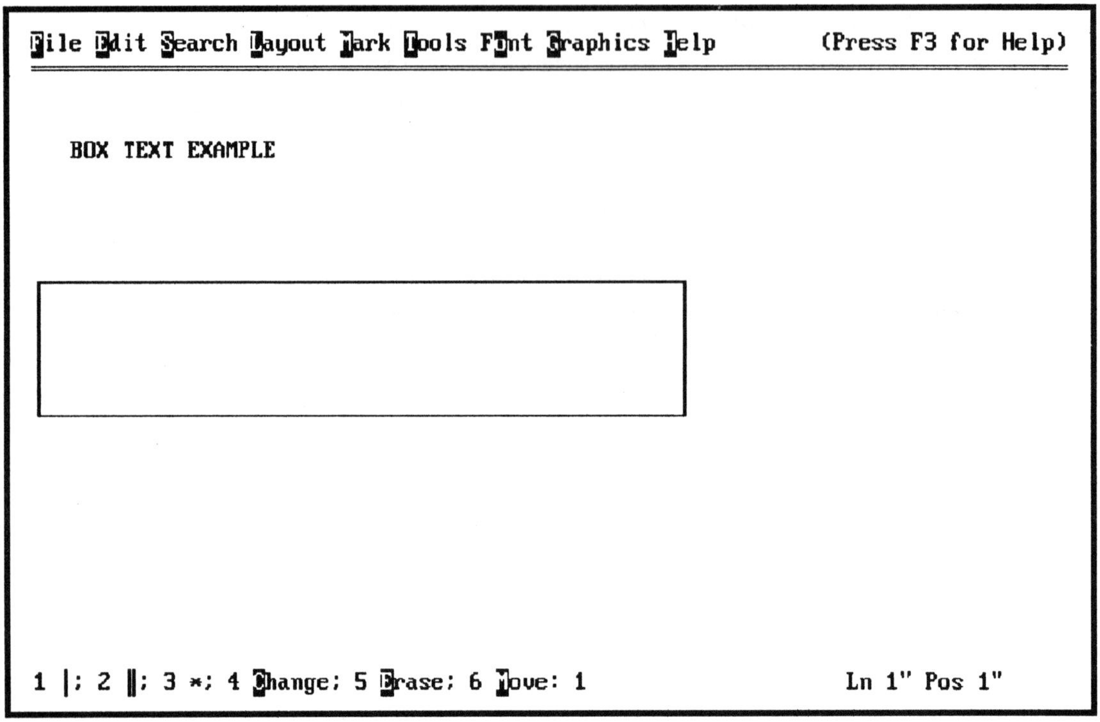

Figure 8-13 Post-Drawn Box in Edit Screen

4. Press **Enter** five times to move the cursor down the screen.
5. Press **(Shift-F8)** and type [**O**], [**A**], [**I**], [**the *line number* you jotted down**], press **Enter**, [**A**], [**P**], type [**the *position number* you jotted down**] and press **Enter**, **(F7)**.

Layout
Other A, I, [line #], <R>, A, P, [position #] <R>, <R>

6. Press **(Ctrl-F3)**, type [**L**], press **Esc**, type [**50**], and press **Right Arrow** to draw the top line of a box.
7. Press **Esc**, type [**5**], and press **Down Arrow** to draw the right side of the box.

Tools
Line Draw

8. Press **Esc**, type [**50**], and press **Left Arrow** to draw the bottom line of the box.

Figure 8-14 Post-Drawn Box in View Document

9. Press **Esc,** type [**5**], and press **Up Arrow** to draw the left and final side of the box.
10. Press **(F7)** to return to the Normal Editing screen.
11. Press **(Shift-F7)**, [**V**] to see that the box shown *below* the text on your Normal Editing screen is positioned *over* the text on the View Document screen. That's the way the box and text would print—even if your font is proportionally spaced. The final result as it appears on the Normal Editing screen is shown in Fig. 8-13. The View Document image of the same result is shown in Fig. 8-14.

File
Print V

ENDNOTES

1. Line draw was available in early releases of WordPerfect before the introduction of the Graphics and Tables features.

8- 6 WORKING WITH EQUATIONS

This module compares equations to other WordPerfect graphical capabilities and describes the equation editor and how it works. Also included are instructions for creating and editing an equation and changing the setup of the equation editor. In the remaining pages are two subsections: (1) an *Overview* that explains what the equation editor is and why you'd want to use it, and (2) a *Procedure* subsection that includes step-by-step instructions for creating, viewing, editing, and saving equations.

Overview

On occasion, you may find it appropriate to include one or more equations in a written assignment to make a point or explain a difficult or abstract idea. Mathematics, after all, is a language that was developed to express complex ideas completely and in a compact way. Opportunities to include equations are most likely to present themselves in economics, statistics, finance, and management science courses. But courses in other disciplines may also be candidates.

If you're like most students, you've avoided including equations in your papers and reports. You don't own a technical word processor, and you just don't have the time and patience to produce equations using a standard word processor—even one as powerful as WordPerfect that has had Greek letters and mathematical symbols in its character set for years. Now in situations when equations *really* should be included in your written work, don't hesitate. Use the equation editor. It's easy to learn, easy to use, and it enables you to produce professional-quality work *very* quickly.

An Equation is a Graphics Box. The equation editor is a member of the WordPerfect family of "graphics" features. In many respects, it resembles the Graphics Box feature of WordPerfect that was first introduced in the 5.0 release. The equation editor is on the same branch of the feature tree that includes figure, table, text, and user-defined graphics boxes and graphics lines. The equation editor produces a graphics box like the older graphics boxes (the equation box is displayed without the borders, just like the user-defined box). It's also possible to change the options of the equation box just as you can change the options of the other graphics boxes; you can put borders around an equation box, shade it, or change the spacing between the box and surrounding text. One final similarity: you can't see an equation created in the equation editor in the Normal Editing screen. To see what your equation will look like on paper, you must display its printer image with the View Document feature.

Generally, equations produced in the equation editor follow typesetting standards. That is, they're centered on a line both horizontally and vertically. Also, variables are set in italic style and functions, numbers, and symbols are set in roman style (straight up and down). For example, in the equation,

$$y = 3x^2 + \beta \sin z$$

the elements y, x, and z are variables and they're set in italics. The elements β, +, and = are symbols, and they're set in roman. The element, sin, a function, is also set in roman. Because all the elements of an equation are graphics, not text, it's easy to change their size and they can be used with any printer that has a graphics capability, even if the printer isn't equipped with a font that includes greek letters and mathematical symbols. It's also easy to number equations when they need to be identified. The default number is shown in parentheses on the right side of the page. The default number style and position are easily changed in the Definition: Equation menu, however.

Using the equation editor. At this point, we describe the characteristics of the equation editor. A little later, we'll walk you through a little exercise to show how it works. (Although you don't need to be sitting at a PC with the equation editor displayed on your screen to understand what follows, it helps.) Here's how to invoke the equation editor. (We assume you know how to run WordPerfect.)

- Type [**WP**] and press **Enter** to run WordPerfect.
- Press **(Alt-F9)** and type [**E**], [**C**] to create an equation.
- Type [**E**] again to toggle the editor.

Graphics
Equation
Create E

The equation editor is shown in Fig. 8-15. It has three windows and a menu at the bottom. The most important window is at the lower left. It's called the edit window, and that's where you build your equation. The window above it is called the display window, and it's used to check the progress of your work in the edit window. When you press (Ctrl-F3), the equation under construction is shown in the display

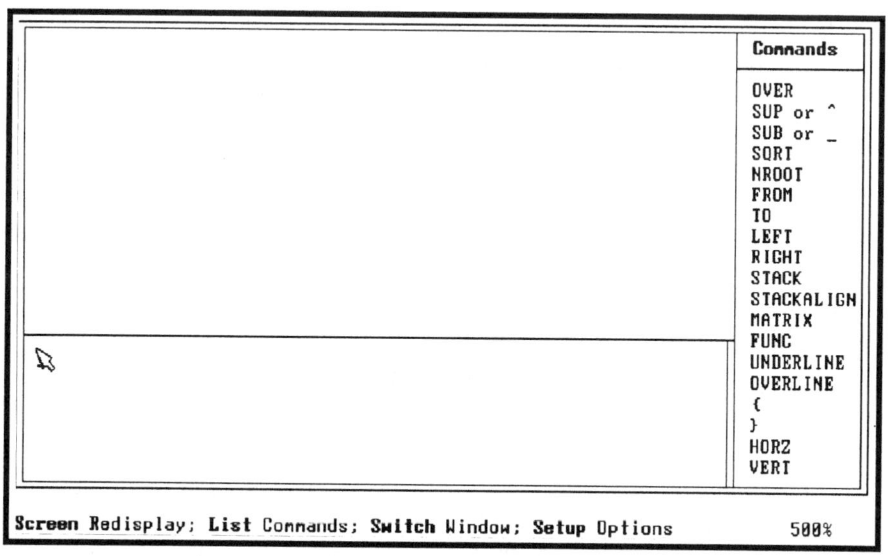

Figure 8-15 Equation Editor Screen

window as a graphic—five times life size (at least to begin with). The window on the right is the equation palette. It lets you select commands, symbols, and functions from a large number of options for insertion into your equation. The menu at the bottom is used to navigate around the equation editor if you're using a mouse.

When you first pull up the equation editor, your cursor is in the edit window. Without further ado, you can begin building an equation by typing characters just as you would in the Normal Editing screen. (In fact, most of the editing capabilities that are available in the Normal Editing screen are also available in the edit window.) If you know the names of all the commands, functions, and symbols available in the palette, you can just type them in without ever using the palette. It's faster.

When you need to grab an equation element from the palette, press (F5). The top cell in the Command Menu is highlighted. Press **PgDn** to cycle through eight sets of options.

- Command
- Large
- Symbols
- Greek
- Arrows
- Sets
- Other
- Functions

Within each set, you move from element to element by pressing the cursor keys. When you've identified the particular element you need, press **Enter,** and it pops into your equation where the cursor is located, bracketed by two spaces. (If you need to return from the palette without picking an element, press **(F7)**.)

As you build your equation, use the display window often. (You have to have a graphics card to see it, however.) Be sure not to wait until you think the equation is complete because it's tougher to ferret out errors if you do. Press **(Ctrl-F3)** to display a graphic image of your equation under construction. Unless you choose to move up into the display and modify the image, it remains unchanged in the display window until you press **(Ctrl-F3)** to check your work again. If you do want to change the appearance of the image, press **(Shift-F3)** to move up. (The double-line at the right of the edit window will move up to the display window.) Press the arrow keys to move the image around and the **PgUp** and **PgDn** keys to make it larger or smaller. (None of this activity has any effect on the *printed* image, by the way. Press **(Shift-F3)** to move back to the edit window.)

Table 8-1 summarizes the keystrokes required to navigate from window to window and within the palette. It also shows how to navigate with a mouse.

TABLE 8-1. EQUATION EDITOR KEYSTROKE SUMMARY

Feature or Activity	Action	Function Keys	Mouse
Review Image		(Ctrl-F3)	Screen
From Edit Window to Display Window	To	(Shift-F3)	Switch
	Return	(Shift-F3)	Switch
From Edit Window to Equation Palette	To	(F5)	List
	Return	(F7)	<R>
	Select	Enter	<L>,<L>
Setup Options		(Shift-F1)	Setup
Cycle through Palette Option Sets		PgUp, PgDn	PgUp, PgDn
Cycle through Palette Options		↑,↓	

We conclude this Overview with some pointers about building equations. First, be sure to include ample space between individual elements and don't be concerned when the equation wraps to the next line down. None of that has any effect on the *graphic* representation of the equation. Second, be sure to include good spacing that will show up in the graphic version. The way to do that is to insert a tilde (~) if you want a whole space and a grave (`) if you want a quarter space (called a "thin" space). Surround =, +, - signs with tildes. Separate symbols and variables set side by side with a `. For example,

$$y{\sim}={\sim}b_0{\sim}+{\sim}b_1\text{`}x{\sim}+{\sim}b_2\text{`}x^2$$

should look good in the display window (and on paper). Third, if you know the names of some of the elements of your equation, type them directly rather than plucking them from the palette. It's faster. You can type in upper case or lower case—it doesn't matter (with the exception of greek letters). Note the names of elements displayed at the bottom left of your screen as you search through the options in the palette. Fourth, use the display window to check your progress often—especially after you make a change you're uncertain about.

Procedure

In this subsection we're going to build a relatively complex equation — it's a demand equation of sorts, actually. Then we're going to do the following things to it:

- Increase its size
- Left justify it
- Give it a number

- Check it
  - In the Normal Editing screen
  - In the View Document screen
- Save it
- Edit it
- Review it again
- Delete it
- Move it

We'll end this subsection with a table that will show you how to create other equations that most business students should find useful. Here's the equation we're going to work with first.

$$q = \alpha + \beta p + \gamma y^2 + \delta\sqrt{a_1 + a_2} + \varepsilon \left(\frac{s_o}{s}\right)$$

where:

q = quantity sold over some time period
p = price
y = income
a_1 = broadcast advertising
a_2 = print advertising
s_o = own selling expenditures
s = competitor average selling expenditures
α, β, γ, Δ, ε are parameters

Here's the second equation:

$$q = \alpha + \beta\left(\frac{p_o}{\bar{p}}\right) + \gamma y_{t-1} + \delta\sqrt{a_1 + a_2} + \varepsilon\left(\frac{s_o}{s}\right)$$

where new elements are:

p_o = own average price
p = competitor average price

We don't pretend to suggest that these are good demand equations or bad ones either. Nor do we have any pretensions as to their accuracy of specification or technical correctness. They were formulated strictly for the purposes of demonstrating how to use the equation editor. We will add parenthetically, however, that they are not unlike the equations with which many business students are familiar —especially students of economics and marketing.

Let's get started. We assume WordPerfect is running and that you have a two-to-three page document displayed on the Normal Editing screen.

1. Press **(Alt-F9)** and type [**E**], [**C**] to create an equation.
2. Type [**E**] to display the equation editor with the cursor in the edit window.

```
Graphics
        Equation
                Create  E
```

3. Build the equation.
   - 3. 1 Type [**q** =].
   - 3. 2 Press **(F5)** and **PgDn** three times to display the greek option set. Since α, the symbol we need, is highlighted, press **Enter** to pop it into the equation.
   - 3. 3 Type [+].
   - 3. 4 Press **(F5)** and highlight the "β" symbol since the greek options are still current. Press **Enter**.
   - 3. 5 Type [**p** +].
   - 3. 6 Press **(F5)**, highlight γ and press **Enter.**
   - 3. 7 Type [**y^2** +].

     NOTE: The carat symbol, "^," means "superscript the next element." We could have used the word, SUP, instead. The result would have been the same. We typed this command instead of picking it from the palette because we knew what it was. You'll know some of the symbols, too. By the way, if you type the greek letters, you should know that the greek alphabet is case sensitive. If you type alpha, an α will be inserted into your equation. If you type ALPHA, however, an A will turn up.

   - 3. 8 Press **(F5)**, highlight δ and press **Enter**.
   - 3. 9 Press **(F5)**, press **PgUp** three times to scroll back up to *Commands,* highlight "SQRT." and press **Enter**.
   - 3.10 Type [**{a_1** + **a_2}**].

     NOTE: The underline symbol, "_," means "subscript the next element," (the 1 and 2 in this case). The braces say, "consider what's between the two of us as a single element."

     NOTE: If you have a left brace, you *must* have a right one, else you'll see an error message.

3.11 Type [+].

3.12 Press **(F5)**, **PgDn** three times, highlight the ε and press **Enter**.

3.13 Type [**{S_0 over S bar}**].

3.14 Move your cursor to the *left* brace you just typed and take the following additional steps:

- Type [**LEFT**].
- Press **(F5)** and then **PgUp** twice to see *Large* options.
- Highlight the left parenthesis and press **Enter**.

Move to the space following the *right* brace in the expression and take these steps:

- Type [**RIGHT**].
- Press **(F5)**, highlight the right parenthesis, and press **Enter**.

NOTE: If you have a "left," you must have a "right," just like the braces.

3.15 Finally, follow the advice given earlier and insert enough ~s and `s to provide good spacing in the *printed* equation.

3.16 Press **(Ctrl-F3)** to review the work in the display window.

4. Change setup options to increase the font size to 14 points and left justify the equation.

4. 1 Press **(Shift-F1)** to display setup options. You'll see four options listed.

1. Print as Graphics
2. Graphical Font Size
3. Horizontal Alignment
4. Vertical Alignment

4. 2 Type [**G**], [**S**], [**14**] and press **Enter** to change font size to 14 point.

4. 3 Type [**H**], [**L**] to left justify the equation.

4. 4 Press **(F7)** to return to the equation editor, leaving the other options as they were.

NOTE: The changes affect only this equation. To change the characteristics for all equations, take the following steps *from the* Normal Editing screen. (Do this later if you think it's necessary.)

- Return to the normal editing screen.
- Press **(Shift-F1)** and type [**I**].
- Type [**E**] to display the Equation: Options menu.

- Make appropriate changes.
- Press **(F7)** to return to the Normal Editing screen.

```
File
      Setup
            Initial Settings  E, <R>
```

5. Number the equations
   5. 1 Press **(F7)** to display the Definition: Equation menu.
   5. 2 Type [**C**] and press **Enter** to toggle on equation numbering.
   5. 3 Press **(F7)** twice to return to the Normal Editing screen.
6. Check the finished equation in the document.
   6. 1 Notice the outline of the top of a graphics box marked with EQU 1. You see the same outline for all graphics boxes that extend all the way across a page. Only the identifiers are different—e.g., TXT for a text box, FIG for a figure box.
   6. 2 Press **(Alt-F3)** (or **(F11)**) to toggle on Reveal Codes and see a code like,

      [Equ Box:1;;[Fish Rgt][Box Num]

   6. 3 Press **(Alt-F3)** to toggle Reveal Codes off.

```
Edit
      Reveal Codes
```

   6. 4 Press **(Shift-F7)** and type [**V**] to see the printer image of the equation. The difference between the equation's size here and in the display window will startle you.

```
File
      Print  V
```

      NOTE: You may want to blow up the image on the View Document screen by typing 1 or 2.

   6. 5 Press **(F7)** to display the Normal Editing screen.
7. Edit the equation.

7. 1 Press **(Alt-F9)** and type [**E**], [**E**], press **Enter** and type [**E**] one more time to display the equation.

```
Graphics
      Equation
            Edit  [1], <R>, E
```

7. 2 Press **(F10)** and type [***filename***] to save the equation.

NOTE: Saving the equation is just a precaution here. But it's helpful to be able to save the equations by themselves—especially if you've taken a lot of time to build them and you plan to incorporate them in some of your other written work.

7. 3 Make the changes in the first equation needed to yield the second equation.

Hint: Treat the price ratio exactly as the ratio of selling expenditures is treated. Surround all three elements of the subscript, t-1, with braces to get the correct result.

7. 4 Press **(Ctrl-F3)** to check the revised equation in the display window.

7. 5 Press **(F7)** to toggle back to the Normal Editing screen.

8. Review your changed equation in View Document.

8. 1 Press **(Shift-F7)** and type [**V**]

```
File
      Print  V
```

8. 2 Press **(F7)** to display the Normal Editing screen when you've finished checking the printer image of the equation.

9. Delete the equation.

9. 1 Press **(Alt-F3)** to Reveal Codes.

```
Edit
      Reveal Codes
```

9. 2 Highlight the code and press **Delete** to delete it. Note that the graphics box outline has disappeared.

10. Move the equation.
    10. 1 Move the cursor to another location in the same document.
    10. 2 Press **(F1)** and type [**R**] to "undo" the previous deletion and retrieve the equation into a new area.

Edit	
	Undelete R

We've covered most of the basic operations you need to do with equations using this example as a vehicle. If you want to become proficient with this great tool, take some time to practice using the examples in Tables 8-2 and 8-3.

TABLE 8-2.—STATISTICAL EQUATIONS

Arithmetic mean	$\overline{x} = \frac{\sum_{i=1}^{n} x_i}{n}$
Overline x~=~{sum from {i=1} to n {x_i}} over n	
Standard deviation	$\sigma = \sqrt{\frac{\sum_{i=1}^{n} (X_i - \overline{X})^2}{n}}$
sigma~=~sqrt{{sum from {i=1} to n (X_i~-~Overline X)^2}over {n}}	
Expected value of a random variable	$E(x) = \sum_{i=1}^{N} x_i p(x_i)$
E(x)~=~sum from {i=1} to N x_i p(x_i)	
Linear regression	$y_i = \beta_O + \beta_1 x_i + e_i$
y_i~=~beta_0~+~beta_1`x_i ~+~ epsilon_i	
Standard error of the estimate	$S_{yx} = \sqrt{\frac{\sum_{i=1}^{n} (y_i - y_i)^2}{n-2}}$
s_yx~=~sqrt{{sum from {i=1} to n(y_i ~-~{{y hat}_i})^2}over {n-2}}	
Prediction interval	$y \pm t_{n-2} S_{YX} \sqrt{1 + h_i}$
{y hat}_i~+-~t_{n-2}`s_YX` sqrt {1``+``h_i}	

TABLE 8-3.—FINANCE EQUATIONS

Cash breakeven analysis BE~=~{FC~-~D} over {P~-~*VC}*	$BE = \frac{FC - D}{P - VC}$
Simple interest SI~=~PV_0 cdot`i cdot`n	$SI - PV_o \cdot i \cdot n$
Future value FV_n~=~PV_0` (1+i) ^n	$FV_n = PV_o(1+i)^n$
Present value PV_O~=~FV_n`left[{(1+i)^n}} right]	$PV_O = FV_N \left[\frac{1}{(1+i)^n} \right]$
Effective interest rate i eff~=~left(1~+~i nom over m right)^m~-~1	$i_{eff} = \left(1 + \frac{i_{nom}}{m}\right)^m -1$
Future value of an annuity FVAN n ~=~ sum from {t=1} to n R over {{(1+i)}^(n-t}}	$FVAN_n = \sum_{t=1}^{n} \frac{R}{(1+i)^{n-t}}$
Present value of an annuity CM~=~{P,~-~VC)	$PVAN_o = \sum_{t=1}^{n} \frac{R}{(1+i)^n}$
Present value of a perpetuity PVPER_0~=~sum from {t=1} to inf R over {(1+i)}^t	$PVPER_o = \sum_{t=1}^{\infty} \frac{R}{(1+i)^t}$
Future value (continuous compounding) FV n~=~PV_0 e^{i nom n}	$FV_n = PV_o e^{i_{nom} n}$
Present value (continuous discounting) PV_0~=~FV_n e^{-i_nom n}	$PV_n = FV_n e^{-i_{nom} n}$

9

Utility Modules

Utility modules are instruction sets for operations that provide generalized support. You will perform some of these operations regularly. Examples are File Management Operations, Importing and Exporting ASCII Text, and Canceling Print Requests. Most casual users can work with these features without instruction because they're almost intuitive given the high quality of WordPerfect menus and on-screen instructions. When you follow the guidelines presented here, however, you'll almost certainly improve your effectiveness both as a WordPerfect user and as a productive writer of well-crafted documents.

Other operations covered in this chapter will be performed infrequently. Examples of these operations are Installing WordPerfect, Defining and Selecting Printers, and Setting WordPerfect Defaults. The primary reason for including these instruction sets is to enable you to install WordPerfect on your own PC, configure it appropriately, and install the drivers needed to correctly match WordPerfect with the printer or printers you'll be using. We expect you to use the set-up and installation modules infrequently, and some readers may not need to use them at all. If you're using laboratory PCs or other machines that are already configured to run the software according to the specifications recommended in WordPerfect documentation, you may need only a few of the set-up and installation instruction sets included here.

9- 1 IMPORTING AND EXPORTING ASCII TEXT

This section explains the nature of ASCII text and describes how to transfer it in and out of WordPerfect. The Overview subsection tells how this feature can be used to link diverse applications to WordPerfect. The Procedure subsection gives instructions for importing ASCII text to WordPerfect, and exporting ASCII text *from* WordPerfect. The Procedure subsection also provides instructions for exporting ASCII data from Lotus 1-2-3, dBASE, and Minitab.

Overview

As you become more proficient with WordPerfect, situations will occur when you'll want to *import* text or tabular information from another software package such as Lotus 1-2-3, dBASE, Minitab, or SPSS/PC+ into a WordPerfect document. You may also find opportunities to *export* text from WordPerfect for use in other applications. Examples would be DOS batch files or dBASE programs coded in WordPerfect for use in DOS or dBASE environments.

The most common method of transferring text or tabular information from a *source* application (such as Lotus 1-2-3) to a *destination* application (such as WordPerfect) is in concept a four-stage process:

1. Convert the text or numbers *from* the source format to an ASCII text file.
2. Export the ASCII file from the source application.
3. Import the ASCII file into the destination application.
4. Convert the ASCII file *to* the destination format.

Using this process, you can create all of the tables for a report in Lotus 1-2-3 and then transfer them to WordPerfect for editing, embellishment and insertion into a report or other long document. Similarly, you can perform a complex statistical analysis in Minitab, write all the output to a file, and then import the file into WordPerfect for editing and addition of interpretive commentary. As a third example, you can generate a sales volume by territory report using dBASE, save the report to an ASCII file, and then import the file into WordPerfect for use as the primary exhibit in a written analysis of sales patterns.

Procedure

In the procedures that follow, we explain how to import and export ASCII data to and from WordPerfect. Then we provide a few brief instructions for exporting ASCII data from Lotus, from dBASE, and from Minitab. Conceptually similar procedures can be used with most other popular personal computer software packages. Just look for coverage of export procedures in the other package's instruction manual.

Importing ASCII data. The first step in the procedure is to create an ASCII file within the *source* package. The file might be called TABLE01.PRN in Lotus, SALESAA.TXT in dBASE, or RESULTS.LIS in Minitab. When the ASCII file has been created, follow these instructions.

1. Press **(Ctrl-F5)** and type [T], [**R**] to retrieve ASCII text with hard returns retained at the end of each line.
2. In response to the WordPerfect prompt,

    Document to be retrieved: ,

    type the drive designation, directory, and name of the ASCII file—e.g., C:\USER\TABLE01.PRN—and press **Enter**. That's all there is to it.

```
File
        Text In
                DOS Text (CR/LF to HRt)  [filename], <R>
```

NOTE: If you're importing an ASCII text file from another word processor, type [E] instead of [**R**] in instruction 1 above. Doing so ensures that the carriage return/line feed (CR/LF) codes at the end of ASCII text lines are converted to soft returns **[SRt]**s in WordPerfect. (Sequences of two or more CR/LF codes are converted to **[HRt]** codes.)

Exporting ASCII data from WordPerfect. To export a WordPerfect document as ASCII text (perhaps for import by another word processor or as a DOS batch program), take the following steps:

3. Press **(Ctrl-F5)**, and type [T], [S]. WordPerfect prompts,

    Document to be saved (DOS Text):.

```
File
        Text Out
                DOS Text [filename], <R>
```

Type a filename in response and then press **Enter**.

When you export a WordPerfect document as an ASCII file, all special formatting codes are stripped out, and any headers, footers, or footnotes/endnotes that were in the original document are removed. The text is unchanged, but the text layout produced in the WordPerfect document by center, indent, and tab align codes is now produced by spaces and tab characters.

Exporting ASCII data from other software. Now we show how to export ASCII files from Lotus, dBASE, and Minitab. The instructions are of necessity quite brief, but they should be meaningful to the reader familiar with the software packages represented. As we mentioned earlier, the procedures described here are meant to be illustrative of what you can do to move text to and from WordPerfect and *many* other packages.

Lotus 1-2-3.

Follow these instructions to export ASCII data from Lotus 1-2-3. (We assume Lotus is running and that a spreadsheet is displayed on your screen.)

1. Type [/], [**P**], [**F**] to signal Lotus that you want to save output to a *printer file*. Lotus then prompts you for the name of an output file. Type an appropriate filename—e.g., [**TABLE01**] and press **Enter**. (Lotus appends the extension .PRN itself.)
2. Type [**R**.], press the cursor control keys to highlight a range that encompasses the information to be exported, and press **Enter**.
3. Type [**O**], [**O**], [**U**], [**Q**] to strip out Lotus formatting codes and return to the Lotus print menu.
4. Type [**G**], [**Q**] to generate the ASCII file and return to the Lotus worksheet.

dBASE.

To export a dBASE report, the report *form* must have been created earlier, and a database with fields matching the fields in the report must be in *USE*. To export a dBASE report as an ASCII file (we assume dBASE is running),

5. Type [**USE** ***filename1***] and press **Enter** in response to the dBASE "." prompt.
6. Type [**REPORT FORM** ***reportname*** **TO** ***filename2***] and press **Enter** again.

For example, if you had a database called "CUSTOMER" and a report form called "BALANCES" to be exported as an ASCII text file named "ARREARS.TXT,"

- Type [**USE CUSTOMER**] and press **Enter** to make CUSTOMER the current database.
- Type [**REPORT FORM BALANCES TO ARREARS**] and press **Enter.** The resulting file is named ARREARS.TXT.

The ASCII file produced is ready to be imported into WordPerfect. Another approach for creating ASCII files in dBASE is to use the SDF (*S*tandard *D*ata *F*ile) format and create a new file. For example,

7. Type [**USE CUSTOMER**] and press **Enter** to make CUSTOMER the current database.
8. Type [**COPY FIELD name, balance TO TEMP FOR balance > 500 SDF**] and press **Enter** to create a file called TEMP.TXT containing the names and balances of all customers with balances greater than $500.

Minitab.

To export Minitab output in ASCII form, you must specify a destination file using the Minitab OUTFILE command before doing any of the statistical analyses you intend to import into WordPerfect. To export Minitab output as an ASCII file (we assume Minitab is running),

9. Type the command, [**OUTFILE TO "*filename*"**] in response to the Minitab "MTB>" prompt, and all the text that scrolls up and off your display screen during a session is written to the ASCII output file. An example of the appropriate command sequence is shown below.

   Type [**OUTFILE TO "MYRESULT.LIS"**] and press **Enter**.

The ASCII file named MYRESULT.LIS can then be imported into WordPerfect. Once the output file has been imported, command lines and other blocks of extraneous matter can be deleted easily, the results can be edited to improve readability, and explanatory prose can be added.

9- 2 FILE MANAGEMENT OPERATIONS

This section includes guidelines to help you manage WordPerfect documents (and other files) so that: (1) you'll be in less danger of losing files if your hard disk fails, and (2) you can find little-used files more easily. The section also tells you how to use the WordPerfect List Files feature to manage files from within WordPerfect. The Overview subsection focuses on good file management practices, while the Procedure subsection shows how to use the options in the List Files screen and menu.

Overview

As you become more familiar with WordPerfect (and other software designed to solve business problems), you're going to create lots of documents, spreadsheets, and other files. If you don't impose discipline on your file organization fairly early, you're sure to lose track of important documents and waste lots of time searching for them.

Principles of organization. Computer users tend to think up filenames that come quickly to mind and are meaningful *at the time of file creation*. Unfortunately, filenames are just as quickly forgotten. For example, if you were writing a paper about *fo*reign *ex*change *ra*te *st*ructures, you might invent "FOEXRAST," a filename with ample meaning *at the time of file creation*. In a few weeks, however, FOEXRAST will become lost in the crowd of your other filenames and, much to your frustration, you will have forgotten the linkage between that particular filename and the contents of the file.

To avoid this problem, adopt five simple file management principles. Following these rules will require some extra front-end work and a bit of discipline, but when you hear the sad stories of others, you'll be glad you did. These are the five principles.

- Back up files on a regular basis.

  This is the first rule of grief avoidance. Save the document on your screen at regular intervals. Copy new or revised documents to a backup diskette prior to leaving WordPerfect, or at some other *regular* interval more in keeping with your schedule.

- Add the extension, ".W51," to all WordPerfect documents.

  Many applications add extensions to output files automatically. For example, Lotus 1-2-3 adds the extension .WK1 to all release 2 spreadsheets; and dBASE appends .DBF to all databases. If *you* add the extension .W51 to all of your WordPerfect documents, you can tell at a glance that they're WordPerfect documents produced with *release 5.1.*

- Create hard disk subsubdirectories for document types and assign meaningful names to them.

  For example, create directories called PAPERS for term papers, CASES, for case analyses, REPORTS for project reports, and CORRESP for letters, memos, and resumes. Creating subdirectories to organize your documents by type should reduce search time and speed up WordPerfect operation. Since diskettes are inexpensive, do the same thing with them. That is, use a separate diskette for each category of documents.

- Develop meaningful file naming conventions using all 8 characters allowable and *apply the conventions religiously.*

  For example, use the first two characters in the filename to designate the *general purpose* of a document:

CA??????.W51	Clubs and Activities
CD??????.W51	Course Documents
JS??????.W51	Job Search
PC??????.W51	Personal Correspondence
MI??????.W51	Miscellaneous
TD??????.W51	Temporary Document

  If the general category is *C*ourse *D*ocuments, use the next two characters to designate specific courses:

CDAC????.W51	Accounting
CDOB????.W51	Organizational Behavior

  Let the third pair of characters designate document type:

JSPLLE??.W51	*J*ob *s*earch *p*lacement *le*tter

CAODME??.W51 *C*lubs and *a*ctivities *OD*K *me*mo
CDMITP??.W51 *T*erm *p*aper for *MI*S

Use the last two characters to identify document types having the same six initial characters. Numbers from 00 to 99 do nicely.

This is our system. Some other, less formal system may work better for you. The important points to remember are that: (1) a system of organization should be developed, (2) the system should be meaningful, and (3) it should be used consistently.

NOTE: If you create large numbers of files, match each filename with a brief description in a directory maintained as a separate file in WordPerfect, Lotus, or Sidekick. A more simple but equally effective approach is to maintain your directory on 3 X 5 cards.

NOTE: We use these filename conventions ourselves because we work with hundreds of files, some of which may not be used for months at a time. Although maintaining the system adds a bit of overhead each time a file is created, the overhead cost is more than offset by savings in search and file duplication time. With a few exceptions, we haven't used the file naming system just described in *WordPerfect Applications* because of its obvious complexity. Simple, easily remembered filenames are more appropriate for the new user.

- If your PC doesn't have a clock chip, enter the date and time whenever you "boot" (start) your personal computer.

  Accurate date and time information are essential if you use WordPerfect's "DATE" feature, but system date and time information appended to newly created and updated files also helps you find important files at a later time.

Use WordPerfect for file maintenance. You can use DOS or WordPerfect for common file maintenance tasks such as copying, deleting, and moving files, but we recommend that you perform all your file management operations within WordPerfect. Doing so is easier than using DOS because the WordPerfect approach is menu-driven rather than command-driven and because the file management operations within WordPerfect are more natural and well integrated with other WordPerfect operations. Let's see how to use WordPerfect to manage documents (and other files).

Procedure

In the following sections we explain how the List Files feature can be used to check the status of directories and files, how to perform operations on directories, and how to perform operations on files. Apart from saving and retrieving files, all operations explained below should be performed from the List Files screen.

NOTE: To save a document displayed in the Normal Editing screen, take the following steps:

- Press **(F10)**. WordPerfect displays the prompt,

  Document to be saved:,

  (followed by drive designator, directory, and filename if the document has been saved previously).
  Type the document name and press **Enter**.

File
Save [*filename*], <R>

To retrieve a document with the Normal Editing screen displayed,

- Press **(Shift-F10)**. WordPerfect displays the prompt,

  Document to be retrieved:,

  Type the document name and press **Enter**.

File
Retrieve [*filename*], <R>

File management operations can be arranged most productively into three categories: (1) status reporting, (2) operations on directories, and (3) operations on files. We consider each category in turn in the paragraphs below.

Status reporting. To display the List Files screen, press **(F5)**, **Enter**.

File
List Files <R>

You should see a three-section display screen with: (1) a banner at the top, (2) a list of directories and files in the center, and (3) a List Files menu at the bottom. (See the example in Fig. 9-1.) The first line of the *banner* lists date, time, and the default directory; the second line shows the size of the *current* document, the amount of free space on the hard disk or diskette, and the amount of space and number of files in the default directory.

```
10-30-90 09:49p              Directory C:\CUT\MODULES\*.*
Document size:    21,793   Free:  4,196,352 Used:  1,485,730      Files:      69

 .  Current     <Dir>                          ..  Parent      <Dir>
GRAFTOOL.WP5     3,329  12-28-89 08:55a  MOUSEBOX.W51     48,266  10-17-90 07:27a
NEWBOX  .W51     4,645  10-11-90 08:19p  SPARPRTZ.W51     42,278  10-18-90 07:37a
WABS0000.W51     4,345  08-22-90 05:11p  WABS0105.W51      5,682  08-22-90 05:11p
WABS0107.W51    11,411  09-25-90 08:10p  WABS0110.W51     18,728  08-22-90 05:12p
WABS0210.W51    67,886  08-22-90 05:13p  WABS0232.W51      5,618  05-23-89 07:50p
WABS0243.W51     4,813  05-23-89 07:52p  WABS0320.W51      6,088  07-26-90 04:27p
WABS0405.W51    11,235  09-25-90 08:25p  WABS0410.W51     40,454  09-26-90 12:04p
WABS0411.W51     6,246  05-11-89 12:24p  WABS0413.W51      7,838  09-26-90 09:33p
WABS0415.W51    35,288  10-18-90 06:44a  WABS0420.W51     31,281  09-26-90 03:43p
WABS0425.W51     6,500  07-26-90 04:06p  WABS0430.W51     31,628  09-26-90 12:06p
WABS0440.W51    21,621  07-26-90 04:07p  WABS0450.W51     33,338  10-18-90 06:44a
WABS0451.W51    44,159  09-14-90 09:02a  WABS0460.W51     37,212  10-18-90 06:44a
WABS0470.W51    21,774  10-18-90 06:44a  WABS0475.W51     59,993  10-18-90 06:44a
WABS0480.W51    48,169  07-26-90 04:08p  WABS0481.W51      3,571  11-18-89 03:33p
WABS0490.W51    20,077  07-26-90 04:09p  WABS0510.W51      4,798  08-22-90 05:15p
WABS0511.W51    17,691  09-26-90 12:27p  WABS0512.W51     24,998  09-26-90 09:33p
WABS0513.W51    16,333  09-26-90 09:03p  WABS0514.W51      5,025  08-19-90 08:27p
WABS0515.W51    20,741  09-26-90 09:04p ▼ WABS0516.W51     7,742  09-26-90 12:32p

1 Retrieve; 2 Delete; 3 Move/Rename; 4 Print; 5 Short/Long Display;
6 Look; 7 Other Directory; 8 Copy; 9 Find; N Name Search: 6
```

Figure 9-1 List Files Screen

NOTE: The *current document* is the document displayed on the Normal Editing screen when List Files is selected. If there's no current document, that is, if List Files was selected from an empty Normal Editing screen, document size is zero.

The *list of directories and files* displays for every file in the current directory: (1) filename and extension, (2) file size in bytes, and (3) date and time when the file was created or updated. Subdirectories of the current directory (if any) are shown at the top of the list. The List Files menu includes ten file management options:

- Retrieve
- Delete
- Move/Rename
- Print
- Short/Long Display
- Look
- Other Directory
- Copy
- Find
- Name Search

We tell how to use most of these options here. To perform most file management operations, first highlight the directory or file of interest and then select one of the List Files menu options. The highlighted bar (called a "highlight cursor") can be moved about by pressing any of the cursor control keys. If you have many files in a directory, press **PgDn**, or **Home**, **Home**, **Down Arrow** to see them. Similarly, press **PgUp** or **Home**, **Home**, **Up Arrow** to scroll back up the List Files screen. If there are too many files in a directory to fit on a single screen, the vertical line in the center of the screen has an arrowhead at the bottom. If you're in the second or later List Files screen in a directory with numerous files, the vertical center line has an arrowhead at the top.

Another way to highlight specific filenames is to use the "Name Search" option on the List Files menu. Type [**N**] and then type the first, second, etc. characters in the filename you're searching for. When you type the first character, the highlight cursor jumps to the first filename beginning with that letter. Type additional characters, and the highlight cursor jumps from filename to filename as WordPerfect closes in on the file you want to see.

You can also switch to other directories from the List Files screen. To switch to the "parent" of the current directory (the next level up), highlight the cell labeled, "<..PARENT>" and press **Enter** twice. The current List Files screen is replaced by the List Files screen of the parent directory, with the current directory shown as one of its subdirectories. To switch to a *subdirectory* of the current directory (subdirectories are at the top of the list with "<DIR>" at the right), highlight the subdirectory name and press **Enter** twice. The List Files screen of the subdirectory replaces the List Files screen of the current directory.

Another way to switch directories is to type [**O**] to select the "Other Directory" option from the List Files menu. In response, WordPerfect displays the name and path for the current directory (C:\SFD\DB3, for example). To select another directory, edit the displayed information and press **Enter** twice or type in the name of the other directory and press **Enter**.

Still another useful option of the List Files feature is printing the List Files screen. The printed screen provides a record of the contents of diskettes or directories for easy reference. Switch on your printer and press **(Shift-F7)** to print the List Files screen displayed on your monitor.

Operations on files. Performing basic maintenance operations on your documents is simple and straightforward when you use the options available in the List Files menu. We describe the most essential operations in the numbered paragraphs below.

NOTE: All of these operations can be performed by moving the mouse cursor to a target filename, pressing the left mouse button to move the *highlight cursor* and then "clicking on" the selected menu option by moving the mouse cursor to the menu option and pressing the left button again.

1. *Retrieve.* Retrieve a document by highlighting its name with the cursor control keys and typing [**R**]. After a few seconds, the selected document is displayed on the Normal Editing screen.
2. *Delete.* Delete a document by highlighting its name and typing [**D**]. WordPerfect prompts you with the message,

   Delete [*filename*] No (Yes).

   Type [**Y**] to purge the document.
3. *Move/Rename.* Highlight the document name and type [**M**] to move a document to another directory. WordPerfect displays the name of the document selected. For example, if you selected MEDIAPLN.W51 in the directory called REPORTS, on drive C:, WordPerfect displays this message,

   New name: C:\REPORTS\MEDIAPLN.W51.

   Edit the prompt, changing the drive designation, directory name, or filename, and then press **Enter**. The selected file is moved to the new location and deleted from the current location.

   NOTE: If all you want to do is change the name of the current document, edit the name and/or extension, leaving drive specification and directory unchanged.

4. *Copy.* To copy a document, highlight its name and type [**C**]. WordPerfect displays the prompt,

   Copy this file to:.

   Type a new filename in response. Also type the drive designation and subdirectory name if the file is to be copied to another subdirectory.
5. *Look.* You may "look" at a document without retrieving it by highlighting its name and pressing **Enter** (*Look* is the default choice on the List Files menu). Since "look"-ing at a document is faster than retrieving it, you can quickly review the contents of many documents. You can't edit the documents you're "looking" at, but you can move about in them by pressing the cursor control keys.

Operations on directories. There are only two operations you can perform on directories from the List Files screen: creation and deletion. Directories are created by typing [**O**] to select the Other Directory option from the List Files menu. In response, WordPerfect prompts with the name of the current directory. Edit the prompt into a new directory name and press **Enter**. WordPerfect prompts again with

Create [directory name] No (Yes).

Type [**Y**] to create the new directory.

To delete an empty directory, highlight the name of the directory and type [**D**]. Type [**Y**] when WordPerfect prompts with the name of the directory.

NOTE: You must delete all the files in a directory before you can delete the directory itself.

9- 3 INSTALLING WORDPERFECT

If you plan to use a laboratory computer, WordPerfect has probably been installed already and you shouldn't have to load and set it up to run on a particular configuration. If you plan to use WordPerfect on your own personal computer, however, you do need to install it. Follow the instructions below to do so.

First, switch on your system and type the date and time to display the C:\> prompt. (If your PC has a built-in clock chip, don't bother with this step.) After you've set the date and time, install WordPerfect on your hard disk.

NOTE: If "C:\>" isn't displayed when you boot up and enter date and time, type [**CD**] and press **Enter** to move to the root directory. *Then* follow the instructions below.

To install WordPerfect, take the following steps:

1. Insert the Install/Learn/Utilities 1 disk in drive A.
2. Type [**A:INSTALL**] and press **Enter**.
3. After you tell WordPerfect that you want to continue with the installation program and install the software to a hard disk, the following list of options is displayed.
    - Basic
    - Custom
    - Network
    - Printer
    - Update

- Copy Disks
- Minimal

We recommend that pick the *Custom* installation at the outset. It's not difficult to do so and the additional directories WordPerfect creates when you select that option help you keep track of the many files you and WordPerfect will create.

When you select the custom installation, WordPerfect prompts you for the location of your files and lists nine file categories:

1. WordPerfect Programs
2. Keyboard/Macro Files
3. Dictionaries/Thesaurus
4. Printer Files and PC Program
5. Style Files
6. Graphic Files
7. Learn and Tutorial
8. Documents
9. Exit

To the right of each grouping should be the directory designator, C:\WP51. Leave option 1 just as it is, but append a subdirectory name to each of the others. We use the subdirectory names shown in Fig. 9-2 because they're simple and meaningful. You might prefer other names, of course. We add a new subdirectory for keyboard and macro files as an example. To make the changes, type [**K**] for Keyboard/Macro files. A prompt is displayed at the bottom of the screen. Press **End** to move to the end of the prompt, type [**KEYMAC**] and then press **Enter.** WordPerfect displays your subdirectory name, tells you it doesn't exist, and asks if you want to create it. Press **Enter** or type [**Y**] to do so. Use the same procedure for the next five file categories.

Leave document files unspecified. Keeping all your WordPerfect files in a single directory is too confining.

After you've specified the subdirectories for file categories, and typed [**E**] to exit the File Location menu, you should be returned to the Custom Information menu. Type [**I**] to install the software from your diskettes. During the installation process, read the screen prompts carefully and follow the directions given there.

The next option is "Check CONFIG.SYS and AUTOEXEC.BAT." Type [**C**] or press **Enter** to let WordPerfect ensure that your operating system environment is configured to handle WordPerfect smoothly.

Option 5, "Select and Install Printer and Exit" is next. This is the step where you first *define* the printer or printers you plan to use. Be sure you know which printer you plan to use and what its model number is. You'll see many options list-

```
Setup: Location of Files

     1 - Backup Files                  C:\WP51\BACKUP

     2 - Keyboard/Macro Files          C:\WP51\KEYMAC

     3 - Thesaurus/Spell/Hyphenation
                       Main            C:\WP51\SPELLER
                       Supplementary   C:\WP51\SPELLER

     4 - Printer Files                 C:\WP51\PRINTER

     5 - Style Files                   C:\WP51\STYLES
              Library Filename         C:\WP51\STYLES\LIBRARY.STY

     6 - Graphic Files                 C:\WP51\GRAPHICS

     7 - Documents

     8 - Spreadsheet Files


Selection: 0
```

Figure 9-2 Example File Directories

ed as you go through the printer definition procedures. Make sure the printer you define is the right one. You can press **PgDn** and **PgUp** to scroll through the list to find your printer, but the faster method is to type [**N**] for Name Search and then type the first few letters of the printer's name to close in on the name you want. For example, to select the Hewlett-Packard LaserJet II from the list of printers displayed,

- Type [**N**]
- Type [**H**] to get close enough
- Press **PgDn** to see the HP LaserJet II
- Type [**6**], press **Enter**, and type [**Y**]

Follow the screen prompts to add other printers. The custom installation is almost complete.

NOTE: You have to install at least one printer driver if WordPerfect hasn't been installed before. Consult Section 9- 5, "Defining and Selecting Printers," in this chapter for additional instructions.

After you've finished defining printers, press **(Ctrl-Alt-Delete)** to restart you computer so that the changes WordPerfect made in your AUTOEXEC.BAT and CONFIG.SYS files can take effect.

9- 4 *SETTING DEFAULTS*

WordPerfect is designed so that the user can change many of the program's features and attributes to fit his or her personal working style, equipment configuration—e.g., display screen resolution, brand and model of mouse—or both. There are literally scores of settings that can be changed, and all of them are accessible by pressing (Shift-F1), System Setup.

To explain every option in detail would require more space than is justified in a book of this nature. Besides, WordPerfect has done an excellent job of creating a standard (or default) environment that serves the average user surprisingly well. In the Procedure subsection below, we do show you how to make some changes, focusing on the settings you're most likely to want to change.

When you have a basic understanding of the kinds of modifications you can make via the system setup options, try experimenting. That's the best way to learn how to design the best configuration for yourself. We also urge you to consult the WordPerfect reference manual if these materials and your experimentation don't answer all of your questions. Finally, if you didn't install WordPerfect on your system yourself and you have reason to expect that many changes have been made to the basic setup, re-install the system by following the instructions in Section 9- 3. It shouldn't take more than a half hour to 45 minutes to do so.

Procedure

Run WordPerfect by typing [**WP**] and pressing **Enter**. Then, press **(Shift-F1)** to display the Setup menu (see Fig. 9-3). The six options on the menu are explained in general terms below in the sequence shown on the screen. Let's go through them.

- *Mouse.* The choices under this option let you identify the specific brand and type of mouse installed on your system. They also let you set the communications port on your PC and set timing parameters.
- *Display.* The choices under this option let you identify the type of monitor you'll be using and allow you to change screen characteristics. Menu options reviewed below as well as View Document and Edit Screen options are changed by selecting options from the Display menu.
- *Environment.* Environment options include document backup options, cursor speed control, and units of measure. Environment options also allow you to: (1) specify whether WordPerfect is to use a more accurate external dictionary or less accurate internal rules to hyphenate your document, (2) specify the degree of control you wish to have over the hyphenation process, and (3) set the conditions under which WordPerfect will signal with a beep. We describe how to set backup options and how to control cursor speed later.
- *Initial Settings.* Initial settings options let you specify many important docu-

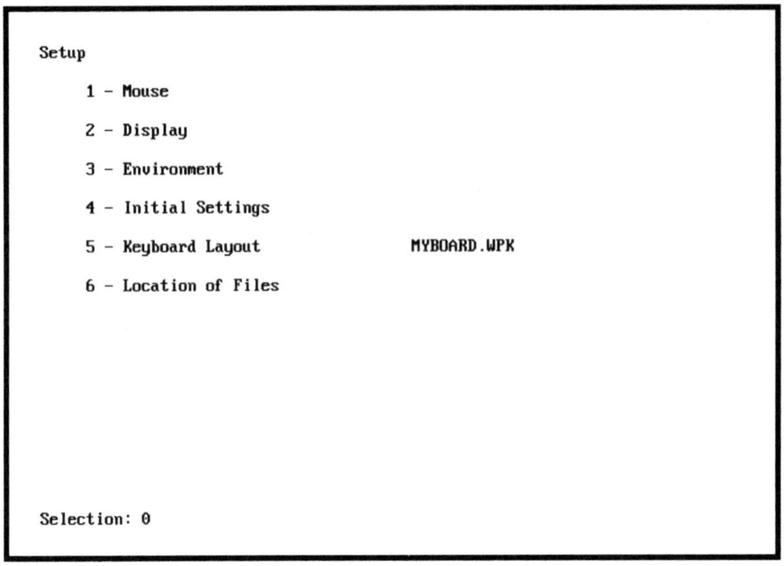

Figure 9-3 Setup Menu

ment characteristics. Settings that are made through this menu can affect some of the characteristics of all of your documents (all of the settings can be overridden at the document level, however). For example, the following characteristics can be specified:

a. *Date format* lets you specify the format of the dates that WordPerfect displays when you press (F5) and type [T] or [C]. You can include days of the week; you can indicate the month in numerical or spelled-out form, and you can change the order of the elements of the date.

b. *Equations* lets you specify font size and the horizontal and vertical position of equations. You can also select an equation keyboard.

c. *Initial codes* is a helpful feature that lets you set default format characteristics such as tab settings, line spacing, and justification for all your documents.

d. *Repeat value* lets you set the repeat value for the Escape key. (When you press the Escape key, a number—the default value is 8—is flashed on your screen. The next keystroke—e.g., the Enter key—is repeated that many times.)

- Keyboard Layout allows you to create, delete, edit, and select alternate keyboard layouts. The keyboard layout feature is a very powerful one that permits you to program your keyboard to perform functions well beyond its standard capabilities. This is an advanced feature that we don't describe here. Turn to the WordPerfect reference manual for appropriate coverage.

- Location of Files lets you specify the subdirectories where your primary file groupings—e.g., macros, graphics, spelling dictionaries—are located. We describe how to create the subdirectories in Section 9- 3, "Installing WordPerfect." If you need to change file locations, select this option.

Now, let's change a few of the options—the more important ones, we think—to see what's involved. First, let's go to the Setup: Mouse menu to make sure we've specified the right type of mouse. (In the following instructions, we always start from the Normal Editing screen.)

1. Press **(Shift-F1)** and type [**M**] to display the Setup: Mouse menu.
2. Type [**T**] to display the brands and models of mice that WordPerfect recognizes (see Fig. 9-4).
3. Note that "Mouse Driver (MOUSE.COM)" is highlighted. MOUSE.COM is the standard mouse driver and it works with mice that follow the Microsoft standard (and that's most of them). Since we use the Keytronic bus mouse ourselves, however, we would highlight that particular option and type [**S**] to select it.
4. Press **(F7)** twice to return to the Normal Editing screen (unless, of course, you want to change some of the other mouse options).

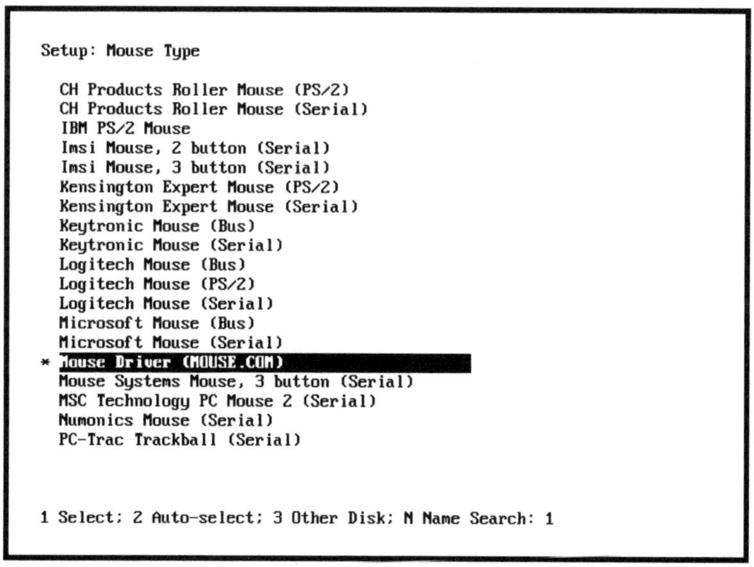

Figure 9-4 Setup: Mouse Type Menu

File
Setup
Mouse T, <R>, <R>

Next, let's change several of the Menu options in the Setup: Menu Options menu. Specifically, we'll include a menu bar separator line and we'll ensure that the menu bar is always visible at the top of the screen. Here's how

1. Press **(Shift-F1)** and type [**D**]. The Setup: Menu Options menu should be on your screen (see Fig. 9-5).
2. Type [**M**], [**S**], [**Y**] to add a separator line between the menu bar and the Normal Editing screen.
3. Type [**V**], [**Y**] to display the menu bar at the top of the screen continuously.
4. Press **(F7)** to return to the Normal Editing screen.

File
Setup
Display M, S, Y, V, Y, <R>

Now, let's change a couple of the options in the Setup: Environment menu. We'll change the backup options slightly, and slow the cursor way down.

```
Setup: Menu Options

     1 - Menu Letter Display               BOLD

Pull-Down Menu

     2 - Pull-Down Letter Display          REDLN

     3 - Pull-Down Text                    SHADW

     4 - Alt Key Selects Pull-Down Menu    No

Menu Bar

     5 - Menu Bar Letter Display           REDLN

     6 - Menu Bar Text                     SHADW

     7 - Menu Bar Separator Line           No

     8 - Menu Bar Remains Visible          Yes


Selection: 0
```

Figure 9-5 Setup: Menu Options Menu

1. Press **(Shift-F1)** and type [**E**] to display the Setup: Environment menu.
2. Type [**B**], [**T**], [**Y**], [**15**] and press **Enter** to display the Setup: Backup menu, select timed backup, toggle (or keep) it on, and set it for 15-minute intervals. (We find 30 minutes to be a little too long between backups.)
3. Press **Enter** once more to display the Setup: Environment menu again.
4. Type [**C**], [**N**] to set the cursor speed to "normal" (10 characters per second).
5. Press **(F7)** to return to the Normal Editing screen.

File
  Setup
    Environment B, T, Y, [15], <R>, <Enter>, C, N, <R>

Finally, we'll change some initial settings in the Setup: Initial Settings menu (see Fig. 9-6 and Fig. 9-7). The only settings we're going to change are the Initial Codes that apply to documents. We show how to change the equation settings in Section 8- 6, and we're satisfied with the default date format. You may want to change the date format, however. That's an area where you can experiment on your own. Merge, the Repeat Value and the Table of Authorities settings are acceptable as is, and we prefer to modify print options when it's time to print a document.

The initial codes feature is quite useful because it lets you set formatting parameters that apply to all of your documents. For example, we prepare many sets

```
Setup: Initial Settings

     1 - Merge

     2 - Date Format                      3 1, 4
                                          November 3, 1990
     3 - Equations

     4 - Format Retrieved Documents       No
           for Default Printer

     5 - Initial Codes

     6 - Repeat Value                     8

     7 - Table of Authorities

     8 - Print Options



Selection: 0
```

Figure 9-6 Setup: Initial Settings Menu

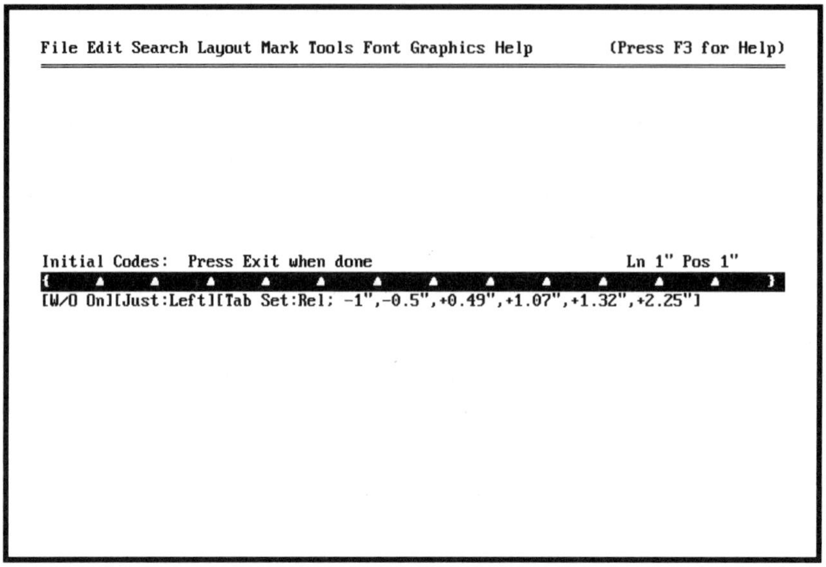

Figure 9-7 Initial Codes Screen

of lectures and case outlines using the same basic format. We've developed a set of tabs that accommodates our outline approach nicely. We also prefer to left-justify our documents, and we always want to trap widows and orphans. By establishing these characteristics using initial codes, they apply to all of our new documents. As we mentioned earlier, they can be easily overridden for any individual document.

Take the following steps to open the Initial Codes screen (see Fig. 9-7). (It looks like the Normal Editing screen with Reveal Codes switched on and nothing typed.)

1. Press **(Shift-F1)** and type [**I**] for Initial Settings.

File		
	Setup	
		Initial Settings C

2. Type [**C**] to display the initial codes screen.
3. Enter the codes just as you'd insert them at the top of a standard document. For example, to insert a left justification code, and toggle widows and orphans on.
    3. 1 Press **(Shift-F8)** and type [**L**].
    3. 2 Type [**J**], [**L**] to toggle left justification.

3. 3 Type **[W]**, **[Y]** to toggle on widows and orphans.

3. 4 Press **(F7)** to return to the Initial Codes screen.

4. Press **(F7)** twice to return to the Normal Editing screen.

> Layout
> Line J, L, W, Y, <R>, <(F7)>, <R>

9- 5 DEFINING AND SELECTING PRINTERS

A printer driver is set of coded instructions in software tailored to a specific printer brand and model such as an Epson LQ-1000 or Hewlett-Packard LaserJet III. The Overview subsection below explains how a printer driver works and describes its purpose. The Procedure subsection includes instructions for installing a printer driver, customizing it to match your work environment, and then selecting it when you're ready to print.

NOTE: You can't print a document without having installed and selected a printer.

Overview

A printer *driver* is a piece of WordPerfect software that translates the WordPerfect formatting and printer control codes into matching codes understood by a specific brand and model of printer. To use a given brand and model of printer with WordPerfect, however, *the driver for that printer must have been installed before it can be "selected" to print a particular document.* The installation process is called "printer definition." (Normally, at least one driver will have been defined when WordPerfect was first installed on your system.)

Every printer brand and model requires a driver, and WordPerfect Corporation provides drivers for most models and brands of printers of the scores available in the market today. Drivers are constituted in large, archived "printer" files found on the WordPerfect installation diskettes labeled "Printer 1," "Printer 2," etc., included in the set of WordPerfect diskettes shipped as part of the total software package. Each file has the extension, ".All." Other drivers for brand new or discontinued printer models may be obtained by calling WordPerfect customer support.

You may have access to two or three different printers in your own work environment, one for draft work, and one or two others for printing through a local area network. If so, you'll want to be able to select a driver for each printer. You may also want to create two or more versions of one basic driver for a particular brand and model of printer. For example, you may need one driver for a Hewlett-Packard LaserJet equipped with the "M" font cartridge and another driver set up to work with downloaded Bitstream Fontware fonts. Depending on the nature of the documents you create and your work environment, you might have a dozen or more drivers in your working set.

After you've selected a working set of drivers from the many available on the WordPerfect distribution diskettes and then tailored them to match your needs, selection of a single driver is straightforward. For example, after writing a draft, you might want to print it on a close-at-hand matrix printer for review and editing. To do so, select the driver matching your draft printer from the driver set created earlier. After editing the draft and incorporating font changes, you might then want to print the final draft on an HP LaserJet on a network. Select another driver from your working set to do that.

Procedure

When a printer driver hasn't been defined previously, printer set-up and selection is a three-step process:

- Defining the printer driver
- Customizing the driver to fit your hardware configuration
- Selecting one driver from a set of drivers

If a driver has already been defined and you only want to change its settings and save it under its old name or change its settings and copy the revised version to a new file, take steps 2 and 3. If you want to select a driver, take step 3. Because the three tasks of printer driver definition, customization, and selection are functionally separate, we describe them separately here.

Printer driver definition. We assume you defined at least one printer when WordPerfect was installed on your system. Follow the instructions below to define *additional printers.* (WordPerfect should be running and the Normal Editing screen should be displayed on your monitor.)

1. Press **(Shift-F7)** and type [**S**] to display the Print menu and choose "Select Printer" from the options shown.
2. Type [**A**] for additional printers. You should see some and perhaps many printers listed on your screen. If the printer you'd like to add is on the list,
   2. 1 Highlight its name by pressing the arrow keys or use name search.
      - Type [**N**].
      - Type the first few letters of the printer name; it should then be highlighted.

   2. 2 Type [**S**] and press **Enter** to display a Printer Helps and Hints message for the new printer.

   2. 3 Press **Enter** to display the Select Printer: Edit menu. Make changes in the default definition by following the instructions in the "Customizing Printer Drivers" subsection that follows this one.

   2. 4 Press **(F7)** to return to the Print: Select Printer menu.

File
Print S, A, N, [*printer name*], S, <R>, <R>, <R>

3. If the printer you'd like to add isn't listed on your screen, follow the installation instructions in Section 9- 3 and select the "Printer" option from the Installation menu.

Customizing printer drivers. Take the steps described next right after defining each printer driver. Also take these steps to modify and re-save an existing driver or modify and add an existing driver as a new driver in the set. (We assume the Normal Editing screen is displayed on your monitor.)

1. Press **(Shift-F7)** and type [**S**], [**E**] to select the Select Printer: Edit screen. Several settings are displayed on the Select Printer Edit screen. We describe some of them here, focusing on the settings of greatest importance to the casual user.

File
Print S, E

Name
This descriptive name can help you remember the driver's purpose. It may be up to 29 characters long.

Port
If your PC communicates with a printer via the PC's *parallel* port, the setting should be LPT1. If your PC talks to your printer via a single *serial* port, the value should be COM1. If your PC has additional communication ports (the link to a network, for example), you may wish to designate the port as LPT2, LPT3, COM2, COM3...

Cartridges and Fonts
Select this option by typing [**C**] to find out if the printer you've selected will let you change the appearance of typed output by selecting from a menu of font cartridges, soft fonts, or print wheels. (Most have some capabilities of this sort.) If cartridges and fonts are available (a font screen will appear when you type [**C**] if they are), you can select one cartridge (if a single cartridge is installed) or two (if two are installed) by highlighting the cartridge line, highlighting choices and typing [*] (uppercase "8"). You can select soft fonts the same way.

NOTE: If downloadable fonts (from Bitstream, Hewlett Packard, or another vendor) aren't available as files on your hard disk, you can select them, *but* *they cannot be downloaded.* If you attempt to download nonexistent soft fonts, WordPerfect displays an error message. The only way to have fonts available for downloading is to buy them from the printer manufacturer or a third-party font vendor such as Bitstream and load or create them on your hard drive.

2. Press **(F7)** to return to the Select Printer: Edit screen if you haven't done so already.
3. Type [**F**] to display the Select Printer Initial Font screen.
4. Your printer's default fonts or the fonts you selected from the Cartridges and Fonts screen are shown. Highlight the font you plan to use most heavily. Type [**S**] to select it and a * pops up beside the font name. The selected font is your "initial font."

Selecting a printer driver. Take the following steps to select a printer driver from your set. (We assume you're starting from the Normal Editing screen.)

1. Press **(Shift-F7)** and type [**S**] to display the Select Printer screen.
2. Press the cursor arrows to highlight the driver to be used with the current document.
3. Type [**S**] to select the driver and a * pops up beside it.

File
Print S, N, [*printer name*], <R>, S, <R>

WARNING: If a driver hasn't been defined previously, you *must* define at least one driver prior to creating your first document.

NOTE: If the driver you've selected for a document requires that soft fonts be downloaded, be sure to type [**I**] on the Print menu (for "*I*nitialize Printer"). When your soft fonts require lots of printer memory for storage, downloading may take several minutes.

9- 6 CANCELING A PRINT REQUEST

If your personal computer is equipped with a graphics adapter, use the View Document feature to check the printer image of your document before printing it. You save lots of wasted time and paper by doing so. If you don't have a graphics adapter, you may not be able to tell you've made an error until the document is printing; then it may be too late. Often, however, you spot something wrong when the document is being printed. If the document is a page or less in length, don't bother stopping. If it's longer than a page and you spot a problem, however, take the following steps:

1. Switch off the printer immediately. That will clear its memory.
2. Press **(Shift-F7)** and type [**C**], [**S**], [**Y**] to select Printer Control and stop the printer.
3. Type [**C**], press **Enter**, and type [**G**] twice to cancel and clear the print job.
4. Press **(F7)** twice to return to the Normal Editing screen.

File
Print C, S, Y, C, <R>, G, G, <R>

5. Switch your printer back on.

NOTE: When you press (F7) to exit the document you're working on, WordPerfect displays the prompt,

Cancel Print Jobs? (Y/N),

if you haven't canceled a print request. To clear out any print jobs that may have resulted from your attempts to avoid printing a flawed document, respond "Y" to the prompt.

INDEX

H

I

J

K

L